4/3/03

MISSION-BASED MANAGEMENT

WILEY NONPROFIT LAW, FINANCE, AND MANAGEMENT SERIES

The Art of Planned Giving: Understanding Donors and the Culture of Giving by Douglas E. White

Beyond Fund Raising: New Strategies for Nonprofit Investment and Innovation by Kay Grace

Budgeting for Not-for-Profit Organizations by David Maddox

Charity, Advocacy, and the Law by Bruce R. Hopkins

The Complete Guide to Fund Raising Management by Stanley Weinstein

The Complete Guide to Nonprofit Management by Smith, Bucklin & Associates

Critical Issues in Fund Raising edited by Dwight Burlingame

Developing Affordable Housing: A Practical Guide for Nonprofit Organizations, Second Edition by Bennett L. Hecht

Faith-Based Management: Leading Organizations that Are Based on More than Just Mission by Peter Brinckerhoff

Financial and Accounting Guide for Not-for-Profit Organizations, Sixth Edition by Malvern J. Gross, Jr., Richard F. Larkin, Roger S. Bruttomesso, John J. McNally, PricewaterhouseCoopers LLP

Financial Empowerment: More Money for More Mission by Peter Brinckerhoff

Financial Management for Nonprofit Organizations by Jo Ann Hankin, Alan Seidner and John Zietlow

Financial Planning for Nonprofit Organizations by Jody Blazek

The First Legal Answer Book for Fund-Raisers by Bruce R. Hopkins

The Fund Raiser's Guide to the Internet by Michael Johnston

Fund-Raising: Evaluating and Managing the Fund Development Process, Second Edition by James M. Greenfield

Fund-Raising Fundamentals: A Guide to Annual Giving for Professionals and Volunteers by James M. Greenfield

Fundraising Cost Effectiveness: A Self-Assessment Workbook by James M. Greenfield

Fund-Raising Regulation: A State-by-State Handbook of Registration Forms, Requirements, and Procedures by Seth Perlman and Betsy Hills Bush

Grantseeker's Toolkit: A Comprehensive Guide to Finding Funding by Cheryl S. New and James A. Quick

Grant Winner's Toolkit: Project Management and Evaluation by James A. Quick and Cheryl S. New

High Performance Nonprofit Organizations: Managing Upstream for Greater Impact by Christine Letts, William Ryan, and Allen Grossman

Intermediate Sanctions: Curbing Nonprofit Abuse by Bruce R. Hopkins and D. Benson Tesdahl

International Fund Raising for Nonprofits by Thomas Harris

International Guide to Nonprofit Law by Lester A. Salamon and Stefan Toepler & Associates

Joint Ventures Involving Tax-Exempt Organizations, Second Edition by Michael I. Sanders

The Law of Fund-Raising, Second Edition by Bruce R. Hopkins

The Law of Tax-Exempt Healthcare Organizations by Thomas K. Hyatt and Bruce R. Hopkins

The Law of Tax-Exempt Organizations, Seventh Edition by Bruce R. Hopkins

The Legal Answer Book for Nonprofit Organizations by Bruce R. Hopkins

A Legal Guide to Starting and Managing a Nonprofit Organization, Second Edition by Bruce R. Hopkins

Managing Affordable Housing: A Practical Guide to Creating Stable Communities by Bennett L. Hecht, Local Initiatives Support Corporation, and James Stockard

OTHER TITLES IN THE *Mission-Based Management Series*
by Peter C. Brinckerhoff

Financial Empowerment: More Money for More Mission
Faith-Based Management: Leading Organizations That Are Based on More than Mission
Mission-Based Marketing: How Your Not-for-Profit Can Succeed in a More Competitive World
Mission-Based Management: Leading Your Not-For-Profit in the 21st Century
Social Entrepreneurship: The Art of Mission-Based Venture Development

Managing Upstream: Creating High-Performance Nonprofit Organizations by Christine W. Letts, William P. Ryan, and Allan Grossman

Mission-Based Management: Leading Your Not-for-Profit in the 21st Century, Second Edition by Peter Brinckerhoff

Mission-Based Marketing: How Your Not-for-Profit Can Succeed in a More Competitive World by Peter Brinckerhoff

Nonprofit Boards: Roles, Responsibilities, and Performances by Diane J. Duca

Nonprofit Compensation and Benefits Practices by Applied Research and Development Institute International, Inc.

The Nonprofit Counsel by Bruce R. Hopkins

The Nonprofit Guide to the Internet, Second Edition by Michael Johnston

Nonprofit Investment Policies: A Practical Guide to Creation and Implementation by Robert Fry, Jr.

The Nonprofit Law Dictionary by Bruce R. Hopkins

Nonprofit Compensation, Benefits, and Employment Law by David G. Samuels and Howard Pianko

Nonprofit Litigation: A Practical Guide with Forms and Checklists by Steve Bachmann

The Nonprofit Handbook, Second Edition: Volume I—Management by Tracy Daniel Connors

The Nonprofit Handbook, Second Edition: Volume II—Fund Raising by James M. Greenfield

The Nonprofit Manager's Resource Dictionary by Ronald A. Landskroner

Nonprofit Organizations' Business Forms: Disk Edition by John Wiley & Sons, Inc.

Planned Giving: Management, Marketing, and Law, Second Edition by Ronald R. Jordan and Katelyn L. Quynn

Private Foundations: Tax Law and Compliance by Bruce R. Hopkins and Jody Blazek

Program Related Investments: A Technical Manual for Foundations by Christie I Baxter

Reengineering Your Nonprofit Organization: A Guide to Strategic Transformation by Alceste T. Pappas

Reinventing the University: Managing and Financing Institutions of Higher Education by Sandra L. Johnson and Sean C. Rush, PricewaterhouseCoopers LLP

The Second Legal Answer Book for Nonprofit Organizations by Bruce R. Hopkins

Social Entrepreneurship: The Art of Mission-Based Venture Development by Peter Brinckerhoff

Special Events: Proven Strategies for Nonprofit Fund Raising by Alan Wendroff

Strategic Communications for Nonprofit Organizations: Seven Steps to Creating a Successful Plan by Janel Radtke

Strategic Planning for Nonprofit Organizations: A Practical Guide and Workbook by Michael Allison and Jude Kaye, Support Center for Nonprofit Management

Streetsmart Financial Basics for Nonprofit Managers by Thomas A. McLaughlin

A Streetsmart Guide to Nonprofit Mergers and Networks by Thomas A. McLaughlin

Successful Marketing Strategies for Nonprofit Organizations by Barry J. McLeish

Successful Corporate Fund Raising: Effective Strategies for Today's Nonprofits by Scott Sheldon

The Tax Law of Charitable Giving, Second Edition by Bruce R. Hopkins

The Tax Law of Colleges and Universities by Bertrand M. Harding

Tax Planning and Compliance for Tax-Exempt Organizations: Forms, Checklists, Procedures, Third Edition by Jody Blazek

The Universal Benefits of Volunteering: A Practical Workbook for Nonprofit Organizations, Volunteers and Corporations by Walter P. Pidgeon, Jr.

The Volunteer Management Handbook by Tracy Daniel Connors

Values-Based Estate Planning: A Step-by-Step Approach to Wealth Transfers for Professional Advisors by Scott Fithian

MISSION-BASED MANAGEMENT

*Leading Your Not-For-Profit in
the 21st Century, Second Edition*

Peter C. Brinckerhoff

JOHN WILEY & SONS, INC

Library of Congress Cataloging-in-Publication Data:

Brinckerhoff, Peter C., 1952–
    Mission-based management : leading your not-for-profit in the 21st century / by Peter
C. Brinckerhoff.—2nd ed.
        p. cm—(Wiley nonprofit law, finance, and management series)
    ISBN 0-471-39013-5 (cloth : alk. paper)
    1. Nonprofit organizations—Management. 2. Associations, institutions,
etc.—Management. I. Title. II. Series.
HD62.6.B74   2000
658′.048—dc21

                                                                          00-038135

Printed in the United States of America.

10 9 8 7 6 5 4 3

This book is dedicated to my mother:
Inger Melchior Hansen Brinckerhoff,
1924–1994
by far the best writer in the family.

Acknowledgments

No book like this is the author's sole product. In my case, much of the theory, case studies, and applications presented here have been developed over my 25 years as a not-for-profit administrator, volunteer, board member, and consultant. My consulting firm, Corporate Alternatives, has worked with thousands of not-for-profits since 1982, and the exceptional efforts of the staff and volunteers of the organizations with which I have worked show up here repeatedly. This book is therefore a compendium of consultation, research, applications, and experience, and like any observer in any field, I have incorporated ideas and experiences of others to apply to the field of not-for-profits. Where appropriate, and when not violating confidentiality, these people have been noted in the text. Where they are not acknowledged, they are still greatly appreciated.

For this second edition, I would also like to particularly thank my technology experts, Ben Brinckerhoff and Dan Mayer. Their understanding of both technology and the potential for technology to help not-for-profits was crucial to major improvements to this text.

About the Author

Peter Brinckerhoff is an internationally known expert on improving the not-for-profit sector. He brings a vast collection of expertise and hands-on experience from his time as a staff member, executive director, volunteer, and board member of local, statewide, and national not-for-profits. In 1982, he founded Corporate Alternatives, Inc. a consulting firm dedicated to improving the business skills of not-for-profits across the United States. In the role of CAI's President, Peter has presented to, trained, and consulted with thousands of not-for-profits in every discipline. He has also written extensively in the not-for-profit press, with over 50 articles published in periodicals as varied as *NonProfit World, Board and Administrator,* the *Whole Non-Profit Catalog, Strategic Governance,* and the international *Journal of Voluntary Sector Marketing.*

Peter's books are used as core texts in over 50 undergraduate and graduate programs in not-for-profit management throughout North America, Europe, and Australia.

A former VISTA volunteer, Peter received his bachelor's degree from the University of Pennsylvania and his masters degree in Public Health from Tulane University. He lives in Springfield, Illinois, with his wife and three children.

Contents

Preface to
the Second Edition

How can so much change in just six years? As I began to review the original text to *Mission-Based Management,* I was repeatedly impressed with how much of the world we live in—the not-for-profit sector—has changed in those few short years. While much of what I wrote in the first edition still holds true, so many of the trends that were just becoming evident then are completely absorbing now. For example, in 1994, I said that technology would become much more prevalent, but no one foresaw the integration into all parts of our lives that the Internet would achieve. Remember, in 1994 very few people knew what a URL was, or understood e-*anything* much less the meaning of .com or .org. E-mail was a novelty, not a nearly ubiquitous way to communicate. If I had told you your organization would have a Web site, you would have either laughed or been totally confused, as in, "What's a Web site?" We were calling them "home pages" then.

Managed care was an important but not yet life-and-death issue for many human services organizations; outcome measures were interesting but, in most cases, not required. The very idea that not-for-profits should, could, and would make money, be businesslike, and set up new ventures was just beginning to take hold.

So much has changed, and it is time for a refreshed set of priorities for the mission-based manager. I've looked at, and changed, the characteristics of a successful mission-based organization. I've given you an updated set of predictions for the next 10 years, added an entire chapter on technology, and brought the chapters on Financial Empowerment, Marketing, and Social Entrepreneurship into agreement with the books I've written on those subjects since *Mission-Based Management* was published. I've also added discussion questions at the end of each chapter, to allow you to read the book with your staff and then generate conversations about which parts of the book most apply to your organization's unique needs.

It is a fascinating and exciting time to be in the not-for-profit world. We have more challenges, more opportunity, and more ways to respond to the increasing community needs that await us than ever before.

A solid U.S. economy, strong federal and state budget surpluses, and a highly valued stock market have provided us a base from which to take the sector, in the catchphrase of the decade, "to the next level." A new *Mission-Based Management* will help you bring your organization to that level.

1

Introduction

Welcome. This book is intended for you, the leadership of our nation's not-for-profit charitable organizations. It is designed to give you a different insight into how top-quality not-for-profits *really* run, what works, what doesn't, and how to ensure that your organization is one of the ones that works, both this year and throughout the new century. It is intended to help you become a mission-based manager.

In this introductory chapter we'll review the core philosophies on which I have based the book, examine the reasons that I feel the book is needed, and then take the first look at what the book holds, and the best ways for you as a reader and a management practitioner to use it. By the end of the chapter, you should have a better understanding of my philosophical perspective, and also be ready to get the most from the book as a whole.

A. CORE PHILOSOPHIES

Before you continue, you need to know that the material in this book is based on three philosophies. These philosophies have been the core of my consulting, training, and writing since 1982, and they express better than anything I have seen my beliefs about what your organization is and what it can become.

FIRST: NOT-FOR-PROFITS ARE *BUSINESSES*

Your organization is a *mission-based* business, not a charity. For-profits chase profits—not-for-profits pursue their mission. But just because you aren't primarily motivated by profit doesn't give you a license to be sloppy or to ignore a good idea simply because it was initially developed

1

for the for-profit sector. Whether you are a paid employee or a volunteer, you are a steward of your organization and its resources. As steward, you are responsible to use all the resources at your command to do more mission, and the techniques of the for-profit world are, in many cases, very applicable. Actually, making the connection between for-profit business techniques and the not-for-profit world is what I have been doing since 1982, and many of those skills show up in this book: good marketing, keeping track of cash flow, good controls management, and focusing on your core competencies.

How many times have you been told that you are a professional? Many, I'm sure. Well, perhaps for the first time, you are now being told that, as a mission-based manager, you are a businessperson as well. If you act in a businesslike manner, you can get more mission for your money, doing more with the limited resources at your disposal.

Using good business skills as a mission-based manager does not, I repeat, *not* mean dropping services simply because they lose money, nor does it mean turning people away because they cannot pay. But it does mean paying attention to the bottom line, having a strategic vision, negotiating in good faith and from a position of strength—in short, being businesslike. Your organization is a business, and the more businesslike you are, the better it will be for your clientele.

For-profit businesses are concerned about one bottom line: the financial return on their investment. If they invest $x, how big is $y return? Not-for-profit businesses need to worry more about their bottom line as well, but you have two returns to consider. On any expenditure (which I consider an investment), the question is: How much mission am I getting back on this investment. What's the mission return? And what is the financial return? We'll talk a great deal about this concept throughout the book. But let's agree that business ideas, concepts, and techniques do have mission application.

SECOND: NO ONE GIVES YOU A DIME

This may come as a surprise, but you do not really get gifts. You do not really receive donations, you do not really get grants. I know that that is what all of us call them, but the problem with thinking of those transactions as gifts or donations is that the organization then acts like a charity. You become stuck in the mentality that you are so poor that the only way you can survive is by the beneficence of people or organizations richer than you.

Technically, that may all be true, but try looking at it this way, and see if you feel differently about yourself and your organization. Let's assume that you come to me for a donation, and you convince me that you really need the money for a service or a building. I write you a check for $100. Am I making the donation to you? Of course not. Am I giving a gift to your organization? You're getting closer. But what I am really doing and what really happens in all of these transactions is that I am *purchasing services for someone who cannot pay.* No one sends you money and expects you to keep it in a vault somewhere. Whether you get a grant from the feds, or a bequest from a local person, it is understood that you will provide services with the money you have. In business terms, I give you my money based on an *expectation of outcome.* When I go to McDonald's, I have an expectation of a burger; when I enter a hotel, I have an expectation of lodging.

In other words, and here is the key: You *earn* all the money you get. It is essential that you and your staff and board understand this and believe it if you are to adopt the characteristics of success that are presented in this book. Why? Because if you keep thinking of yourselves as a poor charity, you will continue to be treated that way and not like the mission-based business that you are.

THIRD: NOT-FOR-PROFIT DOES NOT MEAN NONPROFIT

You have certainly noticed by now that I use the term *not-for-profits,* eschewing the commonly used *nonprofit.* There is a good reason for this—there is a difference. *A nonprofit is an organization that loses money.* Many savings and loans in the 1980s were nonprofits, as were many of our domestic airlines and automakers. Too many not-for-profits are also nonprofits, a situation that we need to correct and soon. There is a reason that so many not-for-profits lose money, and it has to do with the perception that it is illegal and immoral for a not-for-profit to make money.

It is not. Nowhere in any state or federal law, and nowhere in any state or federal regulation dealing with taxation or corporate structures, does it say that a not-for-profit cannot make money, cannot make a profit. In fact, the Internal Revenue Service (IRS) code dealing with 501(c)(3) organizations says, ". . . the profits of the corporation shall not inure to the benefit of. . . ." This clause precludes staff or board from inappropriately benefitting from the organization's profits, but the key to the phrase is that the IRS anticipates and accepts profits. Profits in a not-for-profit are *legal.*

If you or anyone in your organization thinks that I am wrong about profits being legal, consider this. Your organization is considered tax-exempt (by reason of your 501(c)(3) status), but from what kind of *federal* taxes? I know you may not pay sales or property taxes, but those are state or local exemptions. At the federal level, you are exempt from what the IRS terms *income tax.* Now, for you and me, income tax means that we add up all of our income and pay the IRS a portion of that. But the tax your organization is subject to is a business tax. Businesses do not pay tax on what you and I would term *income,* they pay taxes on profits. They add up all their income, subtract all their expenses, and pay, in taxes, a portion of their profits. *Income* to the IRS means *profits* to you and me. Thus, your organization has an exemption against paying taxes on its profits. Here's the question: *If you can't make a profit, why do you need a tax exemption?*

In fact, the entire issue of not-for-profits not being able to make money is just so much smoke, and it runs right in the face of the intention of Congress in giving you the charitable status you have. Congress wanted your organization to keep what it earns and reinvest it in the community. They wanted to encourage our sector and didn't think that we should be taxed for doing good things related to our mission. What have we done? Screwed it all up by not allowing not-for-profits to keep what they earn.

Profits in your not-for-profit are also *essential,* a key element in financial empowerment, a subject that we will cover at length. Without profits, you cannot grow, you can't innovate and try new ways to serve your communities, you cannot recruit and retain excellent staff, and you cannot take prudent risks on behalf of your clientele. You will see in later chapters that I will contend that you need to make money as an organization at least 7 out of 10 years. To do less is not good mission-based management.

These philosophies form the foundation for everything that follows in this book. They are the core of mission-based management. If you agree with them, if you find yourself nodding and saying "That's great!", you are going to enjoy the book and get a great deal out of it. If you are uncomfortable with the philosophies, I hope that the remainder of this chapter and the issues raised in Chapters 2 and 3 will convince you of the validity of these philosophies. If that doesn't work, then I think that the remainder of the book will convince you that there are many, many business applications that can improve your ability to do better mission more efficiently and effectively.

We will return to these philosophies at the end of the book, to look at how your funders can adopt them to give you more leeway to do your job. But for the majority of the book, we will concentrate on how you can make them a reality in your own management style, in your own mission-based organization.

B. WHY IS THIS SECOND EDITION NEEDED NOW?

The 1980s were an extremely turbulent time for America's not-for-profits. During the Reagan Administration years of 1981 to 1989, the vast majority of not-for-profits—those that depend on government funding for the majority of their incomes—had their perspective on life radically changed. No longer could these organizations depend on government (read: taxpayer) largesse to cover their expenses, nor would regular cost of living adjustments (COLAs) solve their problems. No, not-for-profits would have to learn to make do as more independent, more businesslike, entities. Wouldn't they?

Those of us in the field thought so. In many organizations, things did change. New businesses sprang up, inside or outside the traditional organization's array of services. Educational opportunities for not-for-profit staff slowly became available across the country throughout the decade, not only at the continuing education and seminar level, but as graduate degrees in many top-notch educational institutions. More and more staffs sought and received the one type of course work that they had previously never had access to: basic, as well as advanced, management training.

Unfortunately, many organizations continued to do business as usual. After a brief foray into a new idea or service, they returned to their traditional sources of funding, squeezed more work out of their staffs, tried to serve the avalanche of new people needing help. (In the human service not-for-profit, this higher need for service—from homelessness to public health to literacy—was another result of the Reagan years.) They continued to act like charities rather than not-for-profit businesses. Government, foundations, and United Ways for the most part only exacerbated the problems by emphasizing cost controls over strategic planning and marketing, and fund raising over entrepreneurship—two essential components of an excellent organization-for-profit or not-for-profit.

The 1990s have brought some needed change and some new challenges. Hundreds of colleges and universities now have both undergraduate and graduate levels. Management support organizations sprang up in many states and metropolitan areas, ready to help not-for-profits run their organization more efficiently and effectively. Some funders began to move toward fee-for-service contracting rather than grants. But there were also new challenges. Reimbursement structures based on the managed care model took hold in a wide variety of shapes at the federal and state level, requiring measurement of outcomes rather than process for the first times. After decades of punishing "duplication of service," some funders started to worry about costs to such an extent that social service and educational organizations nationwide began a movement to merge. Competition for dollars, for good staff, for good volunteers, and for people to serve became much more intense.

As a result, there is a pressing need for a new way of thinking regarding not-for-profit management. This book is intended to help you put an end to the old way of doing things, to help you make the transition from an administrator of a charity to a mission-based manager. I know, from consulting and training thousands of not-for-profit staff and boards since 1982, that the organizations that *are* succeeding in meeting the needs of their clientele, the organizations that *are* financially stable, the organizations that *will* meet the challenges of the future have the characteristics discussed in later chapters. I also firmly believe that if your organization has those characteristics, or acquires them, *and consistently works to improve them,* that you will succeed in serving the people that are depending on you. Unfortunately, too many not-for-profit managers, not-for-profit board members, and not-for-profit funders are still stuck in the 1970s. And they are getting further behind every day.

Mission-based management is good management. It is more than stewardship, a term that has become widely used in the not-for-profit field in recent years. It is a philosophy that says "I will use all the best tools at my disposal to help my organization excel in the pursuit of its mission. The mission is the reason that we are here, but that is no excuse for sloppy or slipshod management. We would never tolerate poor quality in services. We won't tolerate poor quality in management either."

C. MISSION-BASED MANAGEMENT, SECOND EDITION

You already know that much has changed since the first edition of *Mission-Based Management* in 1994. The format for all of the *Mission-Based Management* series books has evolved as well. There are now more features in the chapters than before that should give you, the reader, more value for your time. The book is designed to be used as a guide and as a reference for you to return to over and over. I know that your time is limited and that you will be tempted to jump right to the parts that you are most interested in, perhaps Developing A Bias For Marketing (Chapter 9) or Financial Empowerment (Chapter 10). To the extent possible, I urge you to read the book from front to back. The chapters are in the order presented for a reason: They build upon one another. Issues raised in the early chapters are discussed further in later ones; problems surfaced in one sometimes reappear in another. To get the most from the book, read it in the order that it is printed.

Because much of what I talk about in the remainder of the book is based on teamwork, and bringing in lots of staff, board, and outside experts to help, I suggest that you work through this book as a team effort. Have a small group of senior managers, middle managers, and direct service staff read a few chapters and then get together to discuss their application in your organization. Ask the group: "Is what is presented appropriate for our organization? If so, what do we need to do to facilitate any needed changes? If it is not appropriate, why not? Are we doing the best we can in this area? How can we be better?" Use the lists of questions that I have included at the end of each chapter to start these discussions. By reading the book as a team, and by reading it at the same time, you will get a more complete, more organization-wide use of the book, and the benefits of the book will be applied to your organization sooner.

Now, let's turn to the format of the book. By giving you an overview of both the format and sequence, as well as a brief peek at the benefits that you will get from each chapter, I hope that you will get more from our time together.

1. THE FORMAT

Each chapter starts with an **OVERVIEW**, intended to give you a brief summary of what the chapter will hold. The body of the text comes next, and I try, as much as possible, to give you illustrations and ideas for immediate use. These illustrations and ideas are highlighted by the terms "❏ **FOR EXAMPLE**" and "☞ **HANDS-ON**," respectively. Look for them in nearly every chapter. Near the end of the chapter is a **RECAP**, which is a brief review of the points that have been covered in the chapter, to allow you to draw all of the material together in your mind. There is also a list of **Questions for Discussion**, which are intended to stimulate group conversations with your staff and volunteers about ways to best use the ideas included in the book.

2. THE CONTENT

The book is broken down into what I call context-setting chapters, working chapters, and the final chapter, which is a call to action for the funders of not-for-profits. Let's look at each chapter briefly.

1. Introduction

   - This is the chapter you are reading now. It includes a look at three core philosophies, who the book is written for, how the book is designed, and how to get the most from reading it.

Context-Setting Chapters

2. Where We Were, Where We Are, Where We're Going

   - A brief history of the not-for-profit world, an examination of the relationship between not-for-profits and their funders, and an updated prediction of the not-for-profit world for the next 10 years.

3. What Works: The Characteristics of a Successful Not-for-Profit

   - An updated list of the nine things that a not-for-profit needs to continue to do its mission well in the twenty-first century.

Working Chapters

4. The Mission Is the Reason

   - How to get the most benefit from the reason that not-for-profits exist. For many, the mission is an underutilized resource. A discussion on updating and then using a motivational mission statement.

5. A Businesslike Board of Directors

   - What an effective board is, and what the board's and the staff's respective roles are. Reducing board liability and recruiting and retaining a board will be covered as well.

6. Managing Your People

   - A new approach to management that succeeds in today's high-speed, information-driven environment, also including better communications, evaluations, and rewards.

7. The Wired Not-for-Profit

   - How to use technology to better manage, inform, market, empower, and compete in today's wired environment.

RECAP

In this chapter we've covered the key philosophies that are the basis for the book and why I think the book is needed. We've also taken the first look at the contents of the book and how it is set up, so that you can make the most use of it to benefit your organization and the people that you serve.

I know that you have a tough and challenging job. As a leader of a not-for-profit, you have to concern yourself with many differing and conflicting needs and demands, those of your funders, your clientele, your board, staff, community, banker, and peers. You need to ensure that your organization is pursuing its mission with zeal, that it meets the changing needs of the community that you serve, and that you have enough money to make ends meet.

The tools to help you do those things are in the following pages. Good reading and good luck!

2

Where We Were, Where We Are, Where We're Going

OVERVIEW

Before we start our journey together, it is important to understand how we got here, and for you to read my vision for the next 10 years. Without those two pieces of context, it will be harder for you to grasp my ideas for what your organization can become and can accomplish.

In this chapter, we will review how not-for-profits in this country came to where they are today, and we will examine the three rules that funders use when they think of you and your organization. We'll then turn to the future and review my seven predictions for trends that will profoundly affect you, your organization, and its ability to perform its mission in the twenty-first century.

A. HOW WE GOT HERE

The United States, more than any other nation in the world, is blessed with a volunteer spirit of helping others. In many developed countries, volunteering or charitable giving (other than to the church) is essentially unheard of. My personal experience with the difference in cultures began early on. My mother is Danish by birth and emigrated to the United States as an infant. There were (and remain) many relatives in Denmark and, during my childhood, many of those relatives came to visit us, often staying at our home.

Often in those years, my parents would need to leave to attend one of the board meetings of the many organizations that they served. (My parents were the original incorporators and first officers of what is arguably the first Association for Retarded Citizens [ARC] in the country in 1951, and served on numerous other not-for-profit boards over the succeeding 25 years.) When the reason for my parents' absence was explained, it was almost always greeted with puzzled expressions and questions from our Danish guests such as, "Why would you *give* your time away?" or "Doesn't the government take care of that for you?", to which my parents would reply, "Here, we have a tradition of trying to help each other."

Whether it sprang from a frontier necessity to help and be helped, from basic Judeo-Christian values, or just from our national economic abundance, Americans have developed a vast network of charitable not-for-profit organizations that assist the poor, rehabilitate the injured, educate the young and old, enrich our senses and sensibilities by providing access to the arts, and fulfill our spiritual needs.

From the beginning of this century until the onset of Lyndon Johnson's "War on Poverty," most of the funding for these organizations came from locally donated funds, raised in the community in which the organization provided services. A few large foundations of national scope such as Ford and Rockefeller provided special projects assistance, but mostly, the not-for-profit community made do with what its local community gave it.

Then, in the sixties, all that changed. Government, particularly at the federal level, began to provide funding, first in the form of grants, and later in the form of "purchase of service" contracts to thousands of locally based, private not-for-profits. The feds, and later the state, county, and local governments, bought such diverse services as preventive health care; mental health screenings; residential community care for the developmentally disabled; breakfasts and lunches for school children; housing for the poor; art for the rich; economic development for minorities; books for libraries; research on a broad array of social, medical, and scientific issues; and specialized transportation throughout the nation.

With this cascade of funding—the good news—came an avalanche of red tape, bureaucracy, fast growth, reduced local control, and a seemingly endless series of priority changes and reversals—the bad news. This period (primarily 1964–1981) also saw the enormous growth in the sheer number of 501(c)(3)s (many created *specifically* to tap funds authorized in a particular piece of federal legislation) and the concomitant development of a huge cadre of vested interests embodied in the emergence of large professional staffs (within the not-for-profits), rapidly growing trade associations, and, perhaps most importantly, a steep rise in the number of government employees whose sole job it was to fund, regulate, and audit these organizations.

This "rise of the staffs," at both the service provider level and within the governments that increasingly were the service provider's single biggest—and sometimes *only*—customer, led to the development of a set of philosophies of funding and oversight that were incredibly damaging to the not-for-profits at the time and are still hampering all of us today. The basic tenets of these philosophies are as follows:

- *FIRST: What we say goes.* While being a logical assumption from the point of view of a major (often the only) customer, this tenet often degenerated into the feeling of "Whatever the staff at the Department of XYZ decides is needed in YourTown, is what we'll fund, and if you don't need it or if you need something else, well, tough." This attitude, of course, flew directly in the face of time-tested marketing theories of *asking* customers (in this case, the people that were ultimately receiving services) what they wanted. Additionally, this philosophy was in direct conflict with reality: No single broad national policy could possibly take into account all of the local variety and uniqueness that shows up in 50 states and 100,000 municipalities. By regularly not recognizing that different communities have different needs, policies and regulations that flowed from this philosophy were and remain doomed from the start.

  But the sheer momentum of dollars flowing from the state and federal capitals spoke louder than the voices of the service recipients. So, organizations acquiesced, services were often funded that people neither wanted nor needed and, when the first budget of the Reagan years came along, these programs were tough to defend against cuts.

- *SECOND: You can't do "well" doing "good."* This tenet is based on the terribly outdated but still overwhelmingly accepted philosophy that not-for-profits must virtually take a vow of poverty in order to not appear to be stealing from those to whom they are providing service. This idea also, of course, nicely justifies minimal funding on the part of the main funders, an abundance of auditing and (in my view) unnecessary oversight, and a policy of "use it or lose it," probably the most shortsighted social policy of our generation.

For those of you not familiar with "use it or lose it," it goes like this: If you negotiate a contract or grant amount for service with a funder—say a state—you get to use what is in the grant during the term of the grant period, usually a fiscal year. You may or may not be able to move funds from one budget line to the next depending on how nice your funder is, but by the end of the year, if you have saved funds (or spent less than expected, through excellent management, hunting for discounts on purchases, etc.), you lose the savings because you can't keep what you didn't spend. Further, if you bring in additional income (from donations, earnings, etc.), it may reduce your income dollar for dollar.

What's the incentive here? To save money? Certainly not. Saving bucks is work, and if your organization can't keep what you save, why go through the effort? To earn more outside income? No, that's more work, and if the money is just going to be taken away, why take the risk? Does this encourage unnecessary spending at the service level? Certainly, and everyone knows it. Why does it continue? Because the feds and the states are not willing to let not-for-profits keep too much money, keep what they earn, or have many, if any, net assets. I call this inane policy "poverty-chic," and it has been beaten into all of our heads for so long that most of us believe it. Funders do, the United Way does, staffs and boards do, and the public in general certainly does. How many times have you been questioned about the purchase of "nice" furniture, or tried to rationalize raising salaries, or not bought a piece of computer equipment because it *wouldn't look right*? I have, and I work with hundreds of not-for-profits who do regularly.

Has poverty-chic saved money? In the short term, certainly. But it has also led in the long term to poorly trained staffs, high staff turnover, a pitiful condition of the national not-for-profit physical plant (usually rented instead of owned), a grievous hole in our technological readiness, and essentially no nonfixed assets with which to address community problems without the funders' further assistance.

The bottom line is that poverty-chic has led to many not-for-profits' becoming—and remaining—virtual indentured servants of their funders at the same time that the funders are urging the not-for-profits to become more independent and self-sufficient. "Use it or lose it" is one way. Under funding or matching requirements—not paying for the full cost of service—is another. Encouraging monopolies is a third. By being encouraged and forced to be poor, agencies think poor and stay poor. They are underfunded so they must fight fires today to stay alive rather than plan ahead for the future: an action that can save money and provide better service. They make do with old, beat-up, inefficient equipment and buildings, losing money on repairs and the inefficiencies. They are never allowed to "have unseemly" fund balances (either by public pressure or regulation) so they can never grow. They have no working capital—without further assistance from the funders.

❑ **FOR EXAMPLE:** Many United Way agencies in this country still have a policy of funding only programs that are in deficit; if you don't have a deficit, you don't get funded. Does anyone seriously think that this encourages agencies to be self-sufficient or to generate enough funds to break even? *Of course it doesn't!* Why would an agency charge more to clients, raise rates elsewhere, or do anything to risk its United Way "free" money? To the surprise of no one, they don't; they simply stay in a deficit condition so that the funding will continue. The United Way contends that it must assure that funds go to the most needy programs, but this policy just perpetuates the problem.

- *THIRD: What is yours is ours.* This is perhaps my favorite, because it underscores so much of what primary government funders really must feel: that not-for-profits that receive their funds are their property. In my work, I see this regularly with auditors of state funds (which may account for, say, 60% of an organization's budget) feeling that they must examine *every* transaction of the organization, evaluate *all* of the assets, look into *all* of the contracts, probe *all* the vendor relationships, even if some or most of those assets and contracts and vendors have nothing to do with the specific programs that the state auditor's department funds. The attitude seems to be that *"because we give you money, we have the right to strip you naked and judge you at our whim."*

This attitude, while not only being insulting, forgets the fact that the not-for-profit is actually *selling* the government agency or foundation a service, and that the payment for this service should not come attached to an unrestricted license to snoop and poke around at will. Remember this: As a for-profit, I contract with many state governments, and they don't audit *me*. Why should they then take your organization apart for inspection? Does being a not-for-profit make you automatically exempt from the constitutional protection from unreasonable search and seizure? I think not.

The most incredible aspect of this attitude is that we all put up with it so willingly. It is a constant amazement to me that there has not been a general revolt against the level of scrutiny, oversight, and general arrogance of the funding sources. How can this have been allowed to evolve? How can the good, intelligent, and well-intentioned people at the local agency level have become so subservient, while the good, intelligent, well-intentioned people at the state and federal level developed policies that, in effect, contradict nearly all of their stated intentions, doing much more harm than good? There are two answers—one psychological and one political.

FIRST: THE PSYCHOLOGICAL ANSWER

The more I think about the relationship between not-for-profits and their funders, the more curious it gets. Look at it this way; how many for-profit companies regularly disparage their best customers? Very few, but how often do you and your peers gripe about the state/feds/foundations at association meetings? Every time you are together, right? I thought so.

Moreover, when was the last time that you went to your state/federal/foundation project officer and asked, "How can we make your job easier and do what you want done better and faster?" Never? Again, I thought so. But understand that in the for-profit world, market-driven companies ask those questions of *all* of their customers, especially the big ones, *all* of the time. They are constantly looking for ways to do things better, faster, easier, and cheaper for their customers. (If you don't think that your funders are your customers, think again. We'll cover this in great detail in chapter 9.)

Over the years, I have developed an analogy of the relationship between not-for-profits and their primary funders that I think (unfortunately) is very apt. It goes like this:

In their relationships with each other, not-for-profits and their primary funders (government or foundations) take on the roles and attitudes of eternal adolescents and parents. Now, this is not to disparage either group, as both have contributed to the situation, but imagine how you would feel as either a teenager or the parent of a teenager if you were going to be stuck in that often frustrating and antagonistic relationship forever?

In this relationship, the not-for-profits (filling the role of the teens) audibly seek more independence, question the wisdom of the funders (who act the parents' part), ask to be left alone (to do their own thing), and generally resent the house rules, but when the car breaks down or when something else goes wrong, they always come to the parent for help/money.

For their part, the funders/"parents" audibly encourage the independence, tolerate the dissension and independence with irritation but benevolence (knowing that they know better) and urge the not-for-profit/"teens" to try new things ("but nothing too new"), experiment ("but not too far out")—but ultimately to always be home by midnight, submit all friends for inspection, and be prepared for a search of your room at any time. House rules.

I'm sure you have seen this relationship and probably been a part of it. Once you recognize the relationship for what it is, it is fairly simple to see how it evolved: People who are giving away the money (particularly those who work for the public) want to control how it is spent. Most not-for-profits and their staff and board really only want to be left alone to do what they do best: service. Neither group really can envision true independence from the other. And no tradition, law, or social norm makes a not-for-profit independent on its twenty-first birthday. Thus, it is easier to grudgingly accept the status quo than to really break apart.

This is *crazy,* and I've been part of it at both a board and staff level. No wonder both sides are so frustrated! And yet, I see it continue over and over and over, even when both sides are aware and acknowledge the problems inherent in not allowing the not-for-profits to grow up and leave home. After all, many not-for-profits *are* over 21.

SECOND: THE POLITICAL ANSWER

With the media excited about any and all "scandals" that they can find, government is reduced to spending millions of dollars to provide oversight to prevent hundreds or thousands of dollars from being misspent. And this is *all* our fault. We don't demand that the media print the whole story. We don't demand a cost–benefit analysis of the fraud prevention section of an agency. We just listen to the story that says "Welfare Mom Cheats Agency of $40,000" and get all worked up about how poorly the agency is run and what a bunch of cheats those welfare moms are. The rest of the story? The mom was one of 110,000 funded, of whom 109,999 *didn't cheat*. The $40,000 was out of $198 million of funding, or less than *2/100ths of one percent!* And then, no one ever asks how much the agency spent to find and recover that $40,000. Given the norm, probably about $200,000. Why do we allow this to happen? Because no government agency official wants to be seen as advocating a lax policy that could allow anyone at all to cheat, and, in reality the $40,000 is a *lot* of money to most voters—no matter that it is an infinitesimal percentage of the total. So we let it go, and waste a whole lot of money chasing a very little.

Thus, not-for-profits spend a great deal of their time and money being accountable for the real or imagined sins of others in order to cover the derrieres of the finders. Because there is a political liability for the funders if the public perceives that even $1 is misspent, the funders want to control *everything*.

These three rules have done more harm than all the budget cuts not-for-profits have endured since 1981. They have prevented stability, empowerment, and dignity in our nation's not-for-profits and steadily eroded our confidence in our ability to manage our own affairs.

❏ **FOR EXAMPLE:** To demonstrate this evolution (and its downfall), I'll use as an example a group of not-for-profits that was created solely to respond to a succession of federal laws in the 1960s and 1970s, who influenced health care policy for a while and faded away with the end of federal largesse in the 1980s: health planning agencies. (The reader should note that I was integrally involved in health planning from 1974 through 1982 as a volunteer, staffer, and executive director, and thus have a somewhat biased view of what happened.)

Most of you will never have heard of HSAs (health systems agencies) or their predecessors, CHPs (comprehensive health planning agencies), but both were funded primarily with federal funds and grew out of federal concern about rising health care costs, duplication of health care services, and a need to control both. CHPs that were funded from 1968 through 1974 were to enable consumer participation in health policy. In over 200 geographic health planning areas of the country, CHPs were to develop health care plans and have limited regulatory authority over hospital and nursing home expansion. HSAs (1974–1984) were the second generation of such agencies, with more money, expanded staffs, a mandate for "consumer" majorities on all boards and committees, and enhanced regulatory powers. The result of this program was over 200 new not-for-profits with anywhere from 4 to 200 staff each, over 100,000 volunteers on boards and committees and an entire federal and state bureaucracy (I have heard numbers in excess of 350 federal staff when all the regional people were accounted for) just to keep tabs on the locals.

Why? To fulfill the federally designed mandates of cost containment, increased access to care, and consumer empowerment. Did it work? No, and in large part because of the three rules: "What we say goes" turned out to be the most deadly. The federal government decided in just one of many broad, national regulations that there should be no more than 6.1 medical surgical hospital beds per 1,000 population. As a result, HSAs were to turn down applications from hospitals for construction that exceeded that amount, and the funding of the HSAs was in part contingent on achieving that goal. This policy allowed for some local variance, but it had to be rigorously justified and never adequately took into account important issues such as patient preference, rural accessibility, and relative quality of hospitals. Since these issues are commonsense ones, even to nonprofessionals, the regulation was derided, resented, and disliked by almost all of the citizen volunteers upon whose service the entire system depended.

"What is yours is ours" and "You can't do well doing good" also had their own impact: HSAs could not fund raise without penalty—whatever money they raised was reduced from the next year's budget allotment. They could not keep assets—they were really the federal government's although HSAs were "independent." The end of the HSAs? Because the federal government funded the program, but never really made it a local one, when David Stockman and President Reagan attacked the program and tried to zero out its budget, even local volunteers were hesitant to come to its defense. The HSAs were dead in the water.

This program cost millions upon millions of dollars, and had good people at the volunteer, board, and staff level committed to its success, but it went aground on the shoals of too much distrust of local control, an overzealous accounting mechanism, and a high resistance to change.

As long as we don't demand some common sense in government, we will have to live with the ludicrous level of oversight that reduces all regulations to catching the 3% of us who are crooks and/or idiots and punishing the 97% who are honest and have a brain cell or two. In this environment, you can't blame the state or federal employees who are caught in the oversight squeeze; they have to assume guilt until innocence is proven, and thus they are never going to fully trust us.

Now, how can we go about breaking both you and your funders out of this relational purgatory? We must, you know, if we are to bring the industry into the twenty-first century in some sort of reasonably effective shape. That's really what the rest of the book is about. Hopefully, by giving you some idea of the world you will be working in, and by increasing your skill base, giving you tools, and showing you how other agencies have broken free of the cycle of codependence (and that is exactly what it is), you'll be better able to do it yourself. Let's start with an examination of the environment you'll be working in.

B. WHAT THE NEXT TEN YEARS WILL BRING

Given the pace of change that continues to ramp up at what is now known as e-speed, predictions a decade out are fraught with danger. No matter where we live, or how large or small our organization is, we've become part of a global economy, and what happens on the far side of the world this morning can affect us in very real ways later today, not in weeks, months, or years, as in the past. What follows is a set of trends that will affect you, and that you, as a mission-based manager, should consider and prepare for.

1. GOVERNMENT IS LESS IMPORTANT, LESS FLEXIBLE, AND LESS LIKELY TO BAIL YOU OUT

Don't believe all the hype you hear about budget surpluses. It is political voodoo. The most optimistic projections don't show a real surplus in the federal operating budget (as opposed to Social Security) until fiscal year 2004, and then there is the small issue of how to pay down the multi-trillion-dollar debt we've managed to accumulate, mostly in the past 20 years. When you combine this fact with the popular phobia that says new taxes make it arithmetically impossible to have either major new domestic initiatives or significant increases in spending, you find that government funding at best will just keep up with the rate of inflation. So, don't bet the farm that the feds, or the states, even those flush with current cash, are going to bequeath it to your organization.

You should also be aware of three important points regarding this prediction. The first is that even though the *overall* rate of funding will remain constant at best, the level of support for the specific programs that your organization provides will vary greatly depending on the political winds. For example, the largest percentage increase in social funding in the past 10 years from the feds has been in areas that prevent or treat substance abuse—in response to the national movement toward semitemperance. Another example is funding for AIDS research, prevention, diagnosis, and treatment, which have flowed to entities as widely varied as health departments, hospitals, child welfare departments, drug centers, medical schools, and arts organizations. Now that AIDS is seen by the public and Congress (falsely) as under control, those funds are dwindling. Our current fundee of choice is schools and crime prevention, which won't last either. If your area of service is in vogue, you will prosper; if not, you may be hurt even more deeply.

The second point is that, although the rate of funding for your organization may stay constant, if you are like the majority of your peers, that rate of payment is probably already woefully short of meeting the needs in your community, and may not even be paying your full cost of service. Thus, the fact that your funding may (at best) stay steady should not be a great deal of comfort. You and your organization will have to look to new sources of income to meet the increasing needs of your community for services. Moreover, if your organization, particularly those in human service or education, gets paid on a fee-for-service basis, wherein you bill the city, county, state, or federal government for services *after* those services are provided, be prepared to be able to come up with more "working capital," the money that you need to pay the bills between the time you provide a service and you get paid. Why? Because you will be providing more such services, and thus floating more receivables, and the government agencies will be paying you later. (One high official of a state welfare agency told me recently, "We postpone payment one day, just *one* day, and we "save" $22 million." That's real money, even in today's inflated environment.)

The third point is related to the second, and it has to do with the need to go outside and look for new sources of funds. The traditional place that not-for-profits do that is in fund raising and foundation applications. These have become much, much more competitive in the past few years as governmental resources stayed static in the face of growing demand. Be prepared to improve your fund-raising and grant-writing skills dramatically or fall by the wayside.

2. THE "BOOMERS" HIT 60

This is both good news and bad news, and it is not a prediction, but a simple fact. Look at it this way—the largest single age cohort in American history (also the best educated, most wealthy, and latest to have children) will be in the middle of middle age. Some of the boomers, depending on national economic conditions, will begin to retire, and certainly they will have more time on their hands as their children leave home. Will this have an impact on people demanding your services? Perhaps, but it certainly will be a huge pool of potential board members and volunteers with time and expertise to donate, and who will leave significant assets in their estates. Most readers will have heard about this huge potential transfer of wealth, but there is also a growing transfer of experience going on. It manifests itself in an unprecedented middle-age career change that is going on within the boomers. More and more of them (actually us, I confess) are either being forced to reconsider where we are because of downsizing or forced early retirement, or are ruminating on our lost youth and idealism, both with the result that huge numbers of boomers are moving from one job to another—and many are moving to the not-for-profit sector, to "do something worthwhile." Think about all that talent, experience, and business skill out there that may be interested in taking a lower-paying job just to feel that they are making a contribution for a change.

On the bad news side, we boomers will suck up more and more government, pension, and health care resources as we age. Whatever entitlements are out there, we'll want, demand, and collectively stamp our self-centered little feet for. This will inevitably leave less government funds for the purchase of services from not-for-profits, which is a nice segue to our next issue.

3. MORE DEMAND FOR SERVICES, EVEN IN A STRONG ECONOMY

The volume of demand will grow irrevocably, irreversibly, and probably faster than you anticipate, in almost every area of not-for-profit service. If you are in education, the national concern with the decay in our educational structure will lead to further privatization, vouchers, and standardized testing, to say nothing of increased demand for classrooms from the demographic phenomena of the boom-echo kids, or the fact that special education services now consume 25% of public education dollars. If you run a religious organization, the continuing return to the church will lead to increased need for services and facilities, as well as increases in competition for dollars, as many reputable ministries vie for the same funding sources. In the arts, a better educated public will want more theater, music, and displays of fine arts nearer and more accessible to them. If you provide a social service, whether to youth, seniors, the homeless, or the mentally or physically disabled, the need for your services will grow faster than the population as a whole.

The reasons for the increase in demand outstripping simple demographic growth are multiple. First, we as a society have turned to not-for-profits increasingly for the past 30 years, and we are used to seeking help there. Second, one of the legacies of the Reagan years is a chronic underfunding of social services, particularly low-income housing and job creation assistance that has led to the large number of chronic homeless and "underclass" citizens who are at significantly higher risk to need services that you provide than the population as a whole. Thus, you should not simply use census projections to predict the need for your services. Even in our (currently) wonderful economy, the disparity between the haves and the have-nots continues to grow. If you are in any field within the not-for-profit sector, this fact should unsettle you and factor into your predictions of demand.

Finally, there is one other key issue to ponder here. Not only is raw demand (the number of people presenting themselves for services) going to continue to climb, but the cost of serving each of those people will also rise, at the same time that income will stay basically static. People are showing up with many, many more needs than ever before, and to adjust to these needs costs money. As a human services administrator told me in February 2000, "The people we see are broken in so many more ways, and all at once. They come with layer upon layer of problems, and digging down through all those layers is an imposing, and expensive task.

4. A MORE COMPETITIVE ENVIRONMENT

This is the biggest single change that you will see during the rest of your career, whether you are 20 or 60. This competition, which began in the early 1990s, is now showing up in everything you do. You are, or will be, competing for clients, students, patrons, or parishioners; for funding from traditional sources and for funding from new sources; for donations; for United Way dollars; for visibility; for donated services such as air time and advertising; for volunteers and for staff.

The most disruptive, nerve-wracking, and positive change will be in the area of competing for people to serve. In the past decade, counties, states, and even the federal government have brought more and more programs into the competitive fold. They did this because of the first two trends listed above: limited funds and nearly unlimited demand for services, many of which are entitlements. Caught on the horns of a fiscal dilemma, the solution many purchasers of service have sought is anathema to our entire sector: capitalism. By this I mean putting agencies, many for the very first time, into the risk/reward cycle that is the engine that runs our economy. This, of course, has challenged the monopoly that you once enjoyed. "Monopoly!?" Absolutely. How many times when asking for funding have you heard the question, "Does this program duplicate anything already serving the same constituency?" Lots, I'm sure. The reason: Funders did not want to encourage "duplicate" funding (i.e., competition). Imagine the same scene with your city council approving only one fast food restaurant, or one grocery store in town—to avoid duplication. They would be run out of office for obstructing commerce, interfering with competition, and in general for being too regulatory. But in the not-for-profit arena this has been considered appropriate.

No more. Funders are looking for the best productivity, the most mission for the money. Volunteers are looking to spend their time wisely. Quality staff want to work with organizations that are financially viable as well as state of the art in terms of service. Businesses that donate services want to associate with top-caliber organizations, not ones that will have their work, finances, or reputation show up in the scandal sheets.

And, here is the good news from the perspective of funder, donor, citizen/taxpayer, and service recipient: This works, and works well. Not perfectly, not immediately, but the result is better services and lower costs. The bad news: From the perspective of the not-for-profit manager, this is hell on wheels. We, as a sector, are not ready for this. And getting ready on the fly is scary and expensive. Much of what is in the remainder of this book is intended to help you get ready.

5. TECH, TECH, AND MORE TECH

This is not news, but even in our e-times, the not-for-profit sector still lags far behind the rest of the economy in using the available technology—in part because the sector is so dominated by social service/educational types, as opposed to techies, and in part because many of our funding sources (and our boards) look at computers as either toys or luxuries. But your field, like any other, needs to adapt, and the costs of that adaptation are coming down every day. Remember that it was only in the 1980s that most of us sat down at our first computer and began playing with a rudimentary spreadsheet or accounting program or word processor. User-friendliness of computers and the availability of off-the-shelf software have both increased dramatically, at the same time that the price of computers has dropped by 90% or more in the past five years. The benefits of using the technology are evident everywhere, from wireless phones to pagers, to e-mail, to doing business on the Web. The question is: Will you and your organization continue to make use of technology to provide the most services for the least dollars? Can you afford not to?

Put simply, rapidly advancing technology is a fact of life, it is economical, and it can help. The not-for-profits that survive into the twenty-first century will use that technology to its fullest to further their mission. Those with technology phobia will be left behind.

6. MORE ACCOUNTABILITY

This is a good thing if it is handled in an atmosphere of making sure that your organization is accountable for what you do, how you do it, and how much you spend—but it can easily turn into a witch-hunt (see my earlier discussion of the basic tenets of funders). It can result in a funder who buys a small amount of services from you, demanding to know all about everything you do, own, think, and plan.

But we have to live with the contracts we sign. Accountability and the seemingly never-ending amounts of paperwork that accompany it will continue to increase, as long as the press and the public wonder about us. Accountability is a fact of life and should be seen as a cost of doing business. The oversight may be frustrating and expensive, but we need to spend less time whining about it and more time figuring out how to use technology to make being accountable easier and less costly.

Also remember that accountability and competition go hand in hand. The funders (who have choices of where to send their money) want more accountability. If you can't do outcome measures in the current environment, you may not get much repeat funding. Better use of technology can help you be accountable more efficiently and effectively, but you have to be accountable, and be resigned to it if not happy about it.

So there are six areas of change you will need to pay attention to, and most likely, accommodate to in the next decade. The remainder of this book will try to give you the tools, techniques, and perspectives to help your organization become more mission-capable and more mission-productive.

RECAP

In this chapter, we have reviewed how not-for-profits came to where they are today, how your funders really think of you, and the six trends that I believe you are going to have to accommodate to stay viable over the next 10 years. These trends are:

1. Government is less important, less flexible, and less likely to bail you out.

2. The "boomers" hit 60.
3. More demand for services, even in a strong economy.
4. A more competitive environment.
5. Tech, tech, and more tech.
6. More accountability.

With these predictions in mind, the next question is: How do we adapt and accommodate to these conditions? Even more difficult is the answer to the next question: How do we adapt and accommodate to conditions that may exist in five years that no one can even foresee today? How do we stay close to our mission, stay solvent, stay flexible, and stay sane—all at the same time? I'm not sure that all of those things are possible, particularly the part about retaining your sanity, but the next few chapters will detail my observations about the key characteristics of the best, most flexible, and yet most focused not-for-profits in the country. By trying to emulate their successes and integrate their strengths with yours, your organization can do much to reach the next century in excellent shape.

3

What Works:
The Characteristics of a
Successful Not-for-Profit

OVERVIEW

This chapter will, in effect, preview the remainder of the book. First, we will turn from the individual to the organization, and I will lay out for you the nine updated characteristics of success that will overcome the problems and environmental changes that we reviewed in Chapter 2. Each of the chapters that follow will detail the ways to attain these characteristics in detail. Then I'll define what I contend are the key characteristics of a mission-based manager. There are four different ways that these stewards show their true colors, and we will go over each. By the end of this brief chapter, you will have a good idea of what is in store for you, and the standards to which I will be holding you and your organization.

A. THE NINE CHARACTERISTICS OF A MISSION-BASED ORGANIZATION

All successful organizations share common characteristics. Since 1982, I have had the opportunity to train thousands and consult for hundreds of not-for-profits. These consultations often included management reviews, strategic planning, and new business development. In the course of this work, I often had the opportunity to talk to staff, board, community members, and the people that the organization served in depth. As a result, I have had the good fortune to see not only work for many, many consistently excellent not-for-profits, but also to talk about their strengths and weaknesses with the people that are most important to their success. It is an examination of those strengths, how they work and how they can work, for you and your organization that make up the rest of this book.

What is striking in these consistently successful organizations is the similarity of the key characteristics of what they are and how they do their job. Over and over, I see the same core foundations on which the organization functions. It doesn't matter whether the not-for-profit is a church, a school, a museum, a hospital, a trade association, or a rehabilitation facility—these key characteristics shine through.

I have attempted to distill these key characteristics into the nine below. Any such distillation is fraught with a certain amount of peril: I may group things in ways that don't fit your organization the best; I may not emphasize a particular item enough. I have tried to put the key components in a logical and workable form, breaking them not only into different segments, but separating them in such a way that I hope you can study each, apply the information to your organization, and then put all the pieces back together to make a cohesive whole.

These characteristics have been updated since the first edition of *Mission-Based Management*, and in the intervening years I have had hundreds of request to put the list of characteristics in priority order. As you will see, mission—which should always come first—is first. After that, I have done my best to order them, but at some peril to the reader. They are *all* important. They work together as a group, like the parts of a fine symphony. You cannot be a good social entrepreneur without planning or be well wired without financial empowerment. Ignore one or more parts and the whole is greatly diminished. Bring them all together and their synergy outstrips the sum of their individual contributions. So don't perseverate on the order. Just attack each one in turn, and try to achieve and maintain your mission-based status.

    1. *A viable mission.*   The first rule of not-for-profits is *mission, mission, and more mission.* A mission-based organization needs to follow its mission, and to do so it needs a mission that motivates, is understandable, supportable, up-to-date and needed. Without the mission, what's the point? Unfortunately, at too many not-for-profits, there is no point, because the mission has become secondary to survival. In Chapter 4 you will learn how to write and use an effective mission statement.

    2. *A businesslike board of directors.* Your organization needs a group of governing volunteers that know, understand, and pursue

the organization's mission, are connected to the community, stick to dealing at the policy level, and are the check and balance on the staff—and on the people who fund the organization. A board needs the information, experience, character, and support to know how to decide key issues quickly and effectively, and, in today's tough environment, they need to know when to say no to a good idea. In Chapter 5, I'll show you how to assess, recruit, and retain just such a board, one that will give you more outcome and policy guidance and less day-to-day manipulation than you thought possible.

3. *A strong, well-educated staff.* Ones who are advocates for the mission, who manage from the bottom up, and who are constantly trained and training. There is no investment more necessary or more neglected than staff education and training. Chapter 6 will show you the best way to treat, employ, manage, motivate, and retain your staff. You will also learn how to most effectively get staff much more integrally involved in the outcomes of your organization.

4. *Wired and technologically savvy.* Not-for-profits who use technology as a way to do more mission sooner, better, and less expensively. Far too many charitable organizations eschew tech as being too expensive, or too impersonal. You can't take that position any longer. E-life pervades every corner of our lives, and it also is changing the ways not-for-profits provide services, buy services, hire, manage, communicate, raise funds, and keep abreast of changes in the state of the art. In Chapter 7, I'll show you how to ride the wave of technology to the benefit of your organization.

5. *Social entrepreneurs.* Organizations that are willing to take risks to perform their mission; to try (and often fail) and try again; to look at markets and provide services to support their mission rather than create bureaucracies to continue past (and often outdated) practices. Chapter 8 will give you the best ideas on how to motivate your staff, board, and community to take prudent risks on behalf of your constituency. It will also show you how to assess your core competencies and match them with the wants of your target markets.

6. *A bias for marketing.* Organizations that understand that *everything* they do is marketing, and see every act, from service provision to how the phone is answered, as a marketing opportunity to pursue their mission. Our marketing discussion will be in Chapter 9, where you will learn who your markets really are, how to give those markets

what they want, and how to provide a marketing edge for everyone in your organization.

7. *Financially empowered.* Organizations that have diversified income, income from non-traditional sources, an endowment, and therefore, the ability to have an impact on their mission without waiting for help. "Sure," you say, "all of that would be nice if it dropped in my lap." Well, it doesn't happen on its own. These organizations make it happen. Chapter 10 will show you how to do it in your organization. We'll look at the characteristics of financial empowerment and how to apply them for you.

8. *A vision for where they are going.* This is so simple, yet so often ignored. A strategic plan, both the process and the document, is a key to success. Without a plan, the only way you get anywhere is by accident: Isn't what you do too important to be left up to chance? Of course it is, and Chapter 11 will show you why you need to have a plan, what kinds of plans there are, and will lay out a process for you to have a useable, meaningful plan.

9. *A tight set of controls.* These include personnel, finance, operations, quality control, and maintenance policies. Good controls free the organization to work on its mission rather than watching its back all the time. In Chapter 12, we'll look at 12 different types of policies and show you where most groups make mistakes, so you don't have to.

In each of the following chapters, we'll discuss the important parts of each of the nine characteristics noted above, and leave you with references for further study should you so desire.

B. WHAT IS A MISSION-BASED MANAGER?

If the outcome that I want your organization to have is to be a mission-based manager, you and your peers obviously should aspire to become mission-based managers. Such managers have four major skills that we will examine here. Balance, innovation, motivation, and communication are the crux of such individuals' tool chests. Let's look at each in a little more detail:

1. *Mission-based managers* balance *the needs of the community with the available resources of the organization.* Balance is such an

important skill. We need to balance our checkbook, our personal and business lives, our priorities with our resources. This has never been more true in not-for-profits than it is today. There are so many people in need, so many community priorities that cry out for attendance. They call to our hearts, and we, as people people, want to respond. But in any organization, even yours, there are only so many resources. Even if your organization won the lottery today, there would still be needs to meet when you got done spending all the money.

Mission-based managers understand that they need to balance pressing needs with available resources and not provide services that they cannot pay for. Does this mean that we accept what we have and don't seek more resources? Of course not. But *mission, mission and more mission* is only the first rule of not-for-profits. It's not the only rule—the second rule is *no money, no mission*. Balance, of money and mission, board and staff, supervision and staff freedom, is a theme and a challenge that you will see over and over in this book.

2. *Mission-based managers are innovative social entrepreneurs, taking reasonable risks on behalf of the people that the organization serves.* True leaders know that consistent innovation is the linchpin of consistent success, and even of continued survival. But innovation is always risky, and it requires an open mind to new ideas and an ability to not fall in love with the way you have always done things— even if you invented that traditional way. Put simply, a socially entrepreneurial organization must be led by social entrepreneurs, and that leadership must role-model the behaviors that they want from the rest of the organization. Organizational risk also always translates to some degree of personal risk: If you make too many bad risk decisions, you'll probably be out of a job. The problem is that if you don't make any risk-taking calls, everyone will lose their job and the mission won't get done. We'll talk a lot more about social entrepreneurism in Chapter 8.

3. *Mission-based managers lead the organization by example, and in so doing motivate their staff, their board, and their community.* Successful organizations have people who lead them through the good times and the bad, who keep them on track when there are lots of distractions, who are able to motivate the rest of the organiza- tion with their energy, their vision, and their example. Successful leaders know that they must lead from the front and walk the talk

first. In not-for-profits leaders are held to an even higher example than in for-profits. We are all on a pedestal, in the hot klieg lights regarding our behavior. Not-for-profit leaders must evidence the values of their organization in their behavior every day, or their staff, their donors, their volunteers, and their community will write them and their organization off. Look at it this way: If a for-profit chief executive officer (CEO) is accused of embezzlement, or sexual harassment, it is a small story on page 5 of your newspaper. And does the for-profit suffer in terms of business? Almost certainly not—people don't feel that management impropriety should affect their use of the organization. But if a not-for-profit CEO were accused of that same behavior, what would happen? Right. Page 1 story, fall-off in donations, community trust, volunteer time, and so on. Your actions as a mission-based manager have major repercussions. You need to lead by your values every day. People are watching, both inside and outside of the organization.

4. *Mission-based managers can communicate effectively to their staff, their board, the public, their funders, and the community at large.* There is no way to lead without being a good communicator, and a mission-based manager has to communicate in many ways every day. You have to tell your staff what you want them to do, inquire of your markets what they want, interact with your board, your funders, your community, all in ways that move your organization forward, not back. The key word here is *effectively,* and that means that the intended message gets to the intended audience. If the wrong message gets out, it means that the organization has taken a small (or huge) step backward. Communications is crucial, and we'll discuss it at length in Chapter 6.

So there are the characteristics of successful organizations and the skills you need to be a competent mission-based manager. As you look at information in the following chapters—information that expands on each of these nine core characteristics of not-for-profit success—ask yourself: How does my organization measure up? Do we *really* do all these things or only pay them lip service? How about me? Am I good at balancing things, or at motivation? As you continue through the remaining chapters, be brutally frank with yourself: This is not a time for self-illusion. That will only lead to ignoring real problems and deferring any needed changes.

RECAP

In this chapter, you have seen the nine characteristics you and your organization need to embrace, adopt and maintain. To recap, these nine are:

1. A viable mission
2. A businesslike board of directors
3. A strong, well-educated staff
4. Wired and technologically savvy
5. Social entrepreneurs
6. A bias for marketing
7. Financially empowered
8. A vision for where they are going
9. A tight set of controls

These nine characteristics, when achieved as a group, can improve your ability to do your mission, improve your organization's long-term viability, and assure the people you serve that you will be there to serve them for the long haul. They don't show up on their own, and they can't be developed overnight. Moreover, once you attain them all, only hard work and discipline will keep them in place.

Then we turned to the essential skills of the mission-based manager. I assume that in reading this book, you are trying to not only improve your organization, but also your own management style. I included four key skills, and we should look at them again:

1. Mission-based managers *balance* the needs of the community with the available resources of the organization.
2. Mission-based managers are *innovative* social entrepreneurs, taking reasonable risks on behalf of the people that the organization serves.
3. Mission-based managers lead the organization by example, and in so doing *motivate* their staff, their board, and their community.
4. Mission based managers can *communicate* effectively to their staff, their board, the public, their funders, and the community at large.

The skills are challenging, and are ones that we will work on throughout the book. The characteristics of success and the skills of the mission-based manager play off each other beautifully, reinforcing one another. So you need them both. In the remainder of this book I'll show you how to achieve and maintain both sets.

Questions for Discussion (Chapters 1–3)

1. How do our funders really view us? How do we know?
2. Do we act like a mission-based business? Specifically, how can we get better? Does our staff view us as a charity or as a mission-based business? What about our board? Our funders?
3. In Chapter 2, Peter makes a number of predictions about the next 10 years. Which apply to us and how?
4. How many of the nine characteristics Peter lists for success do we have here in our organization?
5. Of those that are not fully in place, which is the most important for us to develop?

4

The Mission Is the Reason

OVERVIEW

Let's be realistic: If you are a staff person of a not-for-profit, you are not in this for the money, nor for a low-stress, short-hour job. If you are a volunteer, you are not spending time with this not-for-profit so that you can miss time at home or at work, or avoid getting eight hours of sleep at night. You came and you stay because of the *mission*—what the organization *does*.

If that is true, why is the mission even an issue in this book? Why take up time and space on a topic that we all agree is vital? There are more reasons than you might imagine, and in this chapter we'll cover each of them and provide some examples and ideas for you to better utilize your mission as you move your organization ahead.

In the following pages, we'll first examine the need that you have for a mission statement and how to review and rewrite your mission statement to help you become the organization that you want to be, not merely continue to be the organization you were in the past. We'll then look at the ways that mission statements are misused, underutilized, or completely forgotten. Finally, we will discuss how to use your mission statement as a tool for policy, management, and marketing—in short, how to turn your organization into a mission-based one on a day-to-day basis.

A. THE MISSION STATEMENT IS YOUR LEGAL REASON FOR EXISTENCE

As noted above, the mission statement is not only the reason you work or volunteer for your organization, but it also has important legal implications for staff and board. If you do not perform your mission, the

IRS can take away your tax exempt status under section 501(c) of the Internal Revenue Code. If you bring in too much of your funds from unrelated business income (defined as "income that is derived from activities that do not importantly contribute to the mission of the organization"), you also stand a chance of losing your tax-exempt status, as well as bearing tax liability for any profits from such unrelated businesses.

Many not-for-profits are technically in violation of their mission statement and have unrelated business income that they don't even realize. Usually, this is due to having a prehistoric mission statement (see previous section). For example, if, in 1960 you were set up to provide a service in County A but now, as your community has grown, you provide services in Counties A, B, and C, and if your mission statement specifies only County A, you are technically getting unrelated business income from all of the activities that you perform and are reimbursed for in Counties B and C. The same issue arises for not-for-profits that were originally set up to provide only mental health services but now do substance abuse, were formed to help the African-American community but now assist people from all ethnic backgrounds, or were formed to help senior citizens but now find it useful to provide day care to the elderly *and* the very young. (*Note:* Unrelated business income is covered in detail in Chapter 12.)

All of this is to underscore the importance of having a mission that you know, you can live with, and that accurately portrays not only what your organization does now but what you want it to do in the three-to-five-year range of the future.

B. WRITING OR REWRITING YOUR MISSION STATEMENT

You all have a mission statement. It is in your articles of incorporation and the forms you submitted to the IRS to receive your tax-exempt status. It may also be restated in your bylaws. Every three years (at the same time that you will be writing your strategic plan, discussed in Chapter 10) you need to revisit your mission statement. You need to take the opportunity to get your staff and board input into what your mission should be. In most cases, it will be exactly the same as it is now, only you will have a renewed sense of its urgency as a result of the discussion. There are, of course, a number of steps that I suggest you take in reviewing your mission statement. These are:

1. FIND YOUR CURRENT MISSION STATEMENT

If you are like most of your peers, you may have more than one "mission statement." There may be different language in your bylaws, articles of incorporation, or applications for funding. Gather them all up and review them. See where there are differences and similarities. Take the best of all of them.

2. NOTE ANY SUBSTANTIVE CHANGES

Have you started to provide services in a new geographic area outside of any listed in your mission statement? Have you added services or a new kind of clientele? Make sure to add these to your statement, and make sure that the language you use is up to date.

3. HAVE A BOARD/STAFF REVIEW

At a special meeting or at your strategic planning retreat, go over your current mission and any substantive changes, and then talk through whether your current mission statement is inclusive enough for the kind of organization you are shaping? Does it accurately reflect your core values? Does it restrict your flexibility? *Don't* try to rewrite the mission as a group. You will still be there agonizing over syntax and comma placement in 2105. Do talk through the key points or values you want to include, things like "accessible to all parts of the community," "highest quality of service," and "sensitive to different cultural values." Then redraft your mission statement and take it back to the board for review and adoption.

☞ **HANDS ON:** Once the mission is rewritten, have it formally adopted by the board of directors or voted on by your membership (meeting whatever stipulations are in the bylaws) *and then send it, with the minutes of the board action to your state attorney general and to the Internal Revenue Service.* This is critical, as the IRS will judge you under the Unrelated Business Income Tax provisions of the Code based on the mission statement that they have *on file.* If you do not send the amended mission statement to the IRS, they will never know, and will judge you on your old, outdated mission statement.

Now let's turn our attention to the ways that people misuse or underutilize their mission statement. I have already noted that the mission statement is a resource that you need to use, and, unfortunately, it is a resource that is very underutilized in most not-for-profits.

C. THE FORGOTTEN MISSION STATEMENT

What good is your mission statement if no one knows about it? You and your board and staff may review the mission statement every year or two, but if you are like most not-for-profits, that is the extent of your use of your mission. I think you need to be reminded of it regularly. We need the mission as a beacon, to guide us when we get distracted by the day-to-day ups and downs of life.

❑ **For Example:** All three of my children at one time or another played noncompetitive youth soccer. Since Ben, the oldest, played, his younger brother Adam and younger sister Caitlin started at the earliest age allowed: four. Now at age four, watching soccer is more amusing than exciting, and when Adam started playing, I decided to keep busy by analyzing a little of the group dynamics of the games, practice, and coaching.

Questions sprang to mind. How do you motivate four-year-olds to keep their minds on the game? To compete? To even take the ball away from someone else when all they've heard from parents up to that age is "Share now, Susie." At Adam's first game, I wondered: What does the coach say before the game? Will she say "Win one for the Gipper?" or get technical and say "Remember play 17! Trevor go left, Andrea go right, pass to Sarah and she shoots!"?

Not a chance. What she did, and what all soccer coaches of very young players say is: "Look at me, now WHICH WAY ARE WE GOING???" And most (sometimes all) of the children think and point to the goal and say "THAT WAY!!!" And then the parents line up along the side of the field and remind the kids which way to kick the ball. Why? Because kids get easily distracted, by picking a flower, seeing a friend from school on the other team, waving to Mom or Dad, and often kick the ball toward the wrong end of the field.

The point of the story is that we, in our organizations, often also get distracted from the goal, from our mission, and it is not as easy for us to refocus on the point of what we do as it is for the kids on the soccer field: You can pick them up and show them where the goal is. Your "goal" is the mission statement, and it needs to be as visible and readily available as the goal on the soccer field.

Remember, distractions are a natural part of the busy world we live and work in. We have annual meeting time, budget time, audit time, Monday, Tuesday, Wed. . . . Well, you get the idea. It's easy to get off track. Thus, we need to model ourselves after the parents at the soccer game and constantly be reminding each other that the mission *is* the point. By using the mission statement in management and board decisions, by posting it clearly, by incorporating it into personnel evaluations, you can reinforce and remind people all of the time that your mission is paramount. Otherwise, your mission is forgotten among the ashes of the fires that you are putting out each day.

D. THE MYSTERY MISSION STATEMENT

Can you recite your mission statement right now? Probably not, and that's okay for now. But do you at least know the key elements? Does your mission statement specify a particular group of people, geographic area, or type of service? Or some combination of all three? You do need to know that. When was it written? When was it last reviewed by the board and the staff?

One thing is important to remember: Most mission statements are written to be broad statements of charitable activity—usually drafted by attorneys to be as broad as possible, or by advocates of a particular crusade who do not want to offend anyone. They often say, in effect, *"XYZ of YourTown is a not-for-profit dedicated to be all things to all people everywhere forever, charitably."* That's fine, but realize that along with that broad, all-inclusive mission can come considerable disagreement in *how* to achieve or at least pursue that mission.

☞ **HANDS ON:** Try this. At your next board meeting and next senior management meeting, ask everyone to get out a piece of paper and write down in one sentence *the single most important thing your organization does.* Now have everyone read their answers off and write them on the board or on a flipchart. Compare the answers. How many duplications do you have?

If you are like the overwhelming number of not-for-profits, you'll have few if any duplications. Why? Because *everyone* in the organization comes to it from a different background, perspective or priority. For example, if you are a human service provider, you have staff who are *doing* while your managers are *managing.* It sounds obvious, but look at how their perspectives will be different. The staff will look at the micro (how the mission affects their job and their part of the organization), and the managers *should* look at the macro (the organization as a whole, or at least their larger part of it). You may well have board members or volunteers who have been recipients of one (but perhaps *only* one) of the services you provide, and their perspective on what you do is colored by their individual and often very personal experiences.

This difference of perspective is a key and too often overlooked fact in not-for-profits. We are likely to assume that every one of us comes to the organization because we agree on the mission and good works the organization does. Not so. We come together to support what we perceive the mission to be, and it is that mission (our perceived one) that we will advocate and work toward. Obviously, this phenomenon results in a likelihood that we do not agree on the mission, and that can lead to either major conflicts or major strengthening.

Let's look at some real-world examples of this phenomenon.

❏ **FOR EXAMPLE:** An Association for Retarded Citizens (ARC) in a Great Plains state was a model of a mission-oriented not-for-profit. Formed in the 1950s by parents of retarded children as a voluntary organization dedicated to fighting for funding for their cause, it had, over the years, evolved with the field to provide direct services to persons with developmental disabilities and their families, and employers who employed people with disabilities. The ARC ran 12 residential sites, a vocational workshop, an early childhood assessment program, and recreational outings as well as support groups and outreach into the community.

Economically, 72% of its funding came from state and federal funds, mostly in the form of purchase-of-service, and mostly for less than the actual cost of service provided. The ARC made up for these underpayments by running a traditional (and profitable) "sheltered workshop" where developmentally disabled people do assembly, packaging, and manufacturing for for-profit businesses with assistance from supervisors. The ARC depended on the workshop profits to subsidize many of its other programs.

Then came a change in the philosophy of working with the developmentally disabled, an idea called *supported employment.* In supported employment, agencies like the ARC work with employers to find real jobs in real employment settings, and if the person with the disability needs some assistance, they get the job along with a job coach, who is on site with them some or all of the time to ensure that they stay on task and do the job as it needs to be done.

For the sheltered workshop, this policy was a potential financial disaster. Gone were the least disabled (and thus easiest to work with and most productive) employees. What would be done to keep the workshop profitable? Both the workshop director and the ARC executive director knew that without the profits from the workshop that other services would have to be cut. This would, of course, have an impact on service array, service quality, staff morale, and, eventually, community support and donations.

What should they do? Mandated by the state rules to move people "out into the working community," the ARC was faced with an agency threatening dilemma, unless the staff and board could adjust and adapt. But they did not want to just react, they wanted to respond in a way that they could all support.

The ARC board president called a board/staff retreat to discuss the issue, and started with a review of their mission statement: ***"The Mission of the ARC is to work for persons with mental retardation and other related disabilities and their families to help them achieve their highest potential in school, work, community life, and recreation."*** Even with this broad mission statement, there was stinging disagreement about how to proceed. Some participants wanted to close the workshop, noting that supported employment "works for everyone," no matter how disabled. Some were hesitant about setting a policy (promoting and providing supported employment) that would potentially put clients into a more "risky" job in the real community. Others raised the overall economic impact of potentially reduced profits on the rest of the agency's service array.

The solution? Support the mission. The key phrase? **"WORK FOR PERSONS WITH DISABILITIES."** To the board and staff, this meant allowing clients to choose their options and thus keep both options open. What this resulted in was keeping the workshop open as a work training, transition, and work location, with the eventual goal of having each person with a disability work in the setting *he or she* most liked. To keep profits up, they brought nondisabled staff to supplement the workforce. Thus, the program and the financial viability were preserved, and the solution worked well in light of the mission statement.

Those readers who are professionals or volunteers in the field of developmental disabilities may disagree with the ARC's choices, but the point here is that they let the mission guide them, and didn't just react without thinking.

❑ **FOR EXAMPLE:** A not-for-profit performance auditorium in the South was in crisis. Like all major performance centers, the Hall, as we shall call it, had gone through tough financial times along with the arts community in general. The Hall not only housed the local symphony, ballet, and opera companies (renting to them at a steep discount) but also reached out beyond its traditional white upper-middle-class clientele to the minority and lower-income communities by holding a wide variety of bookings, special performances for children, and so forth.

The financial mainstay of the Hall, however, was its series of Broadway touring productions. The profits from these productions kept the Hall open, and allowed it to subsidize the "fine" arts and community outreach.

But ticket sales for the core Broadway series were down. The Hall needed renovations and upkeep that had been neglected for years. The outreach program had brought new not-for-profit community groups asking to book the Hall—at a discount, of course. The performing arts not-for-profits (symphony, ballet, and opera) were in a financially precarious state as well and could not afford to pay the full cost of the rental of the site, and considered the Hall the only dignified place to perform.

What should be done? The board looked at their mission to gain guidance into what their priorities should be: *"The mission of The Hall Inc. shall be to improve the community and cultural experiences of the people of [this state], to foster improvements and expansion of the arts and to maintain the Hall as a community resource for future generations."*

Now, this broad mission provided some guidance, but there were other barriers to a quick fix. First, several members of the board were also members of the symphony, ballet, and opera boards. Thus, their perspective was that the Hall's board should focus on the phrase "foster improvements and expansion of the arts," which to them meant continuing to subsidize their performing arts groups. Several board members were highly successful CEO's who focused on the "maintain the Hall as a community resource for future generations" part of the mission as a mandate to first and foremost break even financially and keep the Hall in excellent physical condition. The third group on the board were community representatives who wanted more access for their own constituencies.

The solution? There was no perfect one, but all of the people around the table understood finance well enough to know that without financial stability there can be no social good. They agreed to prioritize their social and cultural obligations and budgeted an amount that was affordable for them to subsidize each performing group each year. Then it was up to staff to sell the Broadway series to meet the budget needs. They also set up a five-year capital endowment campaign to facilitate income from a non-arts source each year. Did they satisfy everyone? Not really. But they did acknowledge all of the perspectives around the table and tried to accommodate as many as possible, based on the mission statement.

The important points in these stories are many. First, even with a well-written and up-to-date mission statement, your organization will continue to have healthy (I hope) debate on how to implement the mission, and on what your values are. That's fine, and, as I say, if it is kept on a healthy, positive basis, can help the organization mature and keep up with the times. Second, without some common framework around which to discuss, there would have been no starting point for the ARC's or the performance hall's discussions. Their mission statements provided that framework. Third, everyone at your board table and staff meetings comes to the organization with his or her own history, perspective, and agenda. That can be an enriching fact or a divisive one, depending on how the executive director and board chairperson handle it. Use people's diversity of opinion, experience, and perspective to strengthen your organization; do not require everyone to think and act alike.

E. GETTING MORE FROM AN UNDERUTILIZED RESOURCE

Staff and board members of a not-for-profit have a responsibility to get the most good out of the limited resources that you have. Isn't it ironic that in the day-to-day race to secure more of those resources to allow more of the mission to be realized, people usually forget to use *the mission itself* as a resource.

The mission statement can be a management tool, a rallying cry, a staff motivator, a volunteer recruiter, and a fund raiser. You already have invested in getting the mission statement right for your organization, your community, and current times. Now use that resource in these other areas:

- *Management tool.* The mission statement should be a regular part of staff and board discussions in questions such as: "Which of the three options that we have before us is most responsive to our mission?" or "Will this type of funding gain us dollars but distract us from our mission?" Use the mission statement as a backstop to make better management and policy decisions. Have copies of your mission statement literally on the table at all meetings.

- *Rallying cry and staff motivator.* The mission statement can be used as a rallying cry and motivator for staff, volunteers, and board in tough times.

☞ **HANDS ON:** Try this: When the going gets particularly tough, when morale is low, or it seems people have given up hope, ask your staff or your board to list the good things that have happened in the last three weeks or months as a result of your organization's being in business. Get personal, talking about the impact of your organization's services on individuals. Then turn it around, and ask them what would have happened if you hadn't been around as an organization. Refocus on the mission statement as a higher calling, a cause worth working and sacrificing for. *Note:* you can't use this exercise every day because it will lose its impact. Save it for when you *really* need it.

• *Volunteer recruiter.* Remember the response when President Kennedy called for the formation of the Peace Corps? Or the Red Cross volunteers who flocked to south Florida to help after the devastation wrought by Hurricane Andrew in 1992? Or perhaps the questions you ask when people ask you to serve on a board or special committee? *Mission,* what the organization *did,* was the key in all of these. Kennedy called for assisting in less developed countries as a way of nonmilitary goodwill in an era of military confrontation. After Andrew, the Red Cross made it clear what people could and should do to help hurricane victims. When you are recruited for a board job, you ask what services the organization provides—what it *does.*

• *Fund raiser.* Here, as in the volunteer recruitment area, what you do, what good works are done, and why you do it are all key questions in a donor's mind. The what of what you do is up to you, but the why, the mission, is the linchpin, and should be the first rationale for funding. Donors, particularly big ones, like to see organizations that are focused on their mission, not just taking money for any and all purposes.

F. THE MISSION THAT IS EVERYWHERE

Excellent organizations know their mission. It is on the tip of everyone's tongue, and you can ask nearly everyone in the place what their mission is and they will repeat it verbatim and give you reasons why *they* are the essential link in the chain to get the mission realized. How does this happen? Like the children on the soccer team, it is tough to focus people and it is easy to get distracted. A unified reason for being does not happen by accident. It happens through meaningful repetition. The mission needs to be visible *everywhere.*

Assuming that you have agreed to your revised mission statement, do the following:

- Have your mission statement drawn up in an attractive format (most popular word processing programs are now essentially desktop printing programs and have a wide variety of fonts, backgrounds, and graphics available). Then frame it and place a copy of the framed mission in your reception area(s), staff lounges, and where services are provided. Don't just copy the mission and have people tape it to the wall. Do this right. Also, don't have the first time that the staff people see the mission be the framed copy on the wall. Make sure that they have seen and discussed it in advance.

- Put the mission statement in every document you print. It should be inside the front cover or front and center in at least the following:

  - Your annual report
  - All marketing and public relations material
  - Your board manual
  - Your staff personnel policies
  - Your staff orientation manual (with heavy emphasis on why the mission is so important)
  - Your strategic plan
  - Your Web site, and as a "signature" on your e-mail

- Use the mission daily as a tool (see above).

- One idea that I saw in action recently was to have the mission statement installed as the screen saver on all of the organization's computers. But it has to be short!

The mission that is everywhere is more likely to become part of the culture and part of the mindset of the people who work and volunteer for your organization.

G. PUTTING ACTIONS BEHIND YOUR WORDS

Using the mission statement is a great thing but a perilous risk if not handled correctly. Once you hold the mission statement up as the holy grail, and take time and resources to print it and use it at meetings, you hold yourself to a higher standard, one that invites criticism and interpretation from a variety of places. ("Well, *that* decision certainly does not support our mission" from whoever loses in a choice made by management or board).

The cure for this is threefold: leadership, time, and training. To be more accurate, the real-world components are: leadership, time, training, leadership, training, training, training, and leadership.

❑ **For Example:** Everyone has heard of Ross Perot, the computer services billionaire and former presidential candidate. Perot made his money starting and growing Electronic Data Systems (EDS), a computer data services firm that was the first and, for a time, the largest processor of data in the world. Perot built his organization by doing a number of things, including emphasizing customer service, teamwork, and loyalty to each other and the organization, and by having a simple mission and set of values for everyone to work by.

EDS's mission statement was short and simple. Perot had it reduced to a wallet-sized card, which every employee carried so that they could produce it quickly to use in management discussions. For EDS employees, this worked.

At the same time, General Motors was a giant going nowhere. The new GM CEO, Roger Smith, saw the need for more and more information management to tie together the far-flung outposts of his automotive empire, and he contracted with EDS to set up and run the system. Smith got to know Perot, and he admired the lean, can-do attitude that EDS employees exuded and demonstrated in their work for GM. So, Smith proposed that GM buy EDS, in the hopes that the EDS culture would prove to be a "virus" that would spread throughout GM. He and the senior GM management team analyzed what to do to hasten this spread of entrepreneurial spirit, and they focused on the mission statements that everyone on the EDS team whipped out at the drop of a hat. They paid a consultant to come up with a new mission statement for GM, distributed the cards to everyone, and waited for the new "Entrepreneurial GM" to emerge fully clothed. It didn't. Not only did the two cultures clash, but the inevitable battle and eventual falling out between Perot and Smith has attained the status of corporate legend.

Why didn't the EDS–GM marriage work? There are probably 50 major reasons, and entire books have been written on this subject. Suffice it to say that you cannot change a culture by handing out wallet-sized cards with nice words on them that no one has invested in. (Remember, a consultant had written GM's mission statement.)

1. LEADERSHIP

You need to be seen *living* the mission statement. Once you publicize and invest in your mission statement, you hold yourself up to a higher standard. *You* have to use the mission daily, visibly and consistently. *You* have you embody its ideals. If the mission says to be culturally sensitive, *you* have to be the most educated and sensitive person in the organization. If the mission says for the organization to be an advocate for children, or a service provider to the most disadvantaged or an educator of the best and brightest, *you* have to articulate and be a living symbol of the mission. People will be skeptical of the need or value of a revamped mission, and you have to live the mission: Do it, don't just say it.

2. TIME

After leadership, the next key is the hardest—giving it time. You will need to work for many months and even years before the mission becomes ingrained. If you decide to do this (and you need to), you must lead the charge for a long, long time. As new staff and board people come on, they will know no other organization than one driven by the mission, and it will begin to be culturally ingrained.

3. TRAINING

Next, there is the need for training, training, training. There is no substitute for training. As we will see in later chapters, investing in your workforce is key, and 40 hours per year per person is the minimum acceptable amount. Make at least some of that about the mission: why it is there and hands-on training about how to use it. Remember, if someone has never managed or provided direct service by a clearly articulated mission before, this is new. Do not expect them to know how to do this automatically. Give them a chance to learn, practice, review, and learn more.

❑ **For Example:** In the period from 1986 to 1993, and again from 1996 to 1998, Michael Jordan of the Chicago Bulls in the National Basketball Association was, by a wide margin, the best basketball player in the world. And yet, to stay there, *he practiced every day three hours longer than his teammates.* But in the work world, we say, "Oh I went to a supervision course once, I know how to do that," or "I took accounting in college, I remember that." Wrong. People say "I've got 30 years of management experience, I've seen it all. Remember, OJT (on-the-job training) is not *practice,* it's the *game.* When you screw up, it's for real. If it's just experience you have, it's almost certainly based on outmoded philosophies, techniques, and technologies. Make learning for yourself and for your staff a lifelong pursuit. Train, train, train. More on this in later chapters.

RECAP

In this chapter, we have covered the key points of the central crux of your organization, the mission:

- We've reviewed the way to write or rewrite a mission statement to bring it up to date
- We've reviewed why a forgotten or mystery mission statement is of little or no use
- We've looked at methods of utilizing your mission as a management, motivation, and policy tool
- We've suggested methods for you and your staff and board to *live* the mission, not just parrot it

As you finish this chapter, look around your organization. In how many places can you see and read the mission? Is it on the walls? On people's bulletin boards? Why not? Ask the first five staff you see what the mission is. Listen to their answers. Are they the same? Why not? Look at your marketing material. Is your mission on each and every piece? Why not?

So we agree, I hope, that the mission is a key element in your success. You need to review it, revise it with help from board and as many staff as you can, publicize it, use it daily (starting with your own activities), and train staff and volunteers in how to use the mission as a management and service provision tool. That's the starting point, and if you don't start here, the rest of what's in this book will be of a lot less use to you and your organization.

Questions for Discussion

1. What general improvements would we like to see in our mission statement? Do we have one or many mission statements?
2. Does our mission statement excite us? Is it short enough for us to remember, or does it suffer from comma fault?

3. How can we better use the mission statement to recruit, retain, and motivate staff and volunteers?

4. How can we better use our mission statement in management discussions?

5. What specifically can those of us in leadership positions do to evidence our mission daily?

5

A Businesslike Board of Directors

OVERVIEW

Whether you are a staff member or a board member, you know that the board of directors is a key component of your organization. For starters, you *have* to have one; it is a legal requirement in state and federal statutes. Second, the board can provide an excellent resource of judgment and leadership, a connection with the rest of the community, and a partnership with staff that can strengthen the organization and its services. In other words, the board *should* be a key resource for the organization. Unfortunately, it is often anything but that.

Too often, boards either totally dominate an organization, thus blocking the staff's ability to do their jobs, or are so subservient to staff "expertise" that the staff in effect manipulate the board at will. Neither are effective uses of resources, and both are counterproductive. In the worst case, both problems—board dominance and staff dominance— occur in the same organization. How can that be? Simple, the staff *think* the board is dominating while at the same time the board members *think* the staff is running roughshod over them! Gridlock in governance!

How do you optimize your board as a resource? How do you analyze what your organization needs from a board and then go out and recruit one that meets those needs? What should the respective roles of the staff and the board be? This chapter I'll tell you about those things as well as about how to reduce your board's liability. Chapter 6 I'll show you how to get the most effective board, why board people *really* serve and how you can meet those needs and wants, and how to evaluate your board. With the things you learn in this chapter and the next, you can really turn your board into the effective policy-setting, check-and-balance resource that it needs to be.

A. BOARD EFFECTIVENESS

The first thing you need to do in order to make your board a better-utilized resource is a benchmark of effectiveness against which to measure. An effective board has most, if not all of the following characteristics:

- *It understands the organization's mission, and acts to implement that mission for the benefit of the organization's constituency consistently and professionally.* If they are to be effective, a board must first and foremost understand and support the organization's mission (see Chapter 4). They must also be consistent in the development of policy to implement that mission: If they favor one method of implementation one week and another the next, they will be doing more harm than good.

- *It acts as a policy setter and check and balance with the staff.* With one exception (a start-up not-for-profit in which the board often *is* the staff), the board must act as policy setter and check and balance *only*. It must not allow itself nor any of its members to get seduced into trying to run the day-to-day activities of the organization. If the board hired staff, running the organization's day-to-day activities is what they hired them for. They are supposed to be professionals (if the right people were hired). The board should set the broad policy and let the staff implement it. The board has more important things to do; things that only a board can do.

- *It works primarily with the executive director and evaluates the executive director at least annually.* Rule #1 of not-for-profit management: ***The executive director works for the board, and the rest of the staff work for the executive director.*** The board cannot be effective if it allows itself to be bogged down in both personal and personnel issues that are most appropriate for staff to handle on their own. Thus, board members who acquiesce to letting staff people other than the CEO or executive director call and complain are asking for more trouble than they want. I know that this is not always easy, particularly in small towns where everyone knows everyone else, but it is *the* prime rule of not-for-profit board/staff management. As with any relationship, the one between the board and the Exec can only flourish if both parties let the other know how they are doing. Many, many board people tell me that they are not an expert in the executive director's discipline (i.e, they aren't a minister, teacher or social worker), so they can't evaluate him or her. This, while understandable, neglects what the board *does* know and *can* evaluate. The board can evaluate how the Exec interacts with and supports the board, how close the staff comes to staying within the budget, completing tasks in the long-range plan, achieving fund-raising or outreach goals, reducing staff turnover, and so on. The board can and should set measurable goals for the Exec and then evaluate his or her ability to meet those goals. Moreover, the board should do it annually at the very least. To board members who are reluctant to evaluate, I say this: *You* want to be evaluated in *your* job. If you want to keep your exec, give him or her the same courtesy: let them know how they are doing.

• *It changes over time, filling its membership fully by recruiting new members to meet the changing needs of the organization.* Your organization does not look like it did five years ago in terms of funding, programs, or staff. But it may very well be identical or close to it in board makeup. If the board is a resource, shouldn't its constitution change with the changing needs of the organization? Of course it should. Boards should *not* be perpetual. You should build board turnover into your bylaws. My suggestion is a three-year term, with a maximum of two successive terms before a particular board member goes off for at least a year. Thus, one third of your board is up for renewal each year, and this gives you a chance to evaluate them and recruit both new people and new skills regularly. Also, a three-year term works well with my recommendations on strategic plans (see Chapter 11), which include a planning retreat every three years or at least once in every board member's term of office. The issue of how you assess what kind of board you need and how you recruit them will be covered later in this chapter.

• *It elects qualified officers and appoints qualified committee chairs.* As in so many of life's endeavors, the difference between success and failure can often be leadership. Think of some of the great leaders of key organizations in our past: presidents like Washington, Lincoln, and Franklin Roosevelt, and visionaries like Martin Luther King Jr., Susan B. Anthony and countless others led their groups at a time when they were most needed. Just because you may not be involved with a national or trend-setting organization does not mean you don't need leaders on your board or to head your committees.

It also does not mean that all your leaders need to be officers or committee chairs, but it certainly helps. Effective boards have people in officer and committee chair roles who know their job (and its limitations), get it done effectively, and are willing to commit the time to do so. They show up with their homework done, lead their groups through the decisions that need to be made, and represent the organization without bias with funders, donors, the media, and the public. Your organization needs a leadership development track, where new members are assessed after a time and potential leaders are put onto an "officer track" assigning them first to committee chairs, then officer slots, and finally, if appropriate, the board presidency.

- *It supports the organization in public.* Elaine was elected to the board of the XYZ agency four months ago. She has been to every meeting and has had, in her own words, "a steep learning curve" about the agency, its works, its staff, and its funding problems. Elaine is at a social engagement at a friend's house when she is approached by Phil, whom she has not seen since her election to the board. Phil mentions that he has heard that Elaine is now on XYZ's board. Elaine's response:

> *(Sigh) Yes, I got talked into being on the board. I'm not sure that I won't regret it, what with all of their financial problems. I had no idea how big XYZ is, how many staff and services they have, nor how financially fragile they are. I mean, they are good people and all, but they are working under tremendous strain. I don't really see how they are going to continue at their present pace or their present funding. But I am learning a lot, and I guess I'll be able to help at some point, once I figure out what is really going on.*

OR

> *(Smile) Yes, I started about four months ago, and talk about an education! I had no idea how big and diversified they are. I'm really impressed by the staff. They are good people and are doing miracles with, shall we say, minimal resources. I'm learning a lot, and hope that I can really contribute once I get my feet on the ground.*

As a staff member, which answer would you like to have your board giving? As a board member, do you hear yourself echoed in the first or the second answer? And, just for discussion, what if Elaine's friend Phil happens to be on the United Way allocation committee for this year, or is an officer at XYZ's bank, or is a potential referral source for new clients? What message do you prefer he get?

We will deal more with this in Chapter 9, but it is critical that board people realize that they are "on the team" and must support the team—even if they don't agree with every decision made at every board meeting. Once board members start to criticize board decisions or complain about the agency outside of the boardroom, the ability of board members to act as an effective team starts to go down the black hole of internal conflict.

B. BARRIERS TO BOARD EFFECTIVENESS

What are the main barriers that get in the way? It's always beneficial to highlight the most common places that boards trip up. A board *cannot* be an effective resource for the organization if:

> • *The members of the board don't know basic and up-to-date information about the organization's mission, programs, and purposes.* This sounds so elementary on the face of it that one would think that of *course* people on boards have that kind of information. Don't be so sure. Board members come to the table with different ideas and backgrounds, and their perceptions of the mission (as we discussed in Chapter 4) may be as different as night and day. This also extends to the programs. They may not even be aware of some programs' existence. Thus, orientation, on a consistent basis, is a key to board effectiveness.

> ☞ **HANDS ON:** At *every* board meeting, reserve 15 minutes for ongoing board orientation. Cover a single program, a new state law affecting your organization, or new developments in your field. Orientation should be a continuous, never-ending process. Too often, it is done only at one meeting at the beginning of the board member's term, provided in a language (your jargon) that the board member does not yet understand. Think back to your own orientation when you joined the staff of your employer. How much do you remember? Not much, and you have worked there 40 hours a week ever since. Now add to that "working" only 3 to 4 hours a month as a board member does, and you may get the picture about why they do not keep 100% up to speed. Help them keep current by dedicating 15 minutes per

meeting. (If you don't think you have 15 minutes, see the section of this chapter that deals with more effective committee meetings.)

- *It doesn't get accurate and timely information from staff.* There is no excuse for inaccurate information going out to the board, and even less excuse for not sending it to them in advance. If board members are to set policy, and to be a check and balance for the organization, they need to see the meeting materials in advance— and that does not mean 10 minutes in advance of the meeting. As a rule, three days is the minimum for materials to be *in the hands* of board members before a meeting.

Another part of this barrier is staff not telling board members about key or controversial issues until they read it in the paper. This is, to understate the issue, not smart. Whether the news is good or bad, if you are a staff manager, let the board members hear it from you, not from the grapevine or the press. If the news is good, the board members feel like insiders. If it is bad, you get to tell them the whole story first, not after they have read (and been prejudiced by) whatever spin the paper puts on the story. Keep your board well informed.

- *It frequently is lacking a quorum.* How can you take action without a quorum? You can't. If the board members are not there, three things happen. First, board people who are not present cannot add their contributions to the discussion and decision. Second, if a bare quorum is present, decisions that are made will not have the strength of a wider board ownership and may later be subject to being over- turned, or at least not supported fully. Finally, board members are liable for actions taken in their absence (see section E, Board Mem- bers' Legal Liability).

I tell executive directors all the time what I was told (and did not like hearing) as an exec myself years ago: *If you consistently don't have a quorum, it's your (executive director's) fault, no one else's.* Why, you ask? Because board members are people like all the rest of us. They make choices about how to spend the 24 hours they are given each day. All of us have more things to choose from than we have hours to do them in. Thus, going to a board meeting is a choice, one that competes with family time, work time, TV time, socializing, or sleep, to name a few. As a staff member, you are *competing* for your board members' time and you have to *earn* their attendance by meeting their needs and wants. You need these people at the meetings. It is your job to entice them there and to keep them coming.

☞ **HANDS ON:** You also need a tool to help you entice by enforcement. All boards should have attendance requirements that are discussed during recruitment and enforced rigorously. For example, if you have 12 meetings a year, each board member must come to 9 per year, or not be renewed for membership. Missing three in a row is cause for probation, with one more miss leading to termination. If this sounds tough, it is designed to be. You are a mission-oriented business and you can't get your business done without board attendance. Be up front with your board people and let them know you can no longer have them be casual about attendance. They need to be on or off the board, not both.

Board members are liable for actions taken at meetings that they miss. That fact alone should entice them to come to meetings. This fact will be discussed more later in this chapter.

• *It is not given anything meaningful to do.* I make the assumption that you want talented and accomplished people on your board, ones who can contribute to your organization with their skills, experience, and expertise. Given that, why would you not give these people anything to do that challenges them? Too many boards are perfunctory: Call the meeting to order, take attendance, review the minutes of the last meeting, approve three committee reports, and go home. As the commercial said all too well: "Where's the beef?" If you treat your board as though they are incapable of doing real work, the good board members will leave, and you won't have a quorum, yet again.

• *The board leadership is weak.* Weak leadership often results in internal strife, chaos, and lack of direction. Also, boards sometimes need strong leaders to stand up to strong staffs. Finally, weak leaders do not inspire good people to keep coming to the board meetings, or to contribute or take risks on behalf of the organization.

• *Its meetings have no agenda and are not well facilitated.* The lack of an agenda is an open invitation to anarchy and meetings that go on for centuries. You simply must have an agenda and stick to it. The agenda needs to be mailed out in advance with meeting materials, and, if possible, the agenda should be somewhat standardized from meeting to meeting. Facilitation is another issue. It is a skill, one that your committee chairs and board president need. It requires that they encourage people to speak and allow them to contribute, but at the same time, keep the meeting on track and bring each issue to closure in a timely fashion. That is a big order, and too big an order for a lot of board presidents I have observed.

• *Its committee structure is not effective, and every policy decision comes before the full board for lengthy debate.* There is simply not enough time in a single board meeting (no matter how long it may drag on) to get effective policy and oversight accomplished solely by the board as a whole. To use the board effectively, you need a committee structure that allows for persons on (and sometimes not yet on) the board to use their particular expertise and focus on a particular issue, such as finance, personnel, fund raising, or planning. Then, once the board delegates the details of a particular area to the committees, the board discussion should be limited and, in most cases, perfunctory. If every issue that is discussed at committee meetings is discussed over again at the board level, why have committees? In Chapter 6, we will discuss what committees you need and how to constitute them so that they can be effective, but if the board members will not let the committees do their job, the board won't be able to do its job.

• *The staff lacks the skills to support the board—or worse, makes a systematic effort to ignore the board or undermine its effectiveness.* The staff have a role in making the board work well: They need to be supportive, but guiding (the key functions will be reviewed later). But if the paid staff do not help make the board effective, it won't be; if they undermine the board to try to seize or hold power, the checks and balances get negated and there is a terrible risk of the organization's not keeping to its mission, not keeping up with changes in the community, and thus being out of touch. Additionally, if staff are not supportive, good board members will either walk out or attempt to take over the day-to-day activities of the organization, both of which are situations you want to avoid.

C. BOARD MEMBER RESPONSIBILITIES

In attempting to mold a better board, we need to define the specific responsibilities that they have. As we have already noted, the members of the board of directors are the representatives of the community; they protect the community's interest while advancing the organization's mission in the same fashion that a for-profit corporate board represents the stockholders and promotes the corporate goals.

Even with this philosophical background, it is important to list specifics. The board is responsible for seeing that the items listed below are accomplished; but they may not actually do each of these things personally. If there are paid staff, certain tasks such as filing Internal Revenue Service (IRS) forms are left for staff to do the mechanics, but board members are still responsible for ensuring that they are done.

Other authors have talked extensively about the roles of boards, particularly Brian O'Connell's excellent *Board Member's Book,* Foundation Center, 1999. In this text, O'Connell notes the need for clear definition of roles, particularly between boards and staffs. Barbara Burgess, in *The Nonprofit Management Handbook* (John Wiley & Sons, 1997), lists three governing functions of boards:

1. To preserve the integrity of the trust
2. To set policy
3. To support and promote the organization

Although I agree with this list, I think we need to expand on the roles a bit.

A board of directors must:

- *Fulfill all of the IRS and state not-for-profit reporting requirements.* This includes taxes, FICA, annual reports, Unrelated Business Income Tax (UBIT) estimations, and operating under section 501(c) of the Internal Revenue Code.

- *Set policy and establish organizational goals.* Boards are responsible for broad policy and must do long-range planning to set those policies in place.

- *Hire the executive director.* No one else can or should do this important job.

- *Evaluate the executive director's performance in writing at least annually.* No excuses, accept no substitutes.

- *Assure that fiscal policies are in place and followed.* Boards should be very concerned about financial oversight, and that means good cash, receivables, payables, and budgeting policies.

• *Help develop and adopt budgets.* The board must have final say about how the resources of the organization are allocated, and this is most clearly embodied in the budget. Staff (at all levels) should help draft the budget, but the board has the final say.

• *Review and amend bylaws every two years.* This ensures that they are up-to-date with current regulations and that they reflect current board thinking on attendance, board selection, standing committees and officers, and the like.

• *Ensure compliance with the funding stream's policies and regulations.* Every not-for-profit has at least one major source of funding: government, United Way, foundations. Every funding source has a different way of monitoring expenses and auditing past work. When you sign a contract to take someone's money, you also agree to comply with their regulations. These may include such diverse items as having a drug-free workplace, not discriminating in employment, or keeping all records related to the contract for five years. Read the fine print before you sign, then make sure that you can meet all of the provisions. If you are a board member and you do not fulfill your contractual obligation, it's your head on the platter.

• *Establish personnel policies and monitor their compliance.* More people get in trouble with people problems than any other kind. Have good personnel policies, review them every two years with a professional, and build in checks and balances to ensure that they are followed *to the letter every time.*

• *Nominate and elect officers.* Most bylaws have the board do this function at the annual meeting.

• *Represent the organization in public within the constraints of the media policy.*

• *Help recruit new board members.* The board needs to replenish itself. Good recruitment calls for a board/staff partnership, but board involvement is key.

• *Raise funds.* I used to say that fund-raising oversight was sufficient. No more. This area is so incredibly competitive that there is no place to hide for board members. Not only must they take an active role in fund raising, they themselves must give money to the organization.

• *Perform volunteer program work.* If the organization has a volunteer component, I strongly urge board members to at least try some hands-on volunteer work to get to know the organization better. For example, I tell the school boards I work with that they can't do their jobs adequately unless, at least once a year, they ride a school bus, read to first graders, and serve lunch in the high-school cafeteria. Such hands-on exposure is an integral part of the leadership track.

D. STAFF RESPONSIBILITIES TO THE BOARD

As with any other relationship, "it takes two." Staff have to support the board if the board is to be effective; it is not only the board that must contribute to the overall relationship. What follows are the minimal expectations that the board should have of its staff.

• *The board should expect accurate, timely, honest, and focused information.* The board needs to be able to rely totally on the staff to provide it with honest and unbiased information and to provide that well in advance of meetings. The hired staff are professionals, and the board should solicit their advice and ideas. Too often, I see boards who want "just the facts, ma'am" (like the Dragnet cops) and feel that if they ask for any suggestions from staff they will be overrun. I disagree. The board hired the staff as the paid experts. Let them contribute to the discussion, but make sure that everyone is aware that the board has the final say.

• *The board should be regularly informed of new developments.* As the paid experts, the staff needs to inform the board of new developments in the organization as well as in the field in which the organization operates, such as health care or special education.

• *The board should expect staff to gather information, analyze it, and make recommendations to the board—in essence, to be technical advisors to the board.* As noted above, it is key that the staff be the responsible conduits of information for the board. The staff also need to focus the board on what is essential. Here the staff walk a very thin line, one where they are right on the edge of controlling rather than assisting. If the only information that they provide the board is self-serving, or supports only the staff position, the staff have not done their jobs. In fact, they have violated their trust.

• *The board should expect staff to report fiscal information regularly.* We had a not-for-profit organization a few years ago in my hometown that went out of business very suddenly. Staff (over 100) came to work one morning to find the doors locked and a sign saying "Out of Business." The organization had run out of money and no one—other than the executive director and the financial manager, both staff members—had known it was in trouble. It was a major scandal for our small town, and when I ran into some of the board members, I asked them what had happened. Their (admittedly lame) excuse was that they had not seen financials for a year! I had no sympathy for the board members—none at all. Not providing regular (as in monthly) financials, annual budgets, and cash flow projections to the board is totally unprofessional for staff. Board members—if financials stop being regular, start *demanding* them. This is cause for *extreme* concern and urgency of action. Find out what is going on and accept no excuses. You need to see the financials.

• *The board should encourage staff to make optimum use of the board as a resource.* The staff have a responsibility to be familiar with the skills, connections, and talents of the board and to make use of these skills and talents to the best interest of the organization.

• *The board should expect staff to develop a process for and to educate all new board members and to orient all board members on an ongoing basis.* As noted earlier, board members come to only one or two meetings a month (including committee meetings), so they need regular orientation in addition to their initial overview of the agency.

• *The board should expect staff to provide support for board recruitment and development.* The process I lay out later in this chapter will demonstrate a board/staff partnership in this key area.

• *The board should expect staff to support board committees and provide them with necessary information and expertise they need.* Just as with the board as a whole, someone needs to provide support to the committees, to get them the information and provide technical assistance and advice.

• *The board should expect staff to attend all meetings of the board unless excused therefrom.* I am a strong supporter of board meetings being open to staff—it breaks down the mythical barrier between the board and staff and lets staff know what goes on. I also am a strong advocate of staff, other than just the executive director, making presentations to the board. For example, the financial manager can present the financials, the program director can present items about the programs, and so on.

There is a great deal on both plates, but if the staff do their part, and the board does its part, the relationship will truly benefit the organization.

E. BOARD MEMBERS' LEGAL LIABILITIES

In addition to a long list of responsibilities, boards also have legal liabilities as a result of their board membership. Board members are *fiduciaries,* defined as a person, association, or corporation that has a duty to act for another in a specified area. As such, they have a fiduciary responsibility to the organizations they serve. In financial terms, this means that board members are responsible for the proper utilization, management, or investment of property and other assets placed in their trust. They are legally responsible for the management and control of the organization—and the resulting actions or accidents.

This is a pretty heavy responsibility, but it does not mean that a board member should worry about liability for every corporate loss or mishap that occurs. Most states protect not-for-profit board members from liability for errors of judgment as long as they act responsibly, in good faith, with the best interests of the corporation foremost. All of this must be balanced with the board's overall role. As I have said repeatedly, the board should be interested in results, not details of operation. The board's involvement in programs and operations should be limited to setting overall policy and monitoring results, unless there are extenuating circumstances.

❏ **FOR EXAMPLE:** A medium-sized not-for-profit school found that it was unable to pay its bills. In order to stay afloat, the director began borrowing heavily from employee withholding (FICA) taxes. The board had no idea this was going on until the IRS contacted the board president and demanded payment of the back taxes. By the time the board of directors took action, the school had closed, and the few remaining assets had been liquidated to pay creditors. The IRS, of course, still wanted its money. They took the board to court to pursue the payment of the taxes by the fiduciaries, arguing that the board members were ultimately responsible for the financial actions or inactions of the organization. The lawsuits dragged on for years and there was always the nagging concern that the board members would be held personally liable for the organization's outstanding debts. The answer? Yes, they would, and to the tune of thousands of dollars for each board member.

This is not a scenario you want to repeat. But it is a true story, and one that I hear repetitions of annually. To avoid this and other embarrassments, you need to be aware there are two common violations of fiduciary duties (or of being prudent):

1. *Failure to follow fundamental management principles.* This is the process of making a decision that a prudent person would not make if provided the same information. It occurs when a board:

- Doesn't develop plans or budgets
- Doesn't read staff reports to see if there are problems
- Doesn't pay attention to problems raised in reports
- Doesn't demand a reasonable standard of reporting and control (like the board of the organization that went out of business overnight)
- Ignores repeated warnings from staff, volunteers, or outside experts
- **Does not attend meetings.**

2. *Operating the organization in a way that benefits the board members directly.* This is known as self-dealing or inurement of benefit. You need to have strong conflict-of-interest policies and enforce them.

F. AVOIDING LIABILITY

Let's focus on some proven ways to avoid liability:

- First, if you are a board member, take your responsibility as a board member seriously. Come to the meetings, read the material in advance, and be willing to ask questions.

- Take the time to read and understand the organization's bylaws and mission, and act in accordance with these documents. If actions conflict with either the bylaws or the mission, speak out.

• Stay informed of what is going on within the organization's programs and administration.

• Set policies only after reviewing the facts carefully. Never make decisions in a vacuum; demand documentation.

• Read the financial statements before each meeting. Demand a format that can be understood and some training in how to use the reports in the role as a board member.

• Make sure that your organization has a long-range (three- to five-year) plan and that board and staff contribute to its generation and revisions.

• Make sure that minimum statutory or technical requirements are met: filing annual reports, timely payment of withholding taxes, contracting with a certified public accountant for an independent audit of the agency's books annually, meeting the legal and regulatory requirements of the agency's funding sources, and so forth.

• Demand minutes from all meetings that list who voted which way on all significant items. List dissenting members by name.

• Adopt and enforce a conflict-of-interest policy that discourages any business transactions between directors and the corporation, unless conducted openly and with stringent safeguards.

• Know the state laws regulating voluntary organizations to ensure compliance. The board's attorney should review these laws closely to determine how the state handles the issue of board members' liability. A report to the board should be made on these issues.

• Have directors' and officers' insurance *if* such insurance buys you more than state and federal statutes that protect governing volunteers. Ask your insurance agent to show you why the policy exceeds the statutes in protection.

Following these suggestions should greatly reduce the risk that board members face and make it an acceptable risk for them to continue serving on the board.

Finally, remember that many states have laws that reduce the board members' individual liability for actions taken in good faith. Make a good faith effort, and you will be in much better shape.

G. BUILDING A BETTER BOARD

How can you build a better board? First, you need to look at the needs you have in terms of expertise on the board. Then you should assess when those needs will become critical. For example, if you have in your strategic plan a goal to add a new building in three years, within a year you need to recruit a board member with construction experience and perhaps someone who can help you through the maze of financing options on your board. Finally, you need to develop and implement a recruitment program that fills slots in an orderly and planned manner.

> ☞ **HANDS ON:** Let me say here that I believe that you need a huge and varied skill set on a board, but that a businesslike board should have two broad categories of members. First, you need advocates for your mission—people who passionately believe in what you do. These people keep you honest to the first rule of not-for-profits: mission, mission, and more mission. The second kind of people you need are businesspeople, and these folks keep you honest to the second rule of not-for-profits: no money, no mission. These two groups provide a dynamic and very healthy tension on the board and help the organization balance the needs of the two primary rules.

In assessing the type of board member expertise you need, you should pay attention to three things:

1. Your organization's current programs (what you are now)
2. Your strategic plan (what you want to be in three to five years)
3. Your funding sources' regulations (what the payers' require)

The criteria of need can be objective, such as "race," "age," or "county of residence," or subjective, such as "community leader" or political connections." Exhibit 5-1 allows you to assess those criteria important to you, add your own criteria, and assess your current status.

As you can see from the checklist in Exhibit 5-1, the types of board members that you will need vary greatly and can change over time. I served on a board that, at the time I joined, had no one with finance, architectural, or building skills, and yet the organization had just acquired a 60-bed residential facility and was planning on buying or renting 20

Exhibit 5-1   Board Assessment Tool

Characteristic/ Expertise	On Bd?	Need This Skill			
		Now	1 Year	2 Years	3 Years
Gender					
Ethnicity (various)					
Funder's mandate					
Age group (various)					
Location (county, city, etc.)					
Advocate					
Legislative					
Clergy					
Customer					
Ethnicity					
Legal					
Accounting					
Finance/Banking					
Marketing					
Personnel					
Construction					
Fund raising					
Small business					

small homes within the coming five years. We needed people with those skills and recruited them. Eight years later, as I went off the board, the skills needs had changed again from property acquisition and financing to fund raising, marketing, and property management. Your needs will change too. Don't make your categories for board service static. Review them regularly, at the same time you review your strategic plan.

H. BOARD RECRUITMENT

Now that you have established the board that you want, and the schedule on which you will recruit those skills, you will need to organize a consistent recruitment program to constantly be prospecting for high-quality board members. As noted above, the quality of the board member is as important as the "slot" she or he fills.

There are five keys to good board recruitment and retention:

1. *Consistent recruitment.* This means that you don't just deal with board recruitment the week before the nominations committee meets, or the afternoon before the annual meeting. Finding quality volunteers to sit on your policy-setting board is a constant job, and the process should encourage consistent effort.

2. *The recruitment effort is a joint board/staff task.* Board members need to be involved in the job of recruiting and assessing potential board candidates. So do staff. The effort should be split between the two groups, but if both aren't involved, the outcome will not be optimal.

3. *Provide well-defined and clearly stated expectations of the board members.* There is no substitute for clearly stating to potential board members the expectations of them. That way, if they don't feel that they can meet those expectations, they can decline an offer to serve and save you the trouble of recruiting another person later. Examples of such expectations include:

- You must attend 10 of 12 monthly meetings.
- You must serve on one board committee (most meet monthly) after your first six months on the board.
- You are expected to read your board mailings before you come to the meeting.
- You must work at our annual XYZ (fund-raising) event and either sell 20 tickets or donate $100 dollars yourself.

4. Enforcement of these expectations. Having rules and then not enforcing them is a waste of time, effort, and political capital. If you have these expectations, and board members can't or won't meet them, let them know that they will either be voted off the board or not nominated for renewal. When you let people know in advance, and in writing, about your expectations, then there is little area for them to complain. That doesn't mean that they won't complain or that "firing" a board member is ever easy. It's not, particularly if your culture has not enforced any expectations on them in the past.

5. Evaluation of recruitment efforts. How many of the available board slots did you fill? Did you double up on the important ones? How many of your recruits stayed the first full year? How do you know these things? You track your efforts. As with any good process, you learn from your mistakes only if you know about them. You can build on your successes, but only if you are aware of them. Evaluate, evaluate, evaluate.

I. BOARD ORIENTATION AND EDUCATION

1. ORIENTATION

There are some essential parts of good orientation. First, and unlike the way that most organizations orient boards, orientation should be a never-ending discipline. It should occur at every board meeting, and, in the best-run organizations, extend to brief, focused discussions at committee meetings as well. However, the process does have to start somewhere, and that somewhere is at the interview for potential candidates. At that time, not only does the future board member get an oral briefing into programs, funding, and philosophy, he or she should also get that key document: the board manual. After someone is elected to the board, he or she should get a number of things provided in addition to the board manual, the current budget, the most recent two audits, the last three or four monthly financial statements, and all of the organization's promotional material. If you also want to provide information on key funding sources, fine.

Second, new board members need a personal oral orientation to the organization. That usually means a tour of the facility(ies) hopefully at the time that actual services are being provided. The board member may also choose (or be required) to serve as a volunteer for a short time as a hands-on practicum. A week or so after the tour, the board member should be called to see what questions have popped up.

☞ **HANDS ON:** One technique that I have seen work is to assign a senior staff person, not the executive director, and one veteran board member to each new board member as their "buddies" for six months. These people sit with the new member at the meetings, take them to lunch once or twice to check on whether they are getting what they need, are available by phone to chat, and so on. It is a method to increase the likelihood of meeting the new member's wants and assuring that problems or questions are resolved early. This buddy system does not need to last long—three to six months—but it really works.

Third, make sure that at their first meeting, the board people are introduced to everyone. That is the job of the board president.

2. THE BOARD MANUAL

The board manual (I do not like the term *orientation manual* because board members can regularly return to this document for reference—even after they are veterans) provides board members with an organized, single reference source for questions about your organization. It should include at least the following:

- The organization's bylaws and charter
- The organization's mission statement
- A table of organization with a listing of all key staff people and a *brief* description of what they do for the agency (DON'T send job descriptions unless requested)
- A list of current board members with their addresses, place of employment and title, work and home phone numbers, and what officer or committee chair positions they hold
- A list of the board committees, with a listing of current members and a brief explanation of what the committees do
- A flowchart of funding, where it comes from, where it goes (pie charts are particularly good for this purpose)
- A list of programs with a two-sentence description of each program
- A listing of frequently used acronyms/jargon and their meaning
- A list of board responsibilities (adapted from earlier in this chapter)
- A list of staff responsibilities (adapted from earlier in this chapter)
- A list of officer responsibilities (see next section)

J. COMMITTEES OF THE BOARD

As noted earlier, you need a structure of committees to make the board work. The board does not have the time to review every single issue at length to the level of detail and scrutiny it may merit at every meeting. Thus, the board needs to delegate the "grunt" work to the committees. Your organization needs to determine what type of committees it needs to serve your board of directors. Some committees may outlive their usefulness over time: others, such as your finance committee, will always be needed. Standing committees are those committees that are established on a permanent basis and may be described in the bylaws. Ad hoc committees are those assigned to carry out specific functions, make recommendations to the entire board, and then disband.

It is important to note that committee membership does not need to be solely composed of board members. Committee members can also come from the pool of potential board members (and are an excellent training ground for board membership) and from persons who have a specific interest in helping the organization.

1. AN EFFECTIVE COMMITTEE STRUCTURE

- Provide expertise to the board by gathering a group of experts on a given subject in a committee where they can share ideas and make recommendations based on the issues at hand.

- Alleviate the board's dealing with every detail of operation. Working committees take assignments from the board, deal with them effectively, and return with solutions to recommend to the board. Committees will also come before the board with ideas and recommendations that their committee members have developed.

- Permit broader participation by all board members.

The president, in consultation with the executive director, should make all committee assignments based on each board member's expertise and special talents, as well as personal preference. This should be done on an annual basis. Each board member should know several weeks before the first board meeting of the year which committee(s) he or she will serve on for the year. Board members should be notified in writing on which committee they will serve, who the chairman is, when and where the committee usually meets, and who the other committee members will be.

☞ **HANDS ON:** Some board members will not be happy with their committee assignments. One way to solve this is to ask each board member on which committee they would prefer to serve before the decision is made. At the last board meeting of the year, provide each board member with a written checklist of available committee assignments that must be returned to the president by the deadline noted. (Make it clear that it is not always possible to place them on the committee of their choice, but every effort will be made to do so. If they do not submit the form by the deadline noted, their assignment will be made by the president.) Then, based on this and the organization's needs, make assignments.

As noted in the discussion of board responsibilities, every board member should serve on at least one committee. However, don't ask new members to serve right away. Let them ease into their duties for five or six months and then give them an assignment. Try to keep committee membership small and focused. Five to nine people seems to work well for most groups. An odd number of members provides a tie breaker if you need it.

Finally, I recommend having all committee appointments be one year in length. That way, the president and the committee chair can constantly be improving the committees, adjusting to the changes on the board, on the staff, and in the industry. This does not mean that a particular board member might not serve on one particular committee for six years; it just ensures the maximum flexibility for the president.

2. WHAT COMMITTEES NEED TO OPERATE

Committees, like boards, need certain things to operate effectively and efficiently. As I have noted repeatedly, an effective committee structure is crucial to an effective board, so staff need to ensure that the following elements are present:

- A clear understanding of their role and what their limitations are
- Quality, supportive staffing
- A committee chairperson who is:
  - A leader
  - Knowledgeable
  - Experienced in group leadership
  - Able to encourage participation by all committee members
  - Capable of facilitating a meeting and keeping members on track without inhibiting valuable new discussion
  - Able to bring the group to a timely conclusion and/or a decision

- Committee members who:
    - Complete their assignments on time
    - Do their homework between meetings
    - Are reasonable and thoughtful
    - Understand the importance and impact of their decisions

One last suggestion on committees. If you find that committee reports to the board are simply the basis for rehashing everything at length again, you are not using your committee structure well. I understand that some critical issues will deserve a great deal of board attention and time, but if you see that you are simply holding the committee meeting over again at the board meeting, work to cut short the debate and have the board accept or reject committee recommendations, not reinvent them. One technique that works well for board members who feel the need to know everything about everything is to invite them (in public at the board meeting) to attend the committee meetings and have input there.

RECAP

In this chapter, we have set the stage for building a better board of directors for your organization. You have learned about what makes an effective board and the barriers to that effectiveness. We have reviewed the responsibilities of the board to the organization and listed the expectations that the board should have of the staff. We also went over the legal liabilities of the board and suggested ways to reduce and avoid liability.

A quick review here of the crucial criteria and responsibilities from this chapter is in order. First, the characteristics of a businesslike board:

- It understands the organization's mission, and acts to implement that mission for the benefit of the organization's constituency consistently and professionally.
- It acts as a policy setter and check and balance with the staff.
- It works primarily with the executive director and evaluates the executive director at least annually.
- It changes over time, filling its membership fully by recruiting new members to meet the changing needs of the organization.
- It elects qualified officers and appoints qualified committee chairs.
- It supports the organization in public.

The responsibilities of the board were listed as follows:

- Fulfill all of the IRS and State not-for-profit reporting requirements.
- Set policy and establish organizational goals.
- Hire an executive director.
- Evaluate the executive director's performance in writing at least annually.
- Assure that fiscal policies are in place and followed.
- Help develop and adopt budgets.
- Review and amend bylaws every two years.
- Assure compliance with funding stream's policies and regulations.
- Establish personnel policies and monitor their compliance.
- Nominate and elect officers.
- Represent the organization in public.
- Help recruit new board members.
- Raise funds.
- Perform volunteer program work.

Finally, the staff responsibilities to the board were listed:

- The board should expect accurate, timely, honest, and focused information.
- The board should be regularly informed of new developments.
- The board should expect staff to gather information, analyze it, and make recommendations to the board—in essence, to be technical advisors to the board.
- The board should expect staff to report fiscal information regularly.
- The board should encourage staff to make the optimum use of the board as a resource.
- The board should expect staff to develop a process for and to educate all new board members and to orient all board members on an ongoing basis.
- The board should expect staff to provide support for board recruitment and development.
- The board should expect staff to support board committees and provide them with necessary information and expertise they need.
- The board should expect staff to attend all meetings of the board unless excused therefrom.

Having a board that meets the demands of your organization is essential. But how do you find out what kind of board you really need?

Questions for Discussion

1. Do we have a businesslike board now? How can we get there?
2. Is the list of board responsibilities valid for our agency? How should we improve and amend our list?
3. What about staff responsibilities to the board? Do we do all these things now? Does our board agree? Where can we improve?
4. How can we ramp up our orientation process to be constant and consistent?
5. Is there value in having ongoing board recruitment? Why? How can we move toward that goal?

6

Managing Your People

OVERVIEW

An essential component in successful not-for-profits is building and retaining a strong staff, one that knows the mission, knows the field of endeavor that the organization has embarked on, and manages all of its resources to accomplish that goal. These resources, of course, include the mission and the board, but they also include volunteers, the cash and fixed plant of the organization, and, of course, the staff, which is the subject of this chapter.

In the following pages, I will walk you through the information you need to become a more effective manager of your staff, valuing and empowering them. We'll look at a management style that is literally upside down, some competing management styles and their advantages and disadvantages. We'll look long and hard at ways to communicate better. I'll show you some new thoughts on delegation, how to double your outcomes in evaluations, and how to set up a staff reward program that really rewards rather than punishes. By the end of the chapter, you will have a clearer understanding of how to manage that irreplaceable asset—your staff.

First, some facts to set the framework from which I will advise you: Your staff is one of the "markets" that you need to attend to. As I noted in Chapter 2, you are increasingly in competition for good staff. Second, you can't, and probably never will, pay like the private sector, whether for a secretary, a driver, a line staff person, or an administrator. Thus, you have to give folks who work with you something more than just a check to keep them coming to work for you.

To a certain extent, this something is your mission statement, and we discussed this at length in Chapter 4. But beyond that, it is your culture, the way you as staff treat each other and hang in there together as a team that will keep people wanting to be employed with you.

A. THE INVERTED PYRAMID OF MANAGEMENT

Look at Exhibit 6-1, the traditional management pyramid. This organizational structure, which is familiar to almost everyone, was not, believe it or not, developed at the same time as the pyramids in Egypt or Central America. In fact, it was developed after World War II by the Rand Corporation for the use of global U.S. corporations to help them manage their firms. And it worked for nearly 30 years. Rather, it worked until there was serious competition.

You see, after the war, the United States really had a 20-year window in which it had the only serious manufacturing, medical, research, and higher education capabilities in the world. Much of the industrial world lay in ruins and spent that time rebuilding and recovering from the destruction of the war. America had free rein, until the Europeans and Japanese and then the Koreans and other Asian countries recovered. Then, from the mid-1970s through the mid-1980s, those countries ate our lunch. Remember when the Japanese bought Rockefeller Center and we thought it was a harbinger of things to come?

It wasn't, and one of the many reasons why was the abandonment of the traditional management structure. Companies became flatter (with fewer levels between the line staff and the senior executives) and they also flipped themselves around and realized that the people who were

Exhibit 6-1   Traditional Management Pyramid

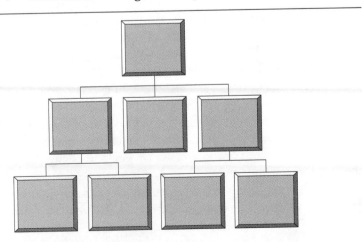

really the most important in any organization were the people who do the actual manufacturing or provide the actual service: the line staff. World-class firms like Cisco Systems, Marriott, Federal Express, Lands End, and Intel all have turned their organizations around by valuing their line staff more and their executives less. This kind of structure empowers staff, pushes decisions to the line of service, and makes use of all of the resources of the organization. In a competitive, globalized marketplace, it is the model that succeeds.

The same holds true for not-for-profits. Most not-for-profits simply copied the for-profit world and still use the old traditional model. Until the not-for-profit world was subjected to serious competition, it worked just fine. No longer. Successful not-for-profits realize that they too must value their staff, educate and empower them, and bring everyone into the effort to provide total customer satisfaction. If they don't, they will not be around much longer.

In this organizational model, the executive director is at the top of the heap, with associate or assistant directors, and assorted middle management between the executive and the line staff who are portrayed at the bottom of the pile.

Note that the box that the executive director would occupy is at the bottom, and the line staff at the top, with the people that you serve at the very top. This symbolism (and that is all it is if you don't live this style of management all the time) is important, because many organizations need to rethink what is the most important thing that they do, who is most important, and where their internal priorities are.

Exhibit 6-2   The Preferred Model

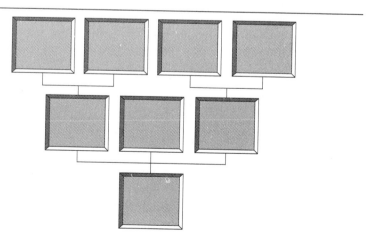

Let's look at the major tenets of my version of the inverted pyramid, and then examine some examples.

• *The only reason there are staff is because there are people to serve. The only reason there are managers is because the staff doing the service need support.* The executive director is not the most important person in the not-for-profit. He or she may be the most *powerful*, but not the most important. If all staff realize that management exists to find and manage resources to allow line staff to do their jobs, then the priorities become much clearer, the roles begin to change a bit, and the organization starts to head in the correct direction.

• *Managers are enablers, not "restrictors."* Good management should be a supportive, assistive function rather than a harsh power game, telling people why they can't do things. As an enabler, your role is to support your staff in accomplishing the goals of the organization. This support means doing what it takes to get the job done. It includes fighting for resources for your people, fixing things that aren't right, getting distractions large and small out of the way, and participating in budget and planning activities, no matter what your level in the organization. This fundamental principle allows you to see your job in very human terms. Your job as a supervisor is to take some of the load off of the people you supervise and let them do their jobs.

• *The supervisor/supervised relationship is two-way.* The relationships you develop with your staff, like any other relationships, are two-way. That means that both the supervisor and the supervised have a responsibility to make things work. Additionally, if the closer you go toward the people you serve, the more important people doing the service are, then the supervisor—instead of spending time restricting and controlling—should be facilitating getting resources to his or her employees. As we all know, relationships will not work if you always talk and never listen, if you only give ideas and are never receptive to those of your staff, or if you make all the decisions and do not delegate. More on these later.

• *Treat others the way you would want to be treated.* Honesty, fairness, and consistency are the key characteristics of a successful manager. Honesty means not promising to do something you cannot deliver ("I'll get back to you on that tomorrow"); fairness means treating all of your staff equally (what goes for Sam has to go for Sally); and consistency means asking for rules to be followed and then enforcing them when you say you will. Say what you mean and mean what you say.

• *Be a leader, but willing to follow.* This means that you are a leader who takes risks on behalf of your staff. It also means you let your staff take the lead when they are right. (This happens more than you or I want to admit.) It also means being very human and part of the team, so that you pitch in and do the most menial task when it is necessary to help support your staff. If there is a rush item to get out, like a mailing, and everyone is hustling around, pitch in: stuff envelopes for an hour, run copies, lug boxes, drive the van. We all know that you are very busy, but these small efforts go a long way with staff people; they remember them and it makes you more accessible to them.

• *If you are going to help your staff, you need to keep in touch.* Knowing what is going on with your line staff has never been more important. The further you are from line work, the more important it is. Make the time to work with line workers. My rule is one day per quarter at the very least, and more if the size and locations that you operate allow it. This task (which too many managers think is a waste of time) is, in truth, an essential component of the job. The most popular term for this was coined by Tom Peters in *In Search of Excellence,* Warner Books, 1982. He called it "Management by Wandering Around." Peters talked about keeping in touch by being on site, on the factory floor, or at the place that service is being provided. In addition to just being there, I also have seen over and over the positive effects of also having management *do* some line work at regular intervals.

☞ **HANDS ON:** Do a monthly stint as a volunteer, a quarterly day as a line worker, or simply have breakfast or lunch with line staff once a week. You've got to keep in touch with your people, and that means starting by understanding what they do. For example, if you run a hospital, work as a security guard, or as a volunteer who greets new patients for a day. If you run a human service organization, open a case, be a meals-on-wheels driver, sit in on an encounter or support group. If you run a school, teach an hour a week or a day a month as guest teacher. The essential philosophy: This is *not* taking time away from your job: *This is an essential part of your job!!!* You will learn more about your organization, how it really runs, and what staff really need to get the mission accomplished than you would ever believe.

Many of the senior staff at McDonald's work one week a year behind the counter at a restaurant, to keep in touch. It doesn't matter that most of them worked at a Mac's as a teenager. They need to work on site *now* to know what works and what doesn't *now*.

• *When you and your staff are praised, pass it around. When you are criticized, take the fall.* You are responsible for the results of both you and your staff. But, when someone praises you (individually or as a group), pass the praise on directly: "Well, thank you, Mayor, for those kind words, but I am just the Exec. The real work, and thus the real praise, should go to our outreach staff." Pass the praise around.

Also, go out of your way to compliment deserving individual and group efforts. Positive reinforcement is always appreciated. This can be constant and informal or may include employee recognition, which we'll discuss later in this chapter.

The reverse is true when you are criticized—as an individual or as your part of the organization: If you are the head person, you take the fall. Never, ever, ever blame someone else. There are three reasons for this. First, even if whatever went wrong is really not your fault, you are in charge. The captain on the bridge is responsible for the actions of his or her people. Second, nothing you do will bring more loyalty or build more morale than stepping in front of the blame bullet for your staff people. "Well, (board president), I know we missed the deadline. I'm doing all I can to minimize the damage, and I've already apologized to the effected people. It won't happen again."

Finally, it is always easy to blame your staff for something that doesn't go right. But remember, *it may really be your fault,* as a result of your not clearly communicating instructions or picking the wrong person to complete a task. We'll look at delegation and communications later in the chapter.

The inverted pyramid works, slowly but surely. However, to make it work, it has to be *lived,* every day in every way. Once you set yourself up as believing this philosophy, it is easy to fall off the pedestal. If you just flip your organizational chart on its head and don't follow it up with real and consistent actions to support the concept, you will lose ground with your staff.

With those tenets in mind, let's look at a couple of applications of the principal of the inverted pyramid and how it works.

❑ **FOR EXAMPLE:** My wife, Chris, is a special education teacher in our local public school district, assigned to one of the 5th–6th-grade centers. All teachers are required to come in for planning days and meetings a few days before the children return in the fall, and these are not days that most teachers look forward to. The schools are still hot, the meetings are dull, the kids are not yet there, and there is too much to get done in too short a time.

This particular fall, Chris went in for her planning days with even more trepidation. The 5–6 center she was assigned to was new; she knew only some of the staff and didn't know the principal at all, although she had heard through the grapevine that the principal was "incredible."

After her first day of meetings, Chris came home, totally pumped up and excited. She almost couldn't tell me the story fast enough. "It was incredible. Our principal (Phyllis) was amazing. She came into our first all-faculty meeting and said: *"I am the principal here. I am the person who ensures that you get the resources you need and the necessary environment to allow you to teach to your maximum potential. You, as teachers, are what this school is all about: teaching children. My job is to get you the resources you need, as well as removing the distractions you don't need. If you need supplies, see me and I'll get them. If you need a disruptive child removed from the room, I'll do it. If you can't get parental support, I'll help you. My job is not to sit on you, it is to help you teach."*

Chris went on: "You could have heard a pin drop. No one had ever been talked to by a principal like that before. I actually heard our union rep say as we walked out, 'Who needs money if we're treated like that?' "

Chris has taught at that school for 11 years as of this writing, and Phyllis has moved on to another school, leaving her successor to carry on the tradition of management that she started. The school is among the most recognized in the nation, and its students are blessed with great teachers, who are well treated, who want to be there every day to teach. The school is a great place to learn. Not only do kids like it there, but their test scores are up, there are innovative teaching techniques being tried, and parents from other 5–6 centers are trying to get their kids transferred.

This example shows what can be done in a short time with a commitment of one person. Admittedly, Phyllis had a clean slate (a new faculty) to start with, but she also had to overcome tradition, past morale problems, and inertia. She did it by letting the teachers know in word and deed that she valued them as professionals and as individuals. What more do any of us really want?

❏ **For Example:** As a result of my work, I travel a great deal. I usually stay in hotels that are the choice of the conference planners at the conventions where I speak, or at hotels close to clients with whom I am consulting. In both cases, someone else decides where I stay. When I am lucky enough to check into a Marriott, I know all of the above needs and more will be met. I know that everything will work, that I will be treated like a valued customer, and that whatever I need will be provided. This is particularly important when I am conducting training, as I need to ensure that the overhead projector, microphone, and room temperature all are working well (and in many places this is an iffy proposition at best), and that other last-minute details are attended to. What I don't want are hassles, bad attitudes, or to be told "can't" or "won't."

In the 20 years that I have been traveling for business, I have probably stayed at 90 Marriotts, and I have never, ever, met anyone (bellhop, waitress, housekeeping staff, convention worker) who works in any of those hotels and not been greeted with a "Good morning, sir, how are you today?" And it was said like they meant it. I can recount dozens of times staff went out of their way to make me feel special or to willingly and immediately fix a small problem that I had. Like the night I arrived at a Marriott in Washington, D.C., at 2:00 A.M. after interminable travel delays, only to find that my reservation was for a different Marriott across town. What did the clerk do? Dismiss me and tell me to go elsewhere? No, first, he called the other hotel to assure that my room was still available, and then, sensing my exhaustion and frustration, offered me a room at "his" hotel—the hotel that I was standing in—even though they had no rooms at my reserved rate. I gratefully accepted the latter offer, and five minutes later was escorted into a three-room suite, complete with fruit basket! On another occasion, I was off to a meeting and walked by a pleasant matronly housekeeping supervisor who greeted me with a cheery "Good morning," then told me to wait while she very tactfully straightened my tie, and added, "Go get 'em!" What a great way to start my day!

Both of these people made my stay memorable, by doing a little extra thing that they were both encouraged and empowered to do. The desk clerk had the authority to upgrade my reservation (or actually to give me one without a reservation), and the housekeeping staff person was simply motivated and pleasant.

Marriott as a corporation believes in the phrase of their CEO: Take care of your employees and they will take care of you. They constantly train and motivate their line staff, drilling into them the concept that they, and not the management, will make the hotel succeed or fail, and to have the line people surface ideas on ways to make the guests more comfortable. The company invests in its people and it pays off.

Other examples abound in the proprietary world. When was the last time you met a curt or unfriendly UPS or Federal Express delivery person? Or talked to a brusque salesperson from Lands End? You don't. Why? Because these organizations value their people, they tell them so all the time, and they show them by their actions. *All* of the staff at the Disney properties are provided costumes—not uniforms—and even the trash collectors at their parks go through a solid week of training in how to interact with customers *before* they get their trash collection training.

Think of each of these and other organizations such as airlines, restaurants, and the like. Who do you deal with nearly all the time in these organizations? *The lowest-paid people in the company.* At the airline, it's the ticket agent or the baggage clerk or the flight attendant. At a hotel, it's the concierge, bellhop, or desk clerk. At a restaurant, it's the greeter or server. It's these people who really shape your experience with the company. And, in successful companies, it is these people who are the most valued.

Who are these people in your organization? Who do your clients, donors, volunteers, and referral sources deal with most? If you are the Exec (unless you are a one-person shop), it's probably not you. Treat the people who actually *do* the mission with respect, and you'll get a lot more out of them.

B. STYLES OF SUPERVISION

There are four broad categories of management styles listed below. In truth, we all fit into at least one, and probably more than one at different times. As you read these, think about how each does or does not fit into our inverted pyramid model.

1. *Attila the Hun.* We've all worked for Attila, or a direct descendant. This person is *the* boss. No question about it. He or she maintains

a "directing behavior," lays down the law and expects it to be followed to the letter. He or she looks at their staff as stepping stones *up* the management ladder. "Attila" is quick to criticize and judge and has never heard of the words "thank you." Attila is obeyed but usually not respected. Attila also gets results, at least in the short term, but when Attila is not present, a great deal of staff time is spent griping.

2. *One of the Gang.* These managers usually come "up from the ranks" but never adjust to the new role. They want to remain one of the gang so they try to minimize or eliminate the distinctions between them and their staff. They never understand that once they cross the bridge to become a supervisor, they never again are peers. They can still be friends with those that they supervise, but they can never be pals. This person has difficulty in completing performance appraisals, and usually cannot discipline at all. Morale is good if you work for one of the gang, but productivity tends to slip, as this person may be liked, but is rarely respected.

3. *All Business.* These managers are thoroughly professional, but distant. They do not fraternize or socialize with the troops, and place great emphasis on plans, goals, objectives, budgets, and performance. They never take the time to truly get to know their people, and this is a key to good communications and effective delegation. I cannot envision this manager stuffing envelopes or filling in at the reception desk in a pinch.

4. *Coach/Conductor.* Both a coach and an orchestra conductor get the job done, but through the actions of others. The coach and the conductor know that they don't play, that others do, and that their success is contingent upon the success of their team. They cajole, praise, and discipline when it is necessary. These managers exemplify team spirit with enthusiasm, but maintain a long-term view of the organization. A coach/conductor helps his or her staff to grow and attain their maximum potential.

Obviously, I would prefer if all of us were coaches or conductors. But it would be naive to assume that everyone can adopt that style. Besides, in the real world, we all need to be Attila once in a while— hopefully for only short periods at long intervals! The most important thing is to adapt your style to let people know you value them. If you are demanding, fine, but be demanding of the right things: things that focus attention on mission and line staff and quality of outcome, not things that inflate your ego or make people cower before you.

Your style as a manager, as well as your priorities in terms of staff and mission, are inherent parts of bringing about the organizational direction that will allow you to succeed.

C. COMMUNICATIONS

To succeed with your staff, you will need to be able to communicate with them: to find out what they need to get their job done, to delegate tasks, plan budgets, figure out what to buy for lunch—all these things require good communications. It often seems that *Communication* is a five-syllable word meaning trouble, as in, "What we have here is a failure to communicate." I can hardly think of one of the not-for-profits that I have consulted with over the past 10 years—even the well-run ones—who didn't complain about inadequate (or poor or awful) internal communications. This seems to be an area where everyone would like to see improvement (or are unsatisfied with the way things are now). Why?

There are a number of reasons. First, many people assume that they need to know everything that goes on in the organization. They don't, but that is irrelevant. They *feel* that they should be better informed, and thus will be discontented until they *feel* that they are being at least adequately informed. (Often, these people will simultaneously complain about too many meetings, too many memos, and not enough time to do their "real" jobs.) The second reason is that many not-for-profits are changing quickly and growing rapidly. As a result, the staff, particularly those who have been employed for a number of years, often feel that they "used to know everything and everyone around here" and now feel isolated. This problem is most acute if the organization has multiple buildings or sites.

Obviously, the issue of communications is essential, not only to good operational management, but also to good morale. Good communications is as much perception as reality, and it is based on the following tenets:

1. TRUST

If the staff don't trust the management to give them full, accurate, and timely information, the rest of these techniques are a waste of time. The staff people will still complain about the lack of communication from top management.

❑ FOR EXAMPLE: A client agency of mine was having problems with employee morale. The executive director had been on the job two years and had instituted a number of staff and organizational changes that I felt were terrific, but that had met with traditional resistance to change from many staff. This agency provided distinctly different services at two separate sites, and thus staff didn't all get to see each other a great deal.

The agency was planning to construct a new building to house some of its services. At the time the events described here occurred, the agency had developed architectural plans, had acquired a site, and had a date for the initiation of construction and a target for completion. They also knew the budget, and which major components of the agency would move to the site upon completion. They were to build the building as a shell first, then later divide the shell into components to house various programs.

As soon as the site had been purchased, all staff who had not been in on the early planning were informed of the project. Approximately two weeks later, I was scheduled to come in to run some focus groups of staff to discuss the results of an employee survey that our firm had administered for the agency. In the survey, communications had come up over and over again as a real deficit in the management area.

During my discussions with staff, one staff person (I'll call her Linda) and I had the following conversation (the notation "PCB" means yours truly.)

LINDA   Senior management never tells us anything 'til after the fact.

PCB   Give me an example.

LINDA   Well, take this new building we just heard about. We just haven't been told anything about the project, and it's important to us.

PCB   Of course it is. What did the management staff tell you specifically?

LINDA   Well, I know that the building is being built at the corner of Adams Street and 15th, and that it will house the Intake, Client Assessment, and Rehabilitation Divisions.

PCB   Did they tell you anything else?

LINDA   No, nothing.

PCB   No information on schedule, budgets or anything else?

LINDA I do know that they are laying the foundation next week and that we are scheduled to occupy next April. I think my division will move in first.

PCB Sounds like you know everything there is to know about this project.

LINDA Well, they always tell us so late. . . .

You get the picture I'm sure. Linda did not trust the management staff, for whatever reason. And, no matter what the management people told her, no matter if she was included in senior management meetings, she would not be happy. If, however, she had trusted the senior management, she would have had a different outlook on the same information.

2. ALL COMMUNICATION IS TWO-WAY

The most important part of communications is not what you say, but what your staff hears. It is not what you send, but what your staff receives. It is not what you write, but what your staff reads. All of us have the mystery filter in our houses; you know the one that comes between you and your spouse or you and your kids. It's the filter that comes between your mouth and their ears and results in the conversation: "No, I didn't say THAT, what I said WAS," etc, etc. etc. There is little protection against miscommunication, but we can do more to check on what people heard so that we correct the initial miscommunication.

☞ **HANDS ON:** To vividly demonstrate this to your management staff, try this exercise with your staff. At a staff meeting, read off the following list (exactly) *without warning*. Read it slowly and deliberately:

**BED, REST, SLUMBER, SNOOZE, PILLOW,
SHEET, NAP, MATTRESS, SNORE, DREAM.**

Now ask the staff to write down as many as they can remember. Give them a minute or two. Ask how many people got six words (ask them to raise hands). Some will have gotten six. Ask if anyone got eight. Compliment them. Ask who wrote down the word "bed", the first word you read. About half will have. Compliment them. Ask who wrote down "dream," the last word you read. About the same number will have. Now, and this is the key, ask whoever wrote down the word "sleep" to raise their hands—and keep their hands up. If your group is like the dozens I've done this with, over half will have written down sleep, and *you never read it*! Have everyone look around to see how many hands were raised.

Make the point with your staff that the reason that they wrote down "sleep" was that they associated it with the rest of the words you read, but that they felt so strongly that they heard it, that they *wrote it down*. Now, if you were to have gone back to them in a week and asked for notes on what you said, they would have proof (documentation) that you said "sleep" because they wrote it down!

We need to ensure that our instructions and communications are understood.

Let's examine the issue of communications from the viewpoint of results. When does one of your staff fail to complete a task correctly? When:

- *They don't know what they are supposed to do.* None of us is very good on this one. Think about it; you tell your staff something and then ask, "Do you understand?" or even worse, "You understand, don't you?" Now, who is going to say to his or her boss, in effect "No, I don't understand; I'm stupid."? We don't give people much of a chance to say no, or to ask for help.

- *They don't know how to do the task.* Same issues as above.

- *They think they are doing it right, but haven't received any feedback.* If you are not around to talk to or observe staff while they are working on the project, you cannot guide them away from mistakes. Thus, little problems become big ones. If people are not given some supervision or observed, the first time they do a job, they may very well, with good intentions, do it completely wrong, and in a way that could have been prevented if you had been around enough to catch the little mistake before it got to be a big one.

- *They don't know* why *they should complete the task.* The *why* is so important. Telling people *why* they need to do something puts it in context; it gives the assignment a rationale, a purpose, and a priority. In terms of accurate communications, think of the difference in the message sent by someone saying, "Please put together a spreadsheet of our cash flow projections" or "Please put together a spreadsheet of our cash flow projections because I need to present them to the finance committee on Thursday night." The first assignment gives the bare bones. The second gives context, and would probably lead to a clearer more complete (and neat) cash flow being presented. Tell people *why* something needs to be done. Don't assume that they don't care about the why. Let them make that choice.

• *They hear something different than what you say and you are not in control of what your staff hears.* Remember our list *without* the word "sleep." Need I say more?

In order to get over the worst of these, when you give instructions to someone, particularly on something new, follow this order:

1. *Explain* how to do it.
2. *Demonstrate* how to do it (if possible).
3. *Request* an explanation of how to do it.
4. *Invite* the employee to demonstrate it for you (if possible).

Now, you can't just treat staff like little kids and say, "What did I just say?" in a condescending voice. But what you can do is ask "Please tell me what we just agreed you'd do, so that I can make sure I didn't tell you wrong." In an inverted pyramid management scheme, and if you agree that you are responsible to get the communications across, ask for feedback with the assumption that you have not communicated whatever needs to be communicated accurately or thoroughly. At the end of meetings, ask everyone at the table to reiterate what it is that they agreed to do at the meeting, and by when. Don't tell them what they agreed to; you want to hear it in their words.

D. DELEGATION

There is enough good material on delegation to fill three shelves at your local library, and we all know that good managers are ones who delegate effectively, so I won't try to convince you that you should be delegating more: rather I'll try to pass on some ideas on how to delegate better. Delegation is particularly tough on first time supervisors who still want to "do" rather than "manage." After all, if you hadn't been good at the "doing," you probably wouldn't have gotten promoted. But since you now are a supervisor, you have a different job, and not enough time to both do and supervise. You need to delegate the jobs that your staff can do now or learn fairly quickly. To be successful, you need to attend to the following rules:

• *Delegate authority with responsibility.* This is critical: Your employees must feel that they have the authority to decide as well as to do. If you require them to get back to you on every little detail, you might as well do it yourself, and your staff person will be very frustrated to boot. The further toward the line staff that decision authority can be pushed, the better.

• *Challenge your staff supportively.* Don't just give them a job and a deadline and then kick them out the door of your office. Learn how to offer support and advice without having them lean on you for everything. Also, push them a bit, forcing them to try new tasks if you feel they can learn them. Back off in the level of supervision as quickly as you can, but let them know that you are there as a safety net.

• *Know your staff.* This is critical for good supervision, delegation, and communications. You just have to take the time to know your people. Learn their strengths and weaknesses, their likes and dislikes, their potential and their pitfalls. You just have to have this information if you are going to use them to their maximum potential. Remember we talked about Peters and "Management by Wandering Around"? Being on site allows you to know your people.

• *Recognize that mistakes will (and should) be made.* It is how we learn. Honest mistakes honestly made are ok. Once. Don't let people make the same mistake twice. But be assuring and helpful, noting that you also have made your share of goof-ups. If people don't make mistakes, and don't learn, they won't ever grow. Adopt the maxim: "DO SOMETHING!" as your credo, and you will have gone a long way toward better delegating.

• *Admit that other people can do some things better than you can.* It really is true. You'll be amazed at how well other people can do what you have always done, often without your help. It will be different, but often—if you are really honest—better than the way you have done it in the past. Remember, be a leader but willing to follow.

☞ **Hands On:** Try this with your staff. Make a copy of the figure below. Hand it out at a staff meeting and tell people *exactly* the following: *"Take this, add one line, and turn this into a six."*

IX

Give the staff people a minute or two to get the right answer, and perhaps 1 in 10 will. The answer, by the way, is:

SIX

I used to use this exercise to teach people to learn how to solve problems in different ways. But, in 1988, my then six-year-old son Benjamin was talking to me as I was preparing for a presentation. He was asking the age-old question, "What do you do at work, Daddy?" and I was trying my best to explain the job of management consultant to not-for-profits in terms that he could understand. While talking, we came upon a copy of my training material that included the "IX" exercise. Aha! Here was a way that I could at least distract Benjamin from my inability to give him a satisfactory answer to my occupation. " Benjamin," I said, showing him the IX just as on the preceding page. "Take the pencil and with one line, turn this into a six." With no hesitation at all, he grabbed the pencil, added an "S" before the IX and said, "Like this?" I was floored. I mean, I knew he was smart (*my* child and all that egotistic drivel), but only about 10 percent of adults get this at all, much less immediately. What was going on?

What was going on, of course, was that Benjamin, as a first grader, had never learned about roman numerals. When he looked at a "IX", he saw an "icks," not a "nine," which is what adults see. In short, we, as adults have *too much information, too much education, too much knowledge* to solve this problem. Later that week, I was visiting Benjamin's classroom, and I asked the teacher if I could repeat the activity with the class. Of 30 kids in the room, all 30 got it immediately.

The point here is, don't assume that because you have a college diploma or a masters or a doctorate or 20 years on the job that you can solve every problem better than someone without those degrees or experience. Sometimes you'll be *too smart to solve the problem.*

❏ POSTSCRIPT TO THE STORY: As I was preparing the first edition of this book, Benjamin, then 11, asked me how the book was coming, and if there were any stories about him in the book. I told him yes and summarized the story for him. When I finished, he asked to see the problem; for me to let him do it again. He couldn't come up with the answer. I laughed and asked him what he saw on the page, and he said, "Dad, how can you turn a 9 into a 6 with one line?" I showed him, and informed him that he now knew too much to solve the problem:

he had learned about roman numerals. At this point, Benjamin's then seven-year-old brother Adam walked in. Benjamin (who like all big brothers thought he knew it *all*) handed Adam the "IX" and asked him to turn it into a 6. You guessed it. Adam, with no hesitation, replayed his brother's actions from five years before. He grabbed a pencil and wrote an "S" in front of the "IX." I still treasure the memory of the look on Ben's face as he realized he did not automatically know more than his little brother just because he was three years older.

Communicate clearly. Back to communications, again. Remember:

- *Explain* how to do it.
- Demonstrate how to do it (if possible).
- Request an explanation of how to do it.
- Invite the employee to demonstrate it for you (if possible).

Good delegation is the path to supportive management: You help people grow by good delegation. They wither without new challenges.

E. EVALUATION

I make the assumption in writing this section that you already have an evaluation policy and an evaluation tool in place. If you don't have such a policy, you need one, starting today.

At a minimum, you and your management team should provide a written and oral evaluation of every staff member, volunteer, and board member every year. Why? Because without evaluations, without confronting the bad and acknowledging the good, people don't grow. It is also the only documentation that you have of a person's capability (or lack thereof), his or her contributions to the organization, and the like. It is the easiest management task to procrastinate on, but it is an essential component of good management.

That having been said, there are some keys to the way we encourage a staff evaluation process to be established and conducted. These may be different than you have seen before, but they are well tested, and they work.

1. ALL EVALUATIONS SHOULD BE TWO-WAY

As discussed in the opening pages of this chapter, the relationship between a supervisor and the supervisee is just that—a relationship. It will not work if both parties don't participate and try to make it work.

For example, if the worker does not get clear instructions from the supervisor, or does not get them in a way that he or she can best understand and follow them, then the worker will fail to do the job up to the supervisor's expectations. In a normal evaluation setting, that problem would be the employee's fault, with no encouragement to the worker to point out the supervisor's communications problem. Therefore, your employee evaluations should have parts where the employee is evaluated, goals reviewed, and so forth, as well as parts where the supervisor is evaluated in terms of his or her interaction with the employee.

There is no question that for many supervisors this is a *terribly* threatening change. Supervisors are used to doing the evaluation, not being evaluated. For staff, this can be very nerve wracking as well. Evaluate my boss? No way! But it does work, can work, and should work in an organization that sees management as support, and staff as critical. We'll cover *how* you do it in the methodology below.

2. EVALUATIONS SHOULD BE ORAL *AND* WRITTEN

You write out evaluations so that you have to think about them, so that people can read and think about them, and so that you have documentation of what was said. You do them orally as well so that each person has to face the other with both the good and bad parts of the evaluation. It opens yet another channel in the communications array.

3. THERE SHOULD BE NO SURPRISES AT EVALUATIONS

If you and your staff are communicating well and regularly, if you are dealing with the good and bad immediately rather than waiting for an annual review, then there should be no bombshells between supervisor and worker. If there are big surprises, then the rest of the communications system is breaking down, and you should use the evaluation process as an early warning sign of that breakdown.

4. SET AND EVALUATE GOALS FOR BOTH PEOPLE

Three or four goals for the next evaluation period are important. If accomplished, they provide a feeling of satisfaction and accomplishment. If not, they provide a challenge for improvement. Again, the goals should be for the supervisor *and* the worker.

5. EVALUATIONS NEVER SHOULD BE JUST NUMERICAL

I feel that the biggest mistake that we all have made in the past 10 years in the area of evaluations is the trend to totally numerical rankings or ratings for evaluations. I understand the need for quantification in many evaluation/compensation systems; you need a number to calculate a bonus or a raise. But numbers without context are meaningless. They provide no guidance for the employee, and a record of no value in the future.

❏ **For Example:** Agency A has a form that asks for a supervisor to rate an employee in 10 categories such as "Enthusiasm," "Attendance," "Work Quality," "Interaction with Clients," "Interaction with Staff," and the like, on a 1–10 scale, with 10 being "Exceptional" and 1 being "Totally Unacceptable." Thus, a supervisor can go down the list and rank John or Mary a 7 for "Interaction with Staff" and a 5 for "Interaction with Clients" and be done with the whole rating in a minute. Now, the supervisor gives the evaluation to John or Mary and tries to compare the rating with last year's. John went from a 7 to an 8 in "Work Quality." But why? The supervisor cannot *really* remember. Worse, if next year there is a new supervisor, he or she will have absolutely no background as to *why* John was rated an 8 as opposed to a 7, or a 2 for that matter.

I strongly prefer written evaluations, with questions that require thought and answers in complete sentences. If you must use a quantified scale, fine, but require written justification for each numerical rating.

6. INCLUDE THE MISSION AS AN EVALUATION CRITERIA

Everyone should have as part of their evaluation criteria an item with wording to the effect of: In what ways did [the person being evaluated] pursue the mission or embody our mission and values this year? This, once again, reinforces the mission statement as a focus for the work ethic at your organization.

7. DEVELOP CRITERIA THAT ARE IMPORTANT TO THE ORGANIZATION AND TO THE INDIVIDUAL JOB BEING EVALUATED

Don't rely on standard evaluation forms. Work with your people to establish criteria that reflect your culture, mission, and values, as well as those that are focused on the job being evaluated. For example, I feel that people who supervise should have a component of their evaluation that deals with how the people that they supervise have evaluated them. This supports the theory of management as a support function. Another example would be to limit an evaluation criterion for "Interaction with Customers" to only those who *have* such interaction.

8. SEPARATE EVALUATION FROM COMPENSATION, IN TERMS OF TIMING

Discussions of money muddy the waters between a supervisor and an employee. Have the supervisor deal with the money portion of this well before the evaluation of work effort, and have it out of the way.

G. CHANGING THE WAY YOU EVALUATE

You may evaluate once a year, twice a year, or quarterly. Never do it any less than annually, and, if you really want to impress your people, do it twice a year. No matter how often you do it, here are some suggestions of how to implement a two-way evaluation system.

1. PLAN AND CONSULT

Before instituting such a major change as going to two-way evaluations, some planning and consultation are necessary—or you will wind up with people very, very upset. Start by establishing a staff committee (of all levels of staff) to review both the evaluation tool and the evaluation process. Discuss the importance of two-way evaluations, what they are and are not, and set the criteria for evaluation as well as the process. If you tie the evaluation process into your compensation package, talk about how that will happen and how worker evaluation of supervisors will not be held against the worker in the compensation area (there are protections against that outlined below).

Write up your new evaluation policy, and the reason it is being instituted, and transmit that to staff in writing and in meetings. I strongly encourage you to stage a role-playing exercise at this point so that people can see how the process is supposed to work. Have two staff act out the entire process.

Try the process for a year, monitoring it closely, and then evaluate and amend it. Understand that it will take time for some staff to adequately trust their supervisors to be willing to take the risk of offering criticism. It will also take time for some supervisors to be able to accept constructive criticism from their workers. Give it time, but monitor the implementation carefully. Have intermittent meetings with supervisors and workers to discuss the program and how it is going, comparing that to the original intent.

2. A SUGGESTED EVALUATION PROCESS

1. The clerical staff (personnel director, etc.) should provide both the supervisor and the worker with their copies of the evaluation form 10 days prior to the evaluation's being due. Each person then fills out his or her part of the form in writing. The supervisor also at this point fills out any salary or bonus recommendation in line with the organization's compensation policy, and hands it in to the appropriate person. That way, the financial part of the evaluation is done and delivered *before* the supervisor gets evaluated by the worker, reducing the chance of retribution by the supervisor if the evaluation from the worker is not perfect.

2. The supervisor and worker meet in private, exchange forms and go over the evaluation as well as the goals that they had set at the last evaluation. They discuss the reason for each criteria rating and, in general, how they are doing as a team.

3. Both supervisor and worker now set their goals for the next evaluation period. This is best done by themselves and then discussed at a second meeting.

4. After meeting to discuss the goals, the supervisor may, as appropriate, inform the worker of compensation changes or bonuses.

5. It is critical that the supervisor and worker informally review the progress toward the goals two or three times during the next evaluation period. I recommend that they both put the times for such an informal review on their calendars to remind them.

H. STAFF RECOGNITION

An often forgotten component of inverted pyramid management has to do with staff recognition—celebrating and rewarding the kinds of behaviors that you want to see the most. There are virtually unlimited ways to do this, but most organizations that try this have problems that could have been avoided. The most common is to adopt another organization's program without checking with their own staff first!

Three critical rules for staff recognition programs are:

1. *The "rewards" should not be punishment.* Don't assume that what you think is a nice reward is received the same way by those whom you are trying to honor. Reward (and punishment) is a very subjective thing.

❏ FOR EXAMPLE: Ten years or so ago, I was running a two-day retreat for a state human services department at which the director and the 15 "highest" level staff were participating. One of the department's training staff who specialized in working with hotels had made all the hotel and meal arrangements, and she was on-site for the two days of the retreat, ready and able to assist us if needed. The staff person, whom I will call Linda, was a very capable and pleasant person and had mentioned to me that, among many other things, in 20 years with the department she had never actually met a director. She also had reserved another training room right down the hall from our meeting room in which she would set up camp to help us if we needed her, and in which she would eat.

Following the afternoon session, the participants broke for dinner in the hotel restaurant, while I remained behind in the meeting room to summarize our afternoon activities so that we could proceed without delay when we reconvened. Linda had made dinner reservations for all the participants, plus me, and now I realized that since I would not be there, there would be an empty seat at the table. I saw the director walking by in the hall and ran out to stop her, suggesting that since Linda had done such a great job on the arrangements that it might be a real treat for her to be invited to dinner with all the department senior staff. The director agreed and said that she would set it up. I returned to my work feeling that I had really done a nice thing for Linda, and that she would be very pleased by the opportunity to visit with the director and other senior staff.

Ten minutes later, Linda stuck her head in the door and said, "Well, I *won't* be down the hall for dinner, if you need me. I have been told to eat dinner with the 'mucky mucks.'" She walked out of the room with a long face, looking completely depressed. I immediately realized that my "reward" to Linda was actually a punishment. While I might want to meet the people at the dinner table, the thought of spending an hour with the "big bosses" terrified Linda. It was the worst thing I could have done to her. I later apologized to her, and we still joke about the incident when we talk.

2. *The system must be seen by staff as fair and impartial.* There is no point to this if the staff people feel that the system is rigged, and that only the "boss's favorites" will be chosen. You simply must have a system that will both actually be and, more importantly, *be seen as* impartial and fair.

❏ **FOR EXAMPLE:** In another statewide agency, a good friend of mine took over as director, following an "Attila the Hun." My friend, whom we'll call Greg, as one of his early actions asked line staff to develop a rewards program that was fair, meaningful, and easy to administer. The results? There is a rewards review committee made up of 10 line staff (the total staff of the department is over 2,000). This review committee has volunteered, and also has made itself *permanently* ineligible from receiving the rewards. Each month, this committee reviews nominations for Employee of the Month, which can be submitted by peers or supervisors. Employees who are selected get a number of things: their picture in the foyer of all agency offices that month, a plaque given to them by Greg, and other "perks" that *they get to choose.* The system has worked wonders in the two years that it has been in place, but it has all the parts essential for success: peer review, impartiality, and rewards that *really* reward.

3. *The system must be understandable and support the mission.* You can't have a reward system that requires a degree in astrophysics to understand. You also need a reward system that rewards behavior that supports the mission. That's why soldiers get medals for valor, and police officers and firefighters get awards for saving citizens' lives; it's the kind of action that we want to encourage in those professions.

In order to do all these things well, have a group of employees from all levels of the organization study the idea of rewards and get back to you on a program. They may even tell you that staff would prefer *not* to have rewards, preferring to remain anonymous, or to have the funds that a reward program would use go into the programs instead. Do not decide from your senior management seat what is meaningful for line staff. You may well waste time, money and morale.

RECAP

In this chapter, we have reviewed the parts of top quality management for your not-for-profit:

- Living the *inverted pyramid*. Valuing your staff, remembering that by increasing the importance of your staff who are closest to the line you will improve morale and productivity. You need to live this attitude, not just put it on your table of organization. You need to be your staff's best advocate.

- Using the *coach/conductor style* of management. Remember that neither the coach nor the conductor plays. You have to get your outcomes completed through the actions of others. You have to know those people and their capabilities well to have them come together and achieve a common, desired outcome.

- Understanding that all *communications* are two-way and that what someone hears is more important than what you say. If you believe, as I do, in the inverted pyramid, you need to act as a facilitator, as a supporter. That means in communications, you need to communicate in the way that your people hear best, not in the way that you feel most important.

- *Delegating* effectively, and how that is a strength—not a weakness. You need to remember that you cannot do it all and, in fact, that others can often do it better than you.

- Evaluating in the best manner: *two-way*. You and your staff should both evaluate the relationship, and your contributions to it. These evaluations will improve your management skills as much as they will help your staff people.

- *Rewarding staff* for their desirable behavior. All of us like to be rewarded. Just remember to make rewards real rewards and not punishments. Ask what people would like, and try to give them that, not something that you would like to have.

Mr. Marriott had it right: "Take care of your employees and they will take care of you." You need your staff to be motivated and committed. You know you can never pay them enough, so keeping the good ones takes a different kind of compensation: what they do and how you treat them. Hopefully, this chapter has provided some insights and some tools for you to apply to that end.

Questions for Discussion

1. What parts of this chapter apply to us? Let's be specific.
2. Do we value our line staff? How?
3. If we had an inverted pyramid, what would we have to change?
4. What are our styles of supervision? What do they say about our values?
5. Should we have two-way evaluations? Why or why not?
6. What about communications? Should we train our staff in this important area?

7

The Wired Not-for-Profit

OVERVIEW

Oh, the wired world. Constant cell phone chatter in public places, endless numbers of cable stations to click through, .com glued to the end of every noun, verb, and proper name, "e-" in front of way too much of the English language. Need something? Information, a friend, a sales venue, groceries, or a reservation for dinner? Go on the Net.

And, of course, that's just the beginning. Luddites aside, we can never go back to the unwired, unconnected, nontech past. You, your staff, your clients, your donors, your funders, your referrers—in short, all the people that matter to your organization—are either wired or on their way there. Think your clientele are too poor or dispossessed to need tech? A friend of mine who runs a homeless shelter told me a story recently about asking a new client the standard marketing inquiry that all not-for-profits should ask: "How did you find out about us?" The answer from this bedraggled, unshaven man who would could fulfill most people's mental image of a homeless person? "Oh, I checked you out on your Web site. I liked what I saw, so I came over." How could a homeless man be able to investigate this organization on the Internet? At the public library.

Technology has gone from being a luxury to becoming a ubiquitous, necessary tool. And in just 10 short years. Quality, speed, the variety of applications, and their ease of use have all improved, and price has gone down, down, down, until we have reached the point where you can get free cell phones, computers, cable installation, and a host of other products and services that five years ago were the mark of only the wealthy. And, the tech is paying off. In large part, the long-term 1990s economic boom was due to all of us finally getting the payoff from our national investment in technology.

Tech has had an impact, of course, in the not-for-profit sector as well. But more than any other part of our economy, we have not yet seen technology's full benefit. As this is written, much of the sector is well behind the tech curve, and suffering from the failure to recognize the revolution for what it was, and to put any of its too scarce resources into tech until very late in the game. But, like it or not, the world has changed. In his wonderful book, *The Lexus and the Olive Tree,* Farrar, Strauss & Giroux, 1999, Tom Friedman notes that in the very near future, there will be only two kinds of organizations: Those who embrace technology and the free market, and those who don't. The first have a long life expectancy, the second next to none.

In this chapter, I will show you many examples of how technology is helping not-for-profits like yours do more service sooner, and better. We'll look at the realities of competing for donors, staff, volunteers, and people to serve in the wired age. We'll examine how to adapt your organization to a tech-friendly model without breaking your budget. I'll give you a technology checklist to examine now, and a review and renewal process to make sure you stay appropriately up to date in using technology to the maximum mission outcome.

I know many readers hate this. Tech is not second nature to many in our sector, and perhaps you, or members of your staff, are tech averse. I understand, and you need to know that you are not alone. At Stanford University, which is located on the north end of the Silicon Valley, the student body breaks itself down into two groups in its slang. "Techies" are engineers, math, and hard science majors. "Fuzzies" are social science, English, art, and history majors. Now think about it. In the not-for-profit world, which would predominate? Of course, the fuzzies. And, there is nothing wrong with being a fuzzy. It's just that all of us fuzzies have to adapt, adjust, and get on with our lives in an increasingly techie world. We can't do the ostrich on this one. The people that we serve depend on us to adapt so that we can continue to pursue our mission.

The tech world is here to stay. Let's figure out a way to use the technology to do more mission, better, sooner, and more efficiently.

A. THE WIRED WORLD WE LIVE IN

When I began considering a new edition of *Mission-Based Management,* I knew immediately that there needed to be a chapter on technology. I knew that being wired was an essential characteristic of a successful mission-based organization, and yet I approached the writing of this chapter with great trepidation: Any discussion of technology on printed paper is doomed to be outdated by the time it is read. I suspect that by the time you read this, this chapter may seem downright quaint.

But I still need to impress you, your staff, and your board members of some realities about the wired world we all now live, work, raise money, and provide service in. Here are a few observations to consider:

1. THE STATE-OF-THE-ART HARDWARE OR SOFTWARE YOU JUST BOUGHT WILL ALWAYS BE OUTDATED IN UNDER 10 MINUTES

Get used to it. When you make your tech purchase, assume that the next day there will be a sale on a better system or set of software. While that is frustrating, you just need to make your best decision, buy the tools you need, and get them in place. I've long lost track of the number of clients who do nothing because they are waiting for the cost to come down further. In the interim, they put up with patched together systems that frustrate everyone, and cost way more in lost time, or poor services, or inaccurate or unusable information than they will ever save. Remember, if you plan well, the benefits of your tech purchases will far outweigh the costs. But to get the benefits, you have to get the equipment and/or software.

2. JUST BECAUSE YOU CAN'T KEEP UP WITH ALL THE CHANGES DOESN'T MEAN YOU SHOULDN'T PAY ATTENTION TO THEM.

Moore's Law, posited by one of the founders of Intel in 1964, states that the computing capacity of microchips will double every 18 months, at no increase in cost. It has proven amazingly true and, although there are some engineering limits on chip capacity, will continue to provide benefits well into the first part of the current century. This fact, and the brutal competition in the technology and telecommunications sector, is what is driving choices up and prices down—a good thing for all of us.

But the choices can be both dizzying and deafening, which can cause us to just stop listening after a while. And that is a mistake. You need to continue to pay attention, as there will shortly be some thing, some piece of equipment, some advance, some software, that will really help your organization in terms of cost, efficiency, and mission. You've got to keep looking and listening.

❏ FOR EXAMPLE: A great example is cell phones. Our family has gone from having a bag phone (Remember those? About four pounds of hardware with 30 minutes of battery life) to in-car phones, to small purse- and pocket-size phones during the past 10 years. First one, then two, now three for the family. In 1995, I had a phone (our second at the time) hardwired into my car so that I could simultaneously talk and drive more safely. Between then and the end of 1999, I watched the phone my wife uses diminish in size and increase in portability, and our eldest son got a phone when he bought his car so that we could all keep in touch. But I kept my car phone, which served me in the car, but did not do much for me on the road.

As you can imagine, I travel a great deal, and I began to hear about services from one national wireless provider that included many more minutes per month and *free long distance from anywhere in the country*. My kind of deal. But, when I checked it out (on the Net), I found it wouldn't help me because it worked only in big cities. So I waited about six more months, and sure enough, our local cell provider offered a real deal. A really cool Nokia digital phone, 600 minutes a month, and free long distance from (really) anywhere in the Continental United States, for *$20 less per month* than my car phone plan, which had only 120 minutes included! And voice mail, caller ID, etc., etc., etc. Such a deal. I now make long distance calls from my office on my cell phone, my cost of telephony has dropped by a third, and I am much more accessible to my family and my clients on the road. But I had to keep paying attention, keep looking until the deal was right. And, I have already put on my calendar a note to remind me to check my rate in six months—I know there will be a cheaper one by then.

The lesson here is that you need to pay attention, because if you see something you want but can't afford today, in a few weeks or months you will be able to. Do you have the time? Probably not. Do you have the interest or expertise? Probably not, or worse, you may even be a technophobe, someone who resists and resents technology issues. But someone in the organization needs to be your tech-head.

☞ **HANDS ON:** You need a CIO (chief information officer). Even if you can't afford to have someone full time in this role, you need to have someone in your organization, someone who understands—and likes—technology, and who also understands what you do, how you do it, and why. This person's job will be to match up the mission with the technology to enhance and support it. In the words of a computer-savvy friend of mine, "You need to get a higher geek quotient." I agree.

3. THE COST-BENEFIT RATIO IS RAPIDLY TIPPING TO THE BENEFIT SIDE—BUT ONLY FOR FLEXIBLE ORGANIZATIONS

Again, Moore's Law and ruthless competition are making what was yesterday's exotic technological breakthroughs today's ubiquitous tools. In 1995, a "home page" was something foreign, somewhat geeky, and no one really knew what a URL (uniform resource locator) was. Remember everyone on TV in 1996 reading a URL in its entirety, starting with "http:// www. . . ." Or when people noted that URL addresses were "something, something, something, *all one word. . . ?*" Or when cell phones were unusual? I vividly remember sitting on airplanes with my early laptop in the late 1980s, or even with a new notebook in the early 1990s and having people come over, look, and ask lots of questions. Now on many long flights, the few people without laptops can't sleep because of the glow of all the laptop screens. On a flight recently with 50 people, I counted 35 laptops going strong on a trip aft to the restroom. How many more were under the seats? What was *so cool* even five years ago is *so normal now.*

E-mail, voice mail, spreadsheets, fund-raising software (even customized), payroll software—outcome measure software, all have become parts of our everyday lives. They are affordable and should be viewed as essential tools, not luxuries. In a competitive environment, you have to compete. Part of that competition is being as responsive and cost effective as your competitors, and tech can help you, now for less money and time than ever before.

However, you can't just buy the hardware or software and have it solve all your problems. You also have to move toward the technology, be a bit flexible, and accommodate to the new situation.

❏ **FOR EXAMPLE:** During the past five years, most of my client organizations have gotten both e-mail and Web sites up and running—some happily, some with a lot of pain and strain. The particular client organization in question wanted me to come out and do a day of training at their annual meeting. They contacted me—by e-mail—in February, to see if I was free for the meeting in October. I e-mailed back saying yes, noting my fees, and that information on topics, agendas, bios, and publicity shots were all available at my Web site. About three weeks later I e-mailed again, asking the status of the session. Two weeks *later,* I got a message that they wanted me but had to finalize the details. A month later, I had not heard from them, and had another client who had called asking for the same date. I e-mailed back *and* called the training director's voice mail, noting that she had a one-week deadline to get back to me or I was giving the date to the second client. On the final day of the week, a different staff person called to "talk over details of your training session for us." This person was totally unaware of all the earlier difficulties, did not know about my ultimatum, and was in the dark about the fact that we didn't even have a contract in place. She had called purely by chance 12 hours before I would have gone elsewhere.

To make a long rest of the story short, I later found out what the problem was: The training director checked her voice mail only *once a week* or so, and her e-mail *once every three or four weeks* "since I don't get many messages, and I hate computers." In fact, her original inquiry to me had been one of the first e-mails she had ever sent. Of course, by using that medium, I assumed that she checked it regularly. Same with her voice mail. Silly me.

Once you adopt the technology, you have to use it, and make sure that your people have enough training and comfort with it to be getting the benefit of it. The technology won't come all the way to you. You have to be flexible enough to meet it part way.

4. TECH CAN GET IN THE WAY OF PROVIDING GOOD MISSION

As you can tell, I am strongly pro-tech, and an advocate for your organization to use the tools that technology provides us to the maximum mission effect. However, I would be naive and would be giving you bad advice if I didn't remind you that tech is just a tool and not a panacea. It won't fix a poorly managed organization that doesn't care about its markets, doesn't value line staff, doesn't recruit and retain good volunteers, or doesn't pay attention to its finances. To think so is the same as assuming that just buying a van will allow you to deliver meals on wheels, or that having a receptionist guarantees prompt customer service. Tech is a tool— a wonderful, flexible, helpful, fascinating tool. But the tool is not the issue. *How well you use the tool* is the issue.

Further, technology can get in the way of good mission, usually without our even realizing it. We can get so enamored of having the newest, coolest thing or of getting tech just to keep up with everyone else that we forget that our investment in technology, just like any other mission-based investment, is supposed to result in *more mission*, not less.

❏ FOR EXAMPLE: When I do my training sessions on marketing and customer satisfaction, I regularly do this little exercise with the participants that demonstrates a very, very common example of good technology run amok. I ask the group the following question, "How many of you really dislike calling an organization and getting one of those automated systems that say something like 'Hello, welcome to XYZ organization, blah, blah, blah. . . . press one to . . . press two to. . . ? Put your hands up if these systems really tick you off." And, of course nearly all, and sometimes every single hand goes up. Then I ask, "Why do you dislike calling into these systems?", and I get answers ranging from "impersonal," to "confusing," to "takes too long to work your way through the system," to "all I want to do is talk to a person." And they don't like having to figure out how to "type the last name of the person you want" into their phone. There is uniform, widespread, consistent dislike that borders on hatred for these systems.

And then I ask the clincher. "So, and be totally frank now, how many of your organizations use these systems?" You got it, nearly all the hands go back up! "And," I ask, "how many of you were at least partially responsible for the decision to purchase and install the system?" Again, most, if not all of the hands go slowly up, accompanied by sad or embarrassed looks.

Finally, I ask the question, "Why? Why did you inflict this on your customers when you yourself despise it? What convinced you to spend money to tick off your clients and funders?" The answers usually focus on the salesperson convincing the staff that they would save money by not having to have a receptionist. So I ask, "How many of you laid off your receptionist or cut your FTE by a person?" Hardly anyone ever puts their hand up.

"So you tick off everyone and don't save any money?" Silence. And I don't even deal with the fact that these systems are terribly difficult, even impossible to use, for people who have hearing problems, or who themselves are technophobic—a large part of the population.

☞ **HANDS ON:** Voice mail is great, but always have your phone answered during regular office hours by a real person. And have your people check their voice mail regularly!

B. USES OF TECHNOLOGY FOR THE MISSION-BASED ORGANIZATION

Put simply, there is no part of our economy that has not been impacted by technology. There is no part of our economy that has not been incredibly impacted by the Net. In the months leading up to my finishing work on this edition, I was constantly struck by the fact that there was hardly anyone I met who would not tell me (often in great detail, and always with more than a little awe) how much and how fast the Net had changed their job, their business, or their industry. And the Net is just the highly visible tip of the tech iceberg. Wireless communications, embedded computer chips, smart appliances, and incredible advances in user-friendly software all chip in (great pun) to build an immense techno wave that is literally lifting our economy to levels of productivity and national wealth never seen before and, frankly, hardly imagined until the late 1990s.

This pervasiveness extends to the not-for-profit sector, of course, as well it should. Here is just a short set of examples gathered from the pages of the not-for-profit press in late 1999 and early 2000. (*Note:* Only starting in 1999 was there regular coverage of tech issues in the not-for-profit press, and even entire publications devoted to not-for-profits and technology!)

❑ **For Example:** Let's start with a subject near to your heart: fund raising. On-line fund raising is growing exponentially, with direct solicitation, accepting donations on secure sites on the Net, and affiliations with larger sites (who make a donation when visitors click on a link). There are numerous books and Web sites covering the issue, including fundonline.com, and fundraising.co.uk. Just before this edition was complete, I did my first two donations over the Net and found it quick, easy, and very appealing. America Online has a site for donors, as do many other portals.

❑ **For Example:** Fund raising, Part II. Specialized fund-raising software, word processors, inexpensive printers, and mailing lists have merged to provide a very, very efficient method of keeping track of, and in touch with, key supporters and donors.

❑ **For Example:** The Net: You can get information on everything—and everyone can learn everything about you, at least about your Form 990. You can find out about federal and state contracts, learn about your competition, search for employees, advertise your wares, and provide a lot of information to your staff, board, and supporters. I have a number of clients who have a staff-only section of their Web site where they can see minutes of senior staff and board meetings, note birthdays, introduce new staff and show their picture, note important internal developments, post financials, and the like. It allows the staff to keep better informed, particularly for organizations with multiple sites, or with workers who are spending more and more time in the community and less and less time at the "home office."

❑ **For Example:** Wireless phones, laptops, and other wonderful tools are ways to keep in touch, but also ways to reduce your costs. If you can combine the cost of a cell phone to keep a staff member in touch with free long distance, why wouldn't you? Also, the ability to connect back to the office allows staff to provide services where more and more people and purchasers want it: in the community.

Getting on the Net doesn't have to be expensive. A huge number of ISP's offer free access to not-for-profits and you can even get your Web site set up free. The cost of access to the Net is going down, and the bandwidth (the speed of access) is going up. By the time you read this, you may well have gotten free access or decided to use a cable modem. Or moved beyond that!

❏ **FOR EXAMPLE:** There are a large number of places to get your Web site developed free. www.WeGo.com is just one example. But be careful. You want to use the Web for more than just putting up a billboard, which is really what a simple site does. You may well need to invest in a bit of help in getting the site you want. We'll talk more about that later in the chapter.

❏ **FOR EXAMPLE:** A sheltered workshop in Massachusetts that sells assembly services to manufacturing to provide jobs for people with disabilities has set up business-to-business Web sites for similar organizations, helping them get their products to market or their services to purchasers, and taking a small commission on the transaction.

❏ **FOR EXAMPLE:** You can link with major e-commerce sites such as Amazon.com, LandsEnd.com, or BarnesandNoble.com to send people from your site to theirs and get a percentage of the sales that this generates. Think about that: You can tell all your staff, all your donors, and anyone else concerned about your organization to go do their online shopping through your site, and get money at no cost to them!

Get the idea? Good. Tech is everywhere, and people throughout our sector are figuring out ways to make it work for them. What about you and your organization? How can you make tech work for your mission?

C. A TECHNOLOGY CHECKLIST

Now that we have set the stage for you to look at your organization's ability to use technology in productive, cost-effective, and mission-increasing ways, let's use a checklist to help you find your way.

1. COMPUTERS

Far too many of us still think of computers as expensive luxuries. They are no longer that. As you consider computer purchases or upgrades, I have five suggestions:

a. Make sure you can easily network.

Two thirds of the benefit of today's computers come from the ability to share information quickly. Remember the tech-related characteristic of success? It was *wired, information rich, and technologically savvy*. Stand-alone computers do not allow you to share calendars, pass projects back and forth, or access information from outside the building. Make sure your computers (desktops, personal digital assistants (PDAs) and laptops) can be both internally networked and that the network server can be accessed from the Internet. Most of my clients who have many offices or work locations have gone to a Net-based intranet.

☞ **HANDS ON:** Your offices need access to the Net. Now. But make sure that each physical office, home, place of worship, school, or other location has only one line to the net. If you have more than one computer at a site, network it, and use one server to access the outside world. It is more economical and easier to secure.

☞ **HANDS ON:** Speaking of security, make sure you have up-to-date software called firewalls on all your computers that connect to the Net. This is particularly important if you have 24/7 access through a cable modem or ISDN line. And assure that you have good virus protection. A great site for this is *www.mcafee.com.*

b. Buy absolutely as much hard-drive storage space as you can afford.

You'll fill it up. If you have to trade chip speed for random-access memory (RAM) or hard drive space, do it. Most businesses don't use the highest chip speed anyway. But everyone fills up their hard drive space.

c. Buy larger monitors.

As more and more people spend more and more time on their computers, and you do more and more graphic design and Web surfing, the larger screens are real eye and headache savers. Particularly if you are buying in bulk, ask for 15-inch or even 17-inch screens. Your staff will love you, and you will get more productivity out of them.

d. Make sure you have a good backup system included.

Computers and their components, particularly the hard drive, are just machines, and machines break. Make sure your computer systems, particularly your network servers, or large hard drives can be easily (and are regularly) backed up.

☞ **HANDS ON:** Make sure that at least one full backup a month gets off-site: Take it home. If the computers don't break but the building burns or floods, that off-site backup will save you. One of the cheapest ways to get this done is with a read/write CD recorder. They are relatively cheap as I write this, and the amount of data you can store is staggering. If you have really fast Net access, through T-1, ISDN, or cable modems, you might do the backup on a remote server. Several Net-based firms offer this service for really low prices. I use one to store some key files such as presentations or samples to access when I am on the road, in case I forget to bring them along. Again, *www.mcafee.com* offers this service, among many others.

e. Make sure each and every computer is fully Internet ready.

The computers need to have an internal modem or a card to connect to the Net. They need an adequate video card to handle Net video, and a set of speakers and an audio card and drivers to handle audio. As I write this, free long-distance calls on the Net are realistic—why not call that way? But you can't without the right setup on the computer. It *has* to be usable on the Net. Without this access, the computers will be junk in a month. Don't waste your money or your time with old, used computers that are donated. Remember, on-line or flat line.

2. SOFTWARE

Not only is there a huge amount of software out there, but it is more and more specific in its application to smaller and smaller markets. For instance, I recently saw accounting software specifically designed for small community foundations.

☞ **HANDS ON:** A caution here: In many cases, general software like Excel or QuickBooks can be adapted to a wide variety of needs, and are much, much cheaper than the custom version. It may well be cheaper to send a staff person to a series of classes on the software (or buy a course on CD-ROM) than to buy custom or high-end software.

When you look at software, remember four things. First, you need to think about the outcomes, the reports, compilations, computations, information, and connectivity that the software provides you. Don't get hooked by all the bells and whistles—make sure you focus on product, not on process. Second, ask around. Talk to your peer organizations about what they use, what they like and don't like about what they have. Third, use print and Net-based resources such as the Chronicle of Philanthropy's Annual Resource Guide, or various on-line reviews at places like Znet. Or join in on a user listserve, and ask lots of questions. There are a whole, whole lot of ways to check things out before you buy. But in the end, remember the fourth thing: There is rarely a perfect match of wants and software. Again, you have to meet the tech part way.

☞ **HANDS ON:** You can get test or demo versions of most software free on-line. Locations like *www.downloads.com, www.freeware.com,* and even most starting portals like Yahoo or Excite offer free download software. If you go to a manufacturer's site, you can download test versions for free. But remember, most of this software stops working in 30 days, or the work you do can't be saved, or printed. So try it, see if you like it, but don't depend on it.

☞ **HANDS ON:** On another note, there is lots of shareware on the Net— and it is free, or very low cost. But you get what you pay for. For some small, focused applications, it is terrific, but for larger things like accounting, it rarely fills the bill. Go to *www.shareware.com* to check this out.

3. COMMUNICATIONS

Wireless digital communications are the name of the game for a hands-on mission-based organization. Whether it is your cell phone, your pager, or wireless access from a laptop or PDA, having wireless access to your organization and your databases is crucial, and a real competitive edge.

❏ **FOR EXAMPLE:** A client of mine is a home health provider in a large, low-population density western state. In 1998, they had the opportunity to bid on being the preferred provider of care for the state's largest health maintenance organization (HMO), but some things stood in their way. First, they would have to enlarge their staff, and those staff would have to be supervised in a new way. Second, while the HMO reimbursement rates were adequate, the home health agency would also work for other providers and private pay. To make the cash flow work, the organization would have to bill the non-HMO work *daily*. The solution? To equip each staff person with a laptop, service reporting software, and a cell phone. Staff had to drive hundreds of miles a day and, on their trip home, they hooked up the laptop to the cell phone and downloaded their day's information and charges to the home network. Each night, the home office developed invoices that were mailed out the next morning. Two years later, they were directly e-mailing their billings to most of the insurers in their network, saving time, postage, and paper.

☞ **HANDS ON:** Another techno-whiz caution: Do not assume that everyone needs every gadget—they probably don't. I saw a stunning piece of research recently that said that fully 25% of people who wear pagers 24 hours a day are paged less than once per month! I know that "needing" a pager is a statement that you are important, and that many people do need them. The question is: Is it ego, or is it essential?

And, of course, there is e-mail. Not only has it supplanted the phone call in many cases, e-mail has changed the way we transmit documents and do business, particularly at long distance, at a great savings and benefit to everyone—except the postal services and overnight shippers!

❑ **FOR EXAMPLE:** From 1997 to 1999, I wrote a series of articles for an international journal that focused on not-for-profit marketing. The entire relationship between this organization and me took place totally electronically. After reading the first edition of *Mission-Based Management*, the editor checked out my Web site and e-mailed me about my interest in writing for the publication. I checked them out at their Web site, agreed by e-mail to write for them, and sent all my articles as e-mail attachments. Editing was done via e-mail attachment, and I was paid by electronic fund transfer directly into my firm's checking account. Three years, six articles, not one long distance call to England, not one cent on postage or shipping. Not one piece of paper or envelope used, at least at my end.

What draft documents can you send to your clients, funders, donors, and the like by e-mail? How about the state and national associations you belong to? A client of mine recently prepared for her organization's strategic planning retreat by e-mailing documents back and forth, saving both of us time and money, but also giving her confidence that we agreed on the key things to be covered and the timing of the agenda. How can you use this technique better, both inside the organization and outside?

The underlying pace of change in communications, in equipment, applicability, price, and service area, is perhaps the fastest of all the areas of technology. So stay tuned in, and when the price gets to where the cost–benefit curve works for you, jump in.

4. INFRASTRUCTURE

The big issue here is internal wiring, both for adequate power and grounding, and to network your computers, printers, scanners, and fax machines. Additionally, you want to make sure that your network can access the outside world through the Net, and that the world can access you. For older buildings, this wiring can be a challenge, but for any new space that you buy, renovate, or rent, make sure that the wiring is up to speed, both figuratively and literally. After all, how can you be a wired not-for-profit without the wiring?

☞ HANDS ON: Having discussed wiring, remember that wireless networks work well, and are much, much cheaper than rewiring a whole building. Some work through your electrical system; some are truly wireless. Check this option out before you hard wire!

5. THE INTERNET

Oh my, oh my, where to start? Can your many markets (funders, referral sources, people to serve, donors, volunteers, and staff) all access the information that they need on the Net? Do you use the Net to its limit for legislative research, communication, networking, continuing education, travel arrangements, hardware and software purchases and technical assistance for same, electronic billing and bill paying, grant and contract research, donor communication, staff recruitment, and to let the people you serve know who, what, where, and why your organization is? If not, why not? If so, go back and check again, because since you started reading this chapter, the Net has improved, and there is probably more you can do.

The Net is the most efficient way to do all of these things. You can update your software, run internal computer diagnosis, make long-distance calls, have group discussions, find out arcane bits of information, and keep up with your competitor, but to do so you have to be wired in. If you are a novice, nearly all the big portals will help you get started. There is tons of technical assistance out there to help you set up a preliminary Web site.

☞ **HANDS ON:** You want your Web site to provide a number of things:

1. *Much more information than is possible in your printed materials.* Don't just scan your brochures into the page. Offer more in-depth information, access to other sites that are concerned about the same issues, more detailed information about your hours, pictures of your staff, information on volunteering, and so forth. You have no limit on what you can put on the Web.

2. *A number of points of contact.* A general e-mail link is essential, but also have feedback loops that go to specific areas, such as intake, or fund-raising staff. And, of course, remember to include phone numbers, addresses, and names!

3. *Specific areas for specific groups.* For example, most of my Web-savvy clients have parts of their site just for board members (with minutes of meetings, glossaries of jargon, contact points for other board members, etc.), others just for staff (who is new, whose birth-day is it, minutes of all meetings, new forms, etc.) and for people concerned with the organization. There are literally limitless ways to use your Web site to build community support and increase donations and volunteer time.

❑ **FOR EXAMPLE:** One client organization of mine runs a residential school for kids with severe disabilities. Many of the kids are from out of state, so in late 1999 they bought a digital camera, and regularly (daily—or weekly at the very least) take pictures of the kids at work, school, field trips, and parties, and e-mail them to the parents. Parental satisfaction rates have skyrocketed—as have donations!

Now let's look at the issue in reverse, from the point of view of your operations. How can you use technology? In many ways.

a. Management.

How about financial reports customized for different levels of the organization? Or having every management team member's calendar on your internal network so that you can schedule meetings more easily?

What about daily or weekly billing of your key customers, or donor reports that are literally up to the minute? Outcome measures? Easy. On-line evaluations for staff? A snap. Communications with staff, peers, and the board? Project planning? So, so easy.

The technology available at this writing—to say nothing of what is out there as you read this—can help you delegate, monitor, and plan better. Ironically, the tech can clear a lot of your drudge work out, so that you can spend more time with your staff, your networking, and your board, instead of less.

Of course, there is a dark side. Turning on your computer and finding 347 e-mails is depressing. And your blood pressure is sure to go up when your computer freezes right after you have spent an hour inputting data and forgotten to back up. But the management benefits are huge, and ones you can ill afford to ignore. You also need to pay close attention to security and the likelihood of data loss at some point.

☞ **HANDS ON:** If you don't have a managers' group on technology sponsored by your local United Way or your state trade association, get them to start one. There should be two types of groups, one for the executive directors, and one for the CIOs. Get together quarterly to talk about hardware, software, and all the applications of technology that are being used to do more mission.

b. Board of directors.

Here the major benefit is communication. Use e-mail to the max. Attach documents as much as you can. Give the board access to special sections of your Web site. And, of course, get them to tell you what kind of financial reports they want, and then get them to them. You can keep boards much more in the loop than ever before.

☞ **HANDS ON:** Don't forget your nonwired board members in a rush to tech-up. Board members should not be punished or treated as second-class citizens if they do not have access to a computer or have e-mail. This problem is rapidly waning in the United States, but will continue in some sectors for a long time. Be sensitive, and check it out!

c. Development.

Can people find out about the different ways to give to you over the Net? Can they give to you directly with a credit card on a secure site? Do you participate in "click and give" sponsorships with your local companies, or your ISP? Do you use donor tracking software? Special event management software? Do you subscribe to development listserves? Or on-line newsletters regarding development techniques?

d. Marketing.

In one of my recent training sessions on marketing, a staff member from FEDCAP, an employer of people with disabilities from New York City, showed the group his PowerPoint presentation for potential customers. The presentation was nice, but the applications were terrific. He could provide it on his laptop or simply give it to the customer on a disk with the free "dumb" player included so that the customer just had to insert the disk and it would play. He also had loaded it on the FedCap Web site so that people could play it there. Very cool. Very efficient. Very effective.

A second and really beneficial technological advance in the marketing area is the advent of inexpensive, high-quality, and user-friendly graphic design software and wonderful inexpensive dot matrix and laser printers. This allows you to cheaply run targeted materials for many of your markets, not just one general-purpose brochure.

☞ **HANDS ON:** Popular word processing programs like WordPerfect and Word come with templates for newsletters, business cards, posters, and brochures already built in. Combine that with the wide array of newsletter, business card, poster, and brochure stock in various designs and colors at all the major office stores, and you have a recipe for quick, inexpensive, and professional-looking marketing materials made to order, *in small quantities,* on demand.

There is literally no end to what you can do in terms of marketing on the Net. People can see your array of services, meet your staff, find out about office hours, payment options, prices, ways to volunteer, available jobs, your history, your accreditations and honors, and on and on and on and on. You need to be on the Net, and you need to make sure your site is regularly updated.

e. Service provision.

In health care—need I say more? Tech, from instant glucose tests, ear thermometers, and remote diagnoses over the phone line, has revolutionized the options for community-based, home health, and rural medicine. In education (in schools, museums, aquariums, and at home), computers and remote learning options have opened up whole new worlds of access. Even in not-for-profits dedicated to political change, such as advocacy and lobbying groups, tech has made access to million of voters and millions of donors instantaneous, and the education of those voters and donors cheaper, faster, and more targeted. Here, the most important thing to do is to talk to your peers and watch your competition. After all, service provision is your closest activity to your mission, so if tech can help, it should, and quickly.

f. Outcome measurement.

In 1972, I was hired by a business that worked for all three television networks (there was just ABC, NBC, and CBS) on election night tabulating votes and transmitting them by phone to the networks. The room I supervised had hundreds of people taking phone calls, and then carrying hand-written results to people who punched the data into cards, which were then hand carried to a computer that read them. Every 15 minutes, the new cards were run by the computer, which whirred loudly, and a thin ticker-tape came out with the results, which were then called orally into the network headquarters. Hundreds of people were employed for the night (and the previous Saturday rehearsal) to get this done, just for the state of Pennsylvania. It was state-of-the-art outcome measurement.

Today, your funders, whether they be government, corporate, foundation, United Way, or donors, all want to see your outcomes, and see them soon. Tech can help both with data entry, data compilation, data display (in written and graphic form) and data access over an internal or Net-based network. You can put up current data on your Web site to show the world how effective your are. Again, look at what your peers and competitors are doing, and integrate your geeks with your contract people. You will make this task much easier.

g. Grant writing.

A big part of grant writing is first finding out that the grant or contract is out there. Here, the Internet brings it all to you (and, of course, to your competition). Good word processing lets you use text over and over (your organizational credentials, for example), and keeps time devoted to the task to a minimum. If you count on grants, or want to get into grant writing, and you are not on the Net, my advice is don't bother until you are wired. The tech is that important.

The point of this section has been to help you begin to think of mission applications through the lens of traditional management disciplines. The point of technology is, after all, to do more mission, sooner, better, and more efficiently. So always focus on outcome, not on the coolest gizmo.

D. KEEPING CURRENT—A REVIEW AND RENEWAL PROCESS

Now you are up to speed. You've done your homework, bought what you need, installed the hardware and software, and trained your staff and volunteers in its mission-based uses. They are using it, and it works! Great. So can you relax? Perhaps coast for a bit?

Nope. Remember my first rule at the beginning of the chapter? It was this: *The state-of-the-art hardware or software you just bought will always be outdated in under ten minutes.* Now, this is not to say that you always have to have the newest of the new, shiniest of the shiny. But it does speak clearly to the fact that the pace of change and—often but not always—improvements is very rapid. So you have to keep an organizational eye out to make sure that some advance does not present you with a great opportunity in mission outcome or cost savings.

But you already have a full-time job, and some days feel like you have 2.5 FTE living inside your skin. What to do? Try these four actions.

1. INCREASE YOUR GEEK QUOTIENT

We touched on this earlier. You need to have a CIO either full or part time, and you need that person yesterday. Beyond just that, you also need to send your staff to tech training. Overall, you need more and more people with more and more technological savvy. You can't have only one person who can reboot the computers or install software, or who knows how to deal with a jammed fax or error message on the printer. You have a lot of tech. You need a ramped-up geek quotient throughout the staff. The more people know, the more they will pay attention to technological advances and understand their implications for your organization. Make sure your techies talk to your fuzzies about what each group does. A lot.

☞ **Hands On:** Ok, so you aren't big enough to get a full-time CIO. I have a solution. Go back to high school. Seriously. High schools are full of bright, tech-savvy kids. In some school districts, they have to have a certain number of community service hours to graduate. In all school districts, the National Honor Society (NHS) kids (the best and the brightest of any school) have to donate at least 50 hours of community service in their junior year and 10 more in their senior year. Go to the high school, talk to the NHS advisor, and get the tech kids to work at your organization!

2. CHECK PRICES, USES, AND OUTCOMES REGULARLY

Set up a schedule to check on communications costs annually. Have someone check for upgrades, patches, and new versions of all your software every 90 days. You do not have to buy every new version, but you do need to know that it is available.

3. TALK TO YOUR PEERS

We've touched on this a number of times. Don't reinvent the wheel. Use the great ideas that your peer organizations have had, and adapt them to your own needs.

4. READ THE NOT-FOR-PROFIT PRESS

Every single one of the major not-for-profit periodicals now have regular features on tech issues, and specific articles as well. You need to get and read at least one of these periodicals anyway. Now, just make sure you read the tech columns as well. Most of these periodicals are also on-line, where you can often find links to useful sites.

RECAP

In this really important chapter, we've talked about ways to make sure that you are using technology to the maximum mission benefit. We first went over the realities of the wired world and I gave you the following observations to consider:

1. The state-of-the-art hardware or software you just bought will always be outdated in under 10 minutes.
2. Just because you can't keep up with all the changes doesn't mean you shouldn't pay attention to them.
3. The cost–benefit ratio is rapidly tipping to the benefit side—but only for flexible organizations.
4. Tech can get in the way of providing good mission.

Next, we went through applications of technology for not-for-profit organizations, and I gave you a large number of examples. Third, we examined a checklist of technology, area by area, and I posed questions for you on how your organization is doing in the tech arena. We looked at things by tech category, such as hardware, software, and infrastructure, and then by organizational division, such as management, development, and outcome measurement.

Finally, I gave you a sequence of actions that will help you keep current with the technology that can enhance your mission and cut your costs of operation. These actions are:

1. Increase your geek quotient.
2. Check prices, uses, and outcomes regularly.
3. Talk to your peers.
4. Read the not-for-profit press.

One last time: The wired not-for-profit can survive and prosper. The nonwired organization is doomed. An investment in technology can, if focused on mission outcomes, greatly benefit the people your organization serves. Don't let the wave pass you and your organization by.

Questions for Discussion: Chapter 7

1. OK, who is our designated CIO? Are we geek-heavy enough?
2. What parts of our system need upgrading? How regularly should we schedule reviews of our website, our internal systems?
3. Are their technological applications that can improve our mission? What are they? Are there funds to pay for them from the people who purchase our services?
4. What is the most technologically advanced not-for-profit in our town? How can we learn more about how they got this way?

8

Creating a
Social Entrepreneur

OVERVIEW

All of us know the common wisdom that small-business entrepreneurs are the hands-on people that generate jobs, develop new products and services, and are the engine of the economy. In truth, so are many not-for-profits today. I must add: All not-for-profits were entrepreneurs in their start-up phase. But how about now? How about your organization? Have you been around long enough that you are no longer flexible, no longer willing to embrace and shape change, no longer willing to take chances with your organization's resources?

I want to you become (or get back to being) a social entrepreneur—an organization that is constantly on the lookout for how to do more and how to do it better, and willing to take prudent risk on behalf of its clientele. This means that you will fail occasionally. But more often you will succeed in both satisfying and mission-oriented ways that serve your community much better.

In this chapter, we'll go over ways to help your organization get comfortable with the idea of social entrepreneurism. We'll talk about how and how not to set up new ventures. I'll show you how to decide how much return on investment is enough, and the 10 biggest mistakes people make in developing their business plan financials. We'll go over how to and how not to seek debt, which can be one of the sources of capital that you may need to expand and prosper. We'll look at ways that your organization can become a culture of new ideas, constantly seeking new thoughts from staff and board, evaluating them and trying the best out. We'll review ways to get comfortable with *prudent* risk. I don't want

122

you to become reckless. Bungee jumping with a rope that is 20 feet longer than the drop is not a good idea. *Prudent* risk is what it's all about.

I hope that by the time you are finished with this chapter, you will be excited about the possibilities open to you if you become a social entrepreneur.

A. THE CHARACTERISTICS OF THE SOCIAL ENTREPRENEUR

To me, the core of social entrepreneurism is good stewardship. Good stewards don't just rest on their laurels, they try new things, serve people in new ways, are life long learners, and try to have their organizations be fonts of excellence. Social entrepreneurs have these characteristics:

- They are willing to take reasonable risk on behalf of the people that their organization serves.
- They are constantly looking for new ways to serve their constituencies, and to add value to existing services.
- They understand that all resource allocations are really stewardship investments.
- They weigh the social and financial return of each of these investments.
- They understand the difference between needs and wants.
- They always keep mission first, but know that without money, there is no mission output.

These are crucial traits for you to mull over as you consider your organizational adaptation to the social entrepreneurism model. How do you, your staff, and board view risk? As something to avoid, or as something that is part of steady improvement of services to the community? What about services? Are you doing the same old thing you were five years ago, or can you specifically list what the organization did to improve services last week, the week before that, and the week before that? Steady, consistent improvement in services, and the constant adding to the value of those services from the point of view of the people you serve and the people who pay for them, is an absolute necessity if you are to become and remain a social entrepreneur.

B. UNDERSTANDING AND ACCEPTING RISK

If you and I and eight other people were to be given $20,000 today, we would do 10 different things with it. Some would buy certificates of deposit, some would pay down our mortgage, or buy a car, or pay off other debt. Some would go on a vacation or try to win big at a casino. Why the variety? Because we all have a different willingness to take risks with money. We are raised differently (some of us are children of the Depression, some self-indulgent baby boomers), we are in different places in our lives (some of us have kids to put through college or big medical costs staring us in the face), and we have different financial situations (to some $10 is a lot of money, to some $250 is pocket change). Some of us are very meticulous, and some are just plain reckless.

But all of us take risks. It is a risk to get in your car and drive to the store. It's a risk to get married, to have a child, to take a job, to buy a house, to buy a stock, to fly on a commercial airliner. Some risks are so small that we just accept them as part of life and stop even calling them risks. Some are so big that we don't take them. We no longer have the stomach for some of the risks that we took when we were younger. Some things we never would have ventured as a child we now do without thinking.

Risk is relative, and our willingness to take it depends on a combination of many things. In not-for-profit organizations, our willingness to take risk—or be reckless—depends on the makeup of the people in charge of the organization, as well as on the organization's history and its financial condition. If, for example, there has been a history of recklessness resulting in big failures (even with another executive director), the board of your organization may be less willing to take on a risk than if you have a stellar record of success. Also, the board's willingness to take a financial gamble will be influenced by how much money is at stake and how financially secure you are. If you are already financially empowered, it is more likely that your board will be willing to use that empowerment for the good of the community.

Your willingness as an organization to take risk also depends on your view of yourself as an organization. The first step is to find out what the people in your organization think about risk, and find it out early in the process.

☞ **HANDS ON:** Try this well-tested method of finding out your risk quotient. Copy Exhibit 8-1 and hand it out to your board, senior staff, and social entrepreneur team. Let them fill it out, tally the result, and then discuss the answers. What you will find may be very interesting and will get the issue on the table.

Obviously, the further down this list of choices you go, the higher your organizational willingness to take risks. Do not assume that there is

Exhibit 8-1   Internal Risk Assessment Tool

This form will help your organization assess its willingness and readiness to take risks. Below are four statements. Read all four and then decide which one best describes your view of the most appropriate role for your organization. Please note that even though your organization is a not-for-profit, your staff and board can interpret the role of the organization differently.

Arm of government: Our organization gets most or all of its funds from some branch of government. As a result, we should provide only the programs that the government asks us to and is willing to pay for.

Government contractor: One or more branches of government contracts with our organization to provide services. Government policy heavily influences us, but we are able to do some things outside of this source of funding.

Local charity: Our organization should provide the services that our community says that they want. We know what they want by what they fund us for, either individually, through United Way, corporate giving, or in fees for services.

Not-for-profit business: Our job is to provide services to support our mission. To accomplish this we may accept funds from the government, local or state funders, corporations, individuals, insurers, or others.

I think that the description that best fits our organization's role is (check only one):

	Arm of government
	Government contractor
	Local charity
	Not-for-profit business

a right answer to the survey: There is only your board and staff's answer. And you need to know it now, before you talk through business ideas with any seriousness. The worst thing that can happen is for you not to realize that the staff to be full of social entrepreneurs, while the board really sees the organization as an arm of government, or vice versa. Ask now, and you will not only find out where people stand, you will generate discussions that will benefit you throughout the business development process.

As you can see, however, the further up the chart you go toward social entrepreneurism, the higher your willingness to take risk is. I would optimally like you to be willing to take prudent risk on behalf of your clientele, but you must understand that you can't do it alone. The most dangerous situation in this area occurs when you feel that your organization should be a social entrepreneur and your board and staff feel that you are an arm of government or a government contractor. Then you and they will address the issue of a new business or a new service in the same manner.

Risk is here, risk is now, and prudent risk is part of your job as a service provider in your community.

C. BUSINESS VENTURES

Nationally, thousands of not-for-profits are turning to outside businesses to supplement and broaden their income streams. Since 1982, I have helped hundreds of not-for-profits throughout the country examine their capabilities in this area and have assisted them in developing their business plans.

The development of good business plans by a not-for-profit is a complex enough issue to merit an entire book by itself, and is in fact the subject of a number of excellent texts listed at the end of the chapter. Here, I want to review the steps of business plan development, focus on the preparation of financials, and review the big mistakes people make in preparing their financials. Hopefully, this advice will help you avoid the big pitfalls in business development and will excite you sufficiently so that you will take the time to read the other resources listed at the end of the chapter.

First, a reality check: No business is going to make you independently wealthy as an organization, nor is it going to make you independent of your current major source of funding. Nearly all of our clients come to us and state that one of their main reasons for wanting a new business is to "become financially independent of the state (feds, county, foundation, United Way)." Sorry, this is not going to happen. The services that your major funders will pay for may not be provided by anyone else, and, in all likelihood, they will continue to be a major part of your income stream far into the future. You can, by expanding your income sources, become *less* dependent on the major funders. But independent? Not likely.

Second, remember that business income is okay and will not result in a threat to your 501(c)(3) status unless it grows to dwarf your charitable functions. Also, most of you will start new ventures that are related to your mission anyway. Why? Because it's what you know, and if you are a professional in education or in the arts or in substance abuse treatment, you are not going to start a Wal-Mart or an engineering firm. People take what they know and find new markets for it. You will too, and so, in most cases (about 90% of our clients), the business that you start will result in more services being provided.

Finally the idea of a business is to maximize profits, and for you this is only slightly diluted (I'll address the issue in a few pages). Suffice it to say here that any profits you make will have a social use: either to fund your mission reserves or to subsidize a money-losing program. You are not just starting this to make a ton of money: There is a social purpose.

D. THE STEPS OF THE BUSINESS PLANNING PROCESS

Let's start the examination of the business planning process by looking at the steps listed below. Note that most people start with number 4, "idea generation," and that this is a big mistake. If you don't do these in order, you are really going to get yourself in trouble. Take them one at a time and you will do fine.

1. ESTABLISH (REESTABLISH) YOUR MISSION

We've already talked at length about your mission statement and the need for it to be up to date and reflective of the organization that you want to become rather than the organization that you were in the past 20 years. If you have not already reviewed your mission with your board and staff, now is a good time. Make sure that your mission statement does not conflict with the idea of your business venture, and that you all agree that a new service fits into the parameters of the mission statement.

2. ESTABLISH THE "RISK LEVEL" OF YOUR ORGANIZATION

Using the figure above, go over your organization's willingness to take on risk with your board and senior staff. How much income do you need from this venture? How much social outcome? Talk this through with great detail and frankness. If you don't, you may wind up leading the charge up the hill and turn around to find that there is no one behind you: They thought it was too risky.

3. ESTABLISH THE MISSION USES OF PROFIT

Of all the steps that people miss, this is the most important. You simply have to specify what you want to do with the money you will earn. If you do, people will be able to rally around the extra work (and risk) involved in the business development process. If you don't, they won't be able to focus on the outcome—they will just question why they have all the extra work.

❏ **For Example:** A number of years ago, I was asked by a large provider of services to the developmentally disabled in the Southwest to come and facilitate a session with board and staff on the development of a new business. The executive director was totally committed to starting a new venture, but it quickly became obvious that the board and staff were anything but excited about the prospect. Questions such as "Why should we try to be in business? We're not IBM!" abounded. After about 45 minutes of this, I asked the group to imagine what they would do with unrestricted funds of $100,000. After a brief pause, the ideas started flying around the room. To make a long evening's discussion short, the focus came to rest on the idea of buying a small residence for three people with mild retardation that the state would not fund.

I then asked the group: "Where are we going to get the money for that?" They immediately chastised me with comments like, "We can't get it, and you said just to imagine what we would do." I said "Okay, but what if a business, one that employed people with disabilities in the community, was able to *net* $100,000 in two or three years, and then its ongoing profits were used to support the home? Would you support the idea of a new business then?"

"YES!" was the answer, with great enthusiasm. The group had gone from staunch resistance to avid support simply because they could now get their hands on a tangible social outcome.

Postscript: The organization started a swimming pool cleaning service three months later, with developmentally disabled persons on the crews. Three years later it had broken even, profited almost $90,000, which was used to buy the house, and contributed over $30,000 in annual profits to subsidize the facility.

Establish the uses of your profit—specifically. For example, name the program that will be subsidized by the profit, and list the amount you need per year and by when to accomplish your social goal. Then, when you finish your business plan, you can look back and see if your business meets your goals for social outcome.

4. IDEA GENERATION

Only once you have done numbers 1 through 3 should you seriously consider what it is that you and your organization can do to earn extra income and provide new services. In developing ideas, use your staff and volunteers. They almost certainly have thought about what the needs are in the community and how you could meet them. They just may, however, never have had the forum in which to voice them.

☞ **HANDS ON:** Get your staff together for a brainstorming session with a facilitator. Explain the need for a business and the social outcome that the business will meet. Then ask for ideas (remember, in brainstorming every idea is a good one). In a minute or two, the ideas will start to flow. If there are problems in getting the group started, use the questions below.

1. What is your organization's primary purpose as a not-for-profit organization?
2. What are your organization's core competencies?
3. What are the markets (the groups of people) you want to target?
4. What do these markets really want?
5. How do those wants match up with your competencies?

When you have your list, develop some criteria against which to weigh each idea. For example, you might want to prioritize businesses that can be started up in less than six months, with no more than $10,000 invested, and have a direct social impact. The combination of criteria will be up to you, but by establishing what is important now, you can fairly weigh all your potential business ideas, and not get the people whose ideas don't get followed up on mad at you.

5. FEASIBILITY STUDY

There are two steps to establishing feasibility: draft and final. In the draft stage, you take three to five pages and review the business, its markets in general and what kind of services are being provided in this market. In the final feasibility study, you go into much greater detail about the market you want to serve, a definition of the service you want to provide, why the market wants this service, how you will provide it, the barriers to success and how you will overcome them, and preliminary financials.

The emphasis in the feasibility study phase is: "Can we do this?", "Do we have (or can we get) the resources to accomplish this?", and "Does it meet our social outcome goals?" If you do your homework and complete the feasibility study well, the majority of the work in your business plan will be done.

Do not, however, automatically proceed to the next stage without considering the key question: "Is this business feasible?" In some cases it will not be, and then your choice is to rework the idea or wait for conditions to improve. For example, if you are considering a recycling business, you might have to wait until the market for recycled goods rebounds to a certain level. Or, if you are in a highly leveraged business (e.g., buying, renovating, and reselling low-income housing), you perhaps could not afford to start the business if mortgage interest rates were high.

Remember my maxim of "prudent risk." The idea of a feasibility study is twofold: to focus you on what the business is and to see if it is feasible. Some businesses will not be and that's okay! Whatever you do, however, do not throw out the idea or the work that you have done. Even the biggest "failure" in today's market may be tomorrow's success.

❏ **For Example:** By now, almost everyone has heard the story of the development of Post-Its—the restickable notes from 3M—and how the developer had to battle against the odds to get his case heard, and how the product is the single most successful product 3M has ever launched. What you may not know is the part of the story about the glue that is used on Post-Its. It is a glue that "failed" all the tests that the chemists put it through. Prior to Post-Its, 3M's criterion for adhesives was that they stick to something and hold things together. This glue failed that test, but was not discarded, and thus was available when the new product idea was presented. The chemists simply kept the formula in case an unanticipated condition developed, which it certainly did.

It may for you too. Don't pitch your work.

6. MARKETING PLAN

The marketing plan portion of a business plan is crucial. Here, all the questions that need to be asked are the same ones we will discuss in detail in Chapter 9: Who are the markets? What do they want? How do we know? How do we let them know we are here? You want your business to be market driven, not service driven, and that means that you will probably have to change the method of service delivery a number of times from your original concept through the business planning process as you ask the market what they want.

7. BUSINESS PLAN

Now that you have done all the preliminary work and found that your business is feasible, why go on? For three reasons:

1. Writing a business plan forces you to take an objective, critical, unemotional look at your business project in its entirety.
2. The finished product is an operating tool that, if properly used, will help you manage your business and work toward its success.
3. The completed business plan is your means of communicating your ideas to others and provides the basis for your financing proposal.

Over half of all new businesses fail within the first two years of operation, and over 90% fail within the first 10 years. A major reason for these failures is the lack of planning. If you have a well-written business plan that takes into account all the variables involved in starting a new business and is based on reality, you can move your venture on the road to success.

8. IMPLEMENTATION

Once the plan is written, reviewed, and adopted, the final step—and certainly not the easiest—is to go and set up and run the business. Obviously, only through the implementation of the plan can you hope to achieve the social outcomes you desire, as well as the new income streams that are so important to your financial empowerment.

Remember, the most successful entrepreneurs fail the first few times before they hit it big. I do not want you to be like them. I want you to develop a sound business plan based on good research and valid marketing and succeed, and in a big way, the first time out. With a solid business plan, you should be taking only prudent risks, not the "leap off the cliff" that so many small businesspeople refer to.

A business plan consists of several parts. The most important components are:

• *A cover letter identifying the business plan as the property of your organization.* This cover letter includes your name, address, and telephone number and the month and the year that the plan is written or revised. One paragraph states in simple terms who the business plan belongs to and the limitations on its distribution. (1 page)

• *A table of contents* (1 page)

• *A summary of the plan with a brief paragraph about your organization.* A four-line description of the product or service; a four-line description of the market; a brief paragraph on production and one on distribution, if needed; and, a short paragraph on the financing requirements (2–4 pages)

- *A description of your organization and its business with the following subheadings (4–6 pages):*

  - The organization
  - The product or service
  - The target consumer
  - The consumer's need for the product or service
  - The sales strategy

- *A description of the market for your product or service,* including information on the competition and cost price comparisons between competitors and your organization (4–8 pages)

- *A marketing plan that includes information on:*

  - The markets
  - Customers
  - Competitors
  - The macroenvironment:
    - Demography
    - Economy
    - Technology
    - Government
    - Culture
  - How each of these areas affects the marketing and selling of your product or service
  - Evaluation of potential pitfalls (10 pages)

- *The financial plan with sources and applications of cash and capital and:*

  - An equipment list
  - A balance sheet
  - Break-even analysis
  - Cash flow estimates by month for the first year, by the quarter for the second and third years, projected income and expenses for the first three years, and notes of explanation for each of the estimates (10–15 pages)

Other reports and statements that can be included in this section (but are not appropriate for all plans) are:

- Historical financial reports for your organization, such as balance sheets for the past three years and income statements for the past three years
- A current audit report
- An annual report if one is available

- *An appendix with:*

  - Management resumes
  - Your organizational brochure and newsletter
  - Other pertinent material about your organization and its work
  - Letters of endorsement
  - Copies of signed contracts for business

E. HOW MUCH "RETURN ON INVESTMENT" DO YOU NEED?

Now that you have a business plan (or are considering developing one), your board and you need to consider a key issue: How much return should we get on our investment, our risk? The answer? It depends.

❑ FOR EXAMPLE: A not-for-profit organization in Colorado was developing a business plan for a janitorial service that would employ some of its clients—people with developmental disabilities. In completing the plan, the staff and board found that they could go two ways. First, they could clean upscale offices with crews made up of both workers with disabilities and those without. If they proceeded this way, they would make about 25 percent return on their investment due to high prices and high profits. Or they could clean factory and warehouse space using crews with a much higher proportion of people with disabilities. If they did this, however, they would make less money. The quandary: Should they earn more dollars and employ fewer people with disabilities, or employ more and make less?

❑ FOR EXAMPLE: A performing arts not-for-profit in Connecticut decided to offer children's theater classes to optimize staff and volunteer talents and to take advantage of the theater building in late afternoon when it was empty. They knew from their financial projections that they could make some money, but their dilemma was whether to charge a high fee—say, $120—for the lessons, turning a larger profit, or charge less—$40—thus making the class affordable to more youngsters but receiving very low returns on the investment.

What should these organizations do? How much return on investment is enough for an organization that is going into a new venture? Are there any benchmarks or ratios that should be followed? Is there such a thing as making too much money? How can you ensure that the staff and board of your organization are getting the most from your limited resources? These questions are among the most commonly asked by not-for-profit staff and board members as they examine the feasibility of new ventures, and rightly so.

Analyzing return on investment (ROI) is not as simple for a not-for-profit as it is for a for-profit organization. This is a good time and place to discuss the options and issues open to you. First, though, some assumptions and definitions. For purposes of this discussion, ROI means the aggregate of the financial and social results of a new venture weighed against the time, cash, and political capital invested. If we make $5,000 a year in profit and receive 100 units of service, the combination of those two is our return on investment. Also, I assume that we are discussing ventures designed to make money *and* provide service; thus, we must consider both these factors as we weigh the options surrounding any venture. Finally, the term *service unit* will be used. This term describes one of whatever an organization does. For a museum, it might be one visitor; for a hospital, a patient day; for a detoxification unit, one outpatient visit. Many not-for-profits have more than one type of service unit, all of which can be used in analyzing ROI.

Instead of looking just at the financial return on its investment, a not-for-profit must look at the social or mission return on its activities as well. Thus, the two organizations in the examples above had to consider not only their earnings but also the social impact of its new venture: jobs for people with disabilities or arts for kids. Having more of one meant having less of the other (although that is not true in all cases). This twin return need makes the analysis more complicated, though still fairly straightforward. Let's look at the way the performing arts organization described in the second example analyzed its ROI.

Before starting the theater classes, the organization staff and board discussed the purpose of the venture. They set goals for the classes and made sure that these goals supported their mission (either financially or in service units). Suppose, for example, that their main goal was to expand appreciation for the theater throughout the community, starting with its youngest members, while, at the same time, not losing money. To accomplish this goal, it would be of the greatest importance to keep tuition low so that the most possible children could attend. If, however, their main goal was to contribute $15,000 a year in related profits to a fund for renovating the theater in three years, the profits become paramount, and tuition may need to be higher (although not so high that no one comes to the classes). In this case, cash return is a higher priority than social return.

It is important to note that putting a higher priority on cash than social return is not only okay in certain cases, it is often essential, even for the most compassionate not-for-profit staff or board member. As we've noted repeatedly, don't associate profits with bad things; making money in one area can help subsidize another area of service that will never pay for itself.

Next, the staff and board developed feasibility studies and a business plan. These documents gave them a good handle on their total investment, including cash, staff time, board time, and volunteer time. They were thus able to make a true comparison of the cost and benefit of various outcomes.

As in any investment decision (and that is exactly what this is), there are options. Our theater group, for example, could start the class with a high price and profit, start with a lower price and profit, leave the money in the bank, or try a different tack altogether. Let's examine how they might view each option.

Assume a cash cost of $25,000 to start the class and a total staff and an investment of volunteer time equivalent to $5,000. Look below to see the results of three options.

Option One—High Tuition

Start-up cost—CASH	$25,000
Start-up cost—TIME	$ 5,000
TOTAL COST	$30,000
Profit per year	$ 2,500
Students per year	100 (service units)

Cash return on investment in year one: $2,500/$30,000 or 8.3%
Invested cost per service unit $30,000/100 or $300 each

Option Two—Lower Tuition

Start-up cost—CASH	$25,000
Start-up cost—TIME	$ 5,000
TOTAL COST	$30,000
Profit per year	$ 500
Students per year	225 (service units)

Cash return on investment in year one: $500/$30,000 or 1.6%
Investment cost per service unit: $30,000/225 or $133.33 each

Option Three—Leave Funds in Bank at 7%

Start-up cost—CASH	$25,000
Start-up cost—TIME	$ 0
TOTAL	$25,000
Net income	$1,750 ($25,000 at 7%)
Students per year	0 (service units)

Obviously, the last option—leaving the money in the bank—is the least risky, but it also offers no return in service units and in visibility. The decision between the first two options (high or low tuition) is tougher, and will depend on the goals the board and staff set earlier; do they want cash or service? And if their goal is to have $15,000 a year in profit for the capital fund, are the outcomes of any of the options good enough? Probably not.

One flaw in this analysis is that we can't consistently quantify the risk associated with the business. Is the risk of failure (and of losing some or all of your investment) high or low? You will need to make some estimates of risk, include these estimates in your analysis, and weigh them in your decision-making process.

The other intangible to consider is the benefit to your organization from exposure. For example, if your museum is offering classes, a low fee will bring more people into the museum and, therefore, provide more exposure for the museum. Greater exposure translates into more potential contributions, visibility, public awareness, and overall goodwill.

Good management is basically resource allocation—making the best use of what you have and committing resources where they will do the most good. By setting and sticking to your goals, carefully accounting for all your costs, and reviewing your options fairly, you and your board can make the best decision possible with the information available regarding your new business. No manager can ask for more than that.

F. PREPARING YOUR BUSINESS FINANCIALS

Now let's turn to the issue of how to prepare your financials. Too many of our clients focus on the markets, on the service, or on the product and forget the key parts of the financials.

There are three steps to go through in developing your financial information. They are listed below:

1. ASSEMBLE YOUR FINANCIAL DATA

In the early stages of product or service selection and feasibility analysis, you should have gathered most of the information you need to prepare your business plan. Your work now is to refine and organize that information, check the accuracy of your estimates, and replace as many estimates as you can with firm figures. For example, for the purpose of your feasibility study, you may have estimated that your rent payment would be $600 per month. In your actual business plan, you may state that you are leasing property at 1124 East Church Street for $675 per month.

Following is a description and listing of the information you need.

a. Sales targets.

In order to make reasonable financial projections, you need to predict as accurately as possible what your volume of business will be. There are two major constraints here: the market and the assets (like money, skill, and time) that can be put into the enterprise. One way to approach these constraints is to estimate, based on your market research, what the potential market for your product or service is if you have restraints on money, skills, or time. The next factor is your internal constraints. This information allows you to estimate with some confidence what your potential sales will be. You should project sales for at least a three-year period.

Be careful not to project growth that cannot be sustained by the market. For example, if you are selling janitorial services in a community of 10,000 people with only 25 business establishments, there are only a limited number of the businesses that may be willing to buy your services. This is true even if you provide top-quality service and beat the price of all the competition. You simply cannot sell any more. Conversely, in a big city, there is an unlimited market for janitorial service at the quality and price you offer. But if your potential workforce is limited to about 10 employees, it makes it difficult for you to reach your entire potential market.

Finally, remember that there is a relationship between price and sales. In general, lower prices mean more sales, *but only to a point.* There is a point at which no matter how low you price your service, no one will buy it. For example, if you clean swimming pools, you can have only as many customers as there are pools: Even if you give services away, you will have no additional customers. So, in your sales projections, remember to consider the impact of price and of the competition.

b. Pricing information.

Pricing is the art of finding the price that your market will pay that will cover your production costs and provide a reasonable return on your investment. By using the information you gathered in your marketing research, you can determine the going price or *price range* for products or services that are similar to yours. Next, set a target for the amount of profit you wish to make during the first three years of operation. This information is used to set the price after you analyze the various costs involved in your operation.

As I have said repeatedly, nearly all not-for-profits are trained to *underprice* their services and thus they do. Do not assume that you will compete solely on price. Perhaps you can do what your competition does better, faster, or with less turnaround time. Consider both the fixed costs and the variable costs in your pricing mix, as well as your profit and your competition. Remember, you will have the tendency to underprice: fight it!

c. Start-up costs.

Capital items. These are the one-time purchase items that you need to operate your business. This category includes the purchase of land, buildings, equipment, and furniture. These are the assets that continue to benefit your business operation. Items like inventory and supplies that are *used up* in the course of conducting business are expenses. With the exception of land, you depreciate your capital assets. Depreciation is simply an accounting method of distributing capital costs to the expense of the business operation. Some not-for-profits do not bother with depreciation because they don't pay taxes and cannot take advantage of depreciation as a business expense deduction. However, depreciation gives you a more accurate picture of the cost of running your business. Large-ticket items should routinely be depreciated even if the business is a not-for-profit; otherwise, you never recover your full costs. For your larger expenses, review one or two financing options even if you plan at this point to pay cash. Borrowing or leasing might be more advantageous, and you need this information to test the financing options.

Other initial costs. In addition to capital items, you have other costs related to getting your business started that are not reflected in your operating expenses. Items such as legal fees, costs incurred to set up an accounting system, licenses, and introductory advertising are included in this section.

d. Operating expenses.

Fixed costs. These are the expenses that you pay whether or not you sell any product or service. They are sometimes called *indirect costs* or *overhead.* These expenses include items like rent, heat and electricity, and salaries. Most of your fixed or indirect costs change at different levels of sales or production. For example, if you operate a mail-order nursery, you produce a certain limited number of plants to sell from one greenhouse. If you wish to sell more, you need two greenhouses. This action increases your capital costs and fixed costs. If you anticipate growth during the first three years of operation, you need to estimate your fixed costs at various sales levels and identify the levels where your fixed and capital costs increase.

Variable costs. These are expenses that vary directly with the number of items or services you sell. Variable costs are also called *direct costs.* These costs vary depending on the type of business. If you manufacture a product, then all of the material costs are considered variable costs. If your product is made by workers who are paid only for contracted work, then their wages are part of the variable costs. If, however, your workers are salaried, you must pay them whether or not there is work to do. This makes salary expense a fixed cost.

2. ANALYZE THE FINANCIAL DATA YOU GATHER

After you organize the critical financial data, you are in a position to analyze the information to help you make decisions about financing and pricing your product or service. There are specific types of analysis you need to perform. Each of these is described below.

a. Start-up costs and working capital needs.

Start-up costs are those costs you have to get the business up and running. Licensing, land, building, equipment, raw materials, and training are all start-up costs.

Your *working capital* is the money you need to operate your business during its start-up phase, and then, when the business is operational, this money becomes what you run the business on between the time you deliver a service or manufacture a product and the time you get paid. Your working capital needs are not fixed. For instance, if you make 1,000 widgets a month and you get paid in 30 days for those widgets, you need to have enough working capital to pay for the direct costs of the widgets plus your operating costs (overhead) for the same period. But what if your customer suddenly decides to pay you in 45 days? Now your working capital needs go up by 50%. As noted before, more businesses go out of money making money than losing money, because they forget that fast growth starves businesses of working capital—of cash. (For more on working capital and some hands-on estimation forms, see Chapter 10.)

b. Break-even analysis.

Break-even analysis provides you with a sales objective that is expressed in either the number of dollars or units of production at which your business is neither making a profit nor losing money. The break-even point is the point where sales income is equal to fixed costs plus variable costs for a certain period of time. Break-even analysis is a technique used to analyze your cost information. The technique helps you to decide how much you have to charge at various levels of sales or how much you have to sell at various prices in order to get a return equal to your expenses. Break-even is calculated by the formula:

$$\frac{\text{Fixed costs}}{\text{(Unit selling price–Variable costs per unit}}$$

You may find that to charge a competitive price, you have to produce an unrealistic number of sales to achieve a profit. In this case, you need to reexamine your cost assumptions to see if expenses can be reduced.

How important is breakeven? See my list of the 10 biggest mistakes people make on their financials later in the chapter. Breakeven is there.

c. Pro forma profit-and-loss statement.

This statement is a projection of your income and expenses. Like the break-even analysis, it provides a further check on the soundness of your venture. Most business plans project income and expense statements for at least three years. I recommend that you project income and expenses for a three-year period, the first by month and the next two quarterly. However, the further you move from present day, the less meaningful your numbers become. To develop your profit-and-loss statement, simply use the figures from your operating expenses form for fixed expenses. Subtract your expenses from your income to show your pretax profit, add taxes if you anticipate incorporating your business as a for-profit enterprise, and subtract any profit sharing or bonuses. The final figure is your retained earnings or fund balance.

d. Pro forma cash flow analysis.

Your cash flow is probably the most important analysis for internal management of your new business, just as it is for your not-for-profit. It is the document that banks are most interested in because it indicates your ability to pay back your debt. The cash flow analysis shows how much cash is needed, when it is needed, and where it comes from. After you develop the cash flow analysis, use it as a check on how your business is doing. If you spend more or take in less cash than you anticipate, you may run into trouble. Variation from your cash flow projection helps you see early on if you are likely to run into cash problems. This analysis gives you a chance to take action and correct the flow of cash before you run into a serious shortage. Do your cash flow by month for the first year and quarterly for the next two. This will give you the most realistic view of your cash situation, and then you can design a credit policy to get you over temporary shortfalls, but *only* if they are temporary.

3. YOUR THIRD STEP IS TO PREPARE THE FINANCIAL DATA TO INCORPORATE IT INTO YOUR FORMAL BUSINESS PLAN

The financial section of your business plan should include the following five displays.

1. Pro forma sources and applications of funds.

This statement identifies where you intend to secure the funds you need to begin your business and how you intend to spend the money. In order to prepare this document, you must first look at your start-up costs and cash flow analysis to determine how much money you need to start the operation and how much working capital you need to carry the business until it generates its own revenue. Next, identify where you anticipate getting your money (your fund sources) in one column. In the second column, list the ways you intend to spend or apply the resources that are available.

2. The financial condition of the owner.

Be sure you include descriptive statements about the financial condition of the organization initiating the new business in this section of your business plan. This includes any information you believe reassures the bank that the financial position of the "parent" not-for-profit organization is sound. It also includes your financial statements for at least three years, audited if possible, and a copy of your annual report if available.

3. Pro forma balance sheet and profit and loss statements.

This statement is prepared to show the anticipated financial condition of your business to bankers and others who wish to help you finance your venture. Many times this statement is completed for three-year periods. We suggest that the first year be month-by-month, and the second two years presented quarter-by-quarter. The first balance sheet shows where the business is on the first day of business and the second a year later. You already prepared your pro forma profit and loss statement for your own analysis of the potential profitability of your business in the future.

4. Break-even analysis.

Include a short section that indicates the number of units you must sell at the asking price in order to break even. If you can find any information about the business you are entering that indicates typical sales for your demography or any other information that shows costs and anticipated sales based on sound information, be sure to include it.

5. Pro forma cash flow.

Include a pro forma cash flow projection for at least three years. The first year is a month-by-month projection. The following years can be done on a quarterly basis. Remember, this is the most important document for your banker. Compile the information with care because it provides you with an invaluable measure of how your business is doing.

Working with these financials will give you a much better idea of how your business will operate, let you have a clearer idea of the risks you will run and make the policy decisions for the senior management and board much more prudent.

G. THE 10 BIGGEST MISTAKES PEOPLE MAKE ON THEIR FINANCIAL PROJECTIONS

Now that we have looked at how to prepare your business plan financials, let's see what not to do. In working with hundreds of not-for-profits developing plans to start or acquire businesses since 1982, I have seen a lot of great plans and a bunch of so-so ones. It seems to me that not-for-profits are quicker to "get" the marketing concept, to understand the idea of meeting market wants than they are to do really good, indeed, useful, financial statements.

I have a week's worth of theories as to why this is, but perhaps the most salient is that all of us in the not-for-profit sector have been trained (by our funding streams) since we were right out of school how to do financials that *don't* cover all of our costs, how to rationalize expenditures that may or may not be related to the program, how to double up, maximize match, make something out of nothing. This accounting alchemy is difficult to overcome in developing a business plan, and it leads to serious business planning problems that I see repeated over and over again.

In order to help you perhaps avoid some of those common and often fatal (to the business) mistakes, I have developed our top ten list below. While it won't make the Letterman Show (on any network), it does bear reading and learning from.

10. MANY PEOPLE DO NOT *READ* FINANCIAL PROJECTIONS AFTER THEY ARE PREPARED

Now why would you spend the time putting together financials and not read them? Well, lots of people do. The financial manager develops the numbers and then the management and board ignore them or give them only a cursory glance. This often leads to a fundamental misunderstanding of how the business will perform. For example, the "bottom line" on an accrual-based profit-and-loss (P&L) projection may be "in the black" starting in six months, but the cash flow may be negative for a year or longer. If the decision makers do not thoroughly read and digest *all* of the financials, the organization is in for trouble.

9. FINANCIAL PROJECTIONS DO NOT SUPPORT THE STATED GOALS OF THE BUSINESS

As I have said repeatedly, the point of your not-for-profit's going into business is to (1) do more mission by having the business be part of the mission; (2) earn money from an unrelated business to then use to buy more mission by supporting another program; or (3) a combination of the two. The trouble with financials for a new business is that too often decision makers get so excited about the business that they forget about the point—the overall mission. If, for example, the new business's financial projections show a profit of $15,000 per year for the second through the fourth year, that may be great. But if the point of the entire exercise is to get a $30,000 per year boost to support a key program, the numbers are not meeting the goals. We have already talked about this a bit, but it bears repeating.

8. NUMBERS IN THE PROFIT-AND-LOSS STATEMENT, CASH FLOW ANALYSIS, AND BALANCE SHEET DO NOT JIBE

This is, yet again, a surprisingly common problem. People put together different financials at different times, the sources and applications one week, the P&L the next, the cash flow after that. They then revise each one a number of times, but don't remember to cross-check the numbers, and wind up with a lot of mistakes. For example, if in revising and fine-tuning your numbers, you merely change the interest rate on a loan from 8.0% to 7.75%, that changes the interest rate shown in the P&Ls, the debt service shown in the cash flow, any calculation that you may do of the cost of capital, and the display of liabilities in the opening balance sheet. If you change one or two and not the others, your numbers no longer jibe, and someone reviewing your plan—particularly a banker who may be considering lending you money—may rethink your business acumen.

Understand that, in my experience, the numbers are not usually off just by a quarter of a percent. I see things like the Sources and Applications noting the purchase of $250,000 of factory equipment and *no* depreciation in the P&L, or a loan for $300,000 in the balance sheet and the appropriate interest line in the P&L, but no debt service payments shown in the cash flow. Little things like that. Little things that can sneak up and bite you. The solution? Have an objective outsider look at your numbers and make sure that they work with each other.

7. PEOPLE DO NOT DO A CASH FLOW ANALYSIS OR CREATE JUST ONE CASH FLOW ANALYSIS EACH YEAR

P&Ls are nice, balance sheets are "cool," breakeven is important; but you live and die by cash flow. Yet, agencies that we work with repeatedly don't do them, or do them only on an annual basis. Particularly in a business start-up, doing a yearly cash flow analysis instead of a monthly one is a recipe for disaster. In truth, it would be better to not have one, because a yearly projection too often provides dangerously out-of-touch information. An annual cash flow predicts the cash at the beginning and end of the year only, with nothing about the status in the middle. It would be comparable to assuming that temperatures are cold year-round if you measured the temperature only on January 1 and December 31.

Do cash flow projections and do them monthly.

6. PEOPLE DO NOT ALLOW AN ADEQUATE NUMBER OF DAYS FOR ACCOUNTS RECEIVABLE

Unless you are a retail business, always assume that people are going to pay you as late as is possible. Then add 15 days for the mail. Then add 15 more for bureaucratic mess-ups and an extra 21 days if you get your funds from the federal government. If you assume you will get paid too soon, you will not set aside enough working capital to get you through. Receivables are part of your cash flow estimation process. Remember to always assume that your expenses go in the category "Sooner" and that your income goes in the category "Later."

5. PEOPLE DO NOT UNDERSTAND THE CONCEPT OF BREAK-EVEN ANALYSIS

Breakeven is *very* important to good business planning for not-for-profits, and yet, few managers and board members really understand how to compute it and, more importantly, what the numbers really mean. First, breakeven is computed by the following formula:

$$\frac{Fixed\ costs}{(Variable\ costs - Price)}$$

This calculates the units of service or number of widgets you need to sell to break even *in a particular time frame.* For instance, if you were selling widgets for $10 that had a variable cost of $4 and you needed to pay off a fixed cost of $3,000 per month, you would need to sell 500 widgets [$3,000/($10 - $4)] *per month* to not lose money *that month.* The value of this projection is to allow you to see how much sales volume is needed to stop losing money, and then to calculate how many months it will take for you to get up to that sales volume. Unfortunately, many people take breakeven to mean the volume of sales that will let you start to make money for the *life of the business,* and it is anything but that. Thus, they make incorrect and overly optimistic assumptions about the business, and assume that the money will start to roll in long before it really will.

4. PEOPLE DO NOT UNDERSTAND MURPHY'S LAW

Here's a news flash: Stuff breaks, people get sick, machines get stuck, storms occur, airline flights get canceled, customers change their minds or get fired or lose their income stream. In other words, and to paraphrase the crude but accurate bumper sticker, "Stuff Happens." If you do not allow for many things to go wrong, you will be very unhappy. In terms of your financials, that means not cutting your working capital so close and your cash so thin that any one of a hundred things could put you under. I recently saw a business plan that had projections of $250,000 income per year and a net profit of $34 each year. And on the basis of these projections they were prepared to borrow $200,000 over 10 years. I did my best to talk them out of it.

3. PEOPLE DO NOT START NEW BUSINESSES WITH ENOUGH CASH RESERVES

This mistake is a combination of nearly all the items that have preceded it. People don't do or understand breakeven, so they do not reserve enough cash. They don't do a cash flow analysis, so they do not know how much cash they really need. They don't allow for a lengthy enough receivable time, so they do not reserve enough cash. They forget the Peter Principle and don't give themselves a cash cushion. Sounds like I'm repeating myself.

If you doubt me, remember this: More businesses go out of business making money than losing it. That's right. How? They get starved for cash and close down.

2. PEOPLE PRICE THEIR PRODUCT OR SERVICE TOO LOW

This is a big-league mistake, and easy to understand given not-for-profits' training in getting paid for work at less than costs. In a new business, you must (1) charge enough to pay all your expenses or (2) have very deep pockets. I have heard people tell me in their business plans on more than one occasion that they will compete based on price, *before* they know what their costs are! You would think they were an airline, the way they talk about cutting costs—and we all know how financially healthy our airlines are.

If you think you can compete on price, great—but read on before you think you can.

1. PEOPLE DO NOT TAKE INTO ACCOUNT ALL COSTS WHEN PREPARING FINANCIAL PROJECTIONS

This is so common it must be a communicable disease. I have lost track of the number of not-for-profit executives who do not add their time into the overhead of the new business even though they will be spending

25% of their time on it for the first six months. Or those who leave out rent as an expense "since our building is paid for." Let me put it this way: If your competition is charging for it, you should be. Or let me put it another way: If you are not accounting for all your costs, you are probably losing money on each sale, and you will *not* make it up in volume.

Be brutal in this area. Compare your business P&Ls to your own organizational books. Are all the same line items there? If not, why? Are the additional things that are different accounted for? Is there a realistic number for depreciation, administration, rent, utilities, support services, accounting, and bad debts? If you are manufacturing, is there a contingency for wasted raw materials? Put everything in, or you don't have a realistic view of what's really going on.

So there they are. The 10 big mistakes that you can avoid if you try. They are easier to make than you might imagine.

H. CREATING A CLIMATE OF NEW IDEAS

One of the most important things that you need to do if you want to develop or enhance your social entrepreneurism is to develop a climate of endless new ideas, one in which suggestions are encouraged, ideas are fairly weighed, and the best ones implemented.

In line with our theory of the inverted pyramid of management, this means *everyone's* ideas—board staff, management, and line. You need these ideas to stay fresh, to see new methods of providing service, to keep in line with the changes in your many markets' wants.

To create this climate of ideas, you must constantly be asking. Do at least these things:

1. *Talk to all staff—particularly managers—about the need to use people's ideas.* Let all staff know that ideas are welcome, valued, and will be evaluated fairly and objectively. Let them know that no idea is too small, and that all suggestions—even those that are not used—are appreciated.
2. *Create a number of ways for people to offer ideas.* Have something such as a suggestion box. Ask for ideas at staff meetings. Make a new idea or process a reward item on people's evaluations and a time during the evaluation for discussion of new ideas. The freer people feel, and the more opportunities they have to offer their thoughts, the better.
3. *Develop an objective review system.* People need to know that their ideas will be reviewed impartially. For small suggestions,

the managers can probably do this; for larger ideas, you perhaps can adopt the criteria you developed in your business development process to weigh varying suggestions.

4. *Close the loop—get back to people.* Let anyone who puts forth a suggestion know what happened to their idea—it was implemented, it will be implemented, or it cannot be implemented and why. And *always* thank people for their ideas.

5. *Consider a reward/recognition system.* Whether you do this or not on a systematic basis, if someone makes a suggestion, or does a great deal of work on a particular idea, at least recognize them publicly, and consider rewarding them financially. If you feel the need to systematize this, just make sure the reward is a reward, not a punishment. (For more on rewards systems, see Chapter 6.)

You need your staff to use all their synapses and neurons on your organization's behalf all the time. Creating a climate in which new ideas are valued, recognized, and encouraged will not only make you able to be more entrepreneurial, it will also keep you flexible.

RECAP

Life is full of risk, and all of us learn to accommodate a certain level of risk every day. It is no different for mission-based managers. The skills that you have learned in this book will help make it easier for you to take risk on behalf of your clientele. Building a better board, a stronger staff, becoming market oriented, having strong controls, and becoming financially empowered all build your ability to evaluate and take risks. Some of these skills increase your strengths, some reduce unnecessary risks, and others build an important financial cushion—all of which leads us to the skills you have been learning in this chapter: how to be more entrepreneurial for the benefit of your community.

I hope that in this chapter I have given you food for thought on how to become better risk takers and more entrepreneurial. We have reviewed how to assess and take risk, and how to accept its presence in your organization. We have looked at new sources of income and have reviewed the steps necessary to start an outside business venture.

The next decade is a risky one for you and for your organization. You need to meet those risks with an ability to think and act like an entrepreneur.*

*For much more on this subject, see my book *Social Entrepreneurship,* also published by John Wiley & Sons.

Questions for Discussion

1. Do we meet the characteristics of a social entrepreneur? How?
2. Are there business ideas that would make both mission and money sense for us?
3. How do we look at expenditures now? As investments in mission? How can we be better at this and communicate it to our staff?
4. What risks are we taking now? How can we incorporate the idea of good risk into our culture more?

9

Developing a Bias For Marketing

OVERVIEW

This chapter is central to your success. If you don't know who you are serving, if you don't know what they want, if you don't know how to ask them how to improve, if you don't know how to let people know that you are around—how can you stay in business? You can't. You need to adopt a culture of marketing and this chapter will show you how. We'll talk through the benefits of marketing, and then go through each of the seven key steps in the marketing process, which are:

1. Identifying your target markets
2. Assessing what the market wants
3. Developing and redeveloping the product or service
4. Pricing
5. Promotion
6. Distribution
7. Evaluation

After that, we'll look at the best ways to ask your markets what they want, and then show you the ways to evaluate your marketing efforts. By the end of the chapter, you'll have a new understanding of who your markets *really* are, what they *really* want, and how to satisfy their wants.

A. WHY MARKET?

Marketing is essential, integral to your success, and yet, in many ways, foreign to not-for-profits. Let's start this critical component with a short quiz:

- You are a not-for-profit, so you don't have to worry about marketing, right? *Wrong.*
- The people who you serve are your primary markets, right? *Only partly.*

Successful not-for-profits know that their continued success, even their continued existence, depends on living, breathing, eating, and sleeping this slogan:

"EVERYTHING THAT EVERYONE HERE DOES EVERY DAY IS MARKETING."

This means that the way the phone is answered, the way the staff dress, the way the trash is picked up and the lawn is cut, the quality of your printed material, the knowledge of the board, to say nothing of how services are provided. All these activities go into the marketing mix. You have to assume that every interaction with a client, patron, donor, funder, community member, or politician—even those that you are totally unaware of, have an impact on some part of your organization: a decision to come to you for services, a decision to refer someone else to you, a decision to donate, or a decision to fund.

This maxim is not just applicable to management, or to service provision staff, but to every employee and volunteer that is associated with your organization. Remember the story I told in Chapter 5 about the new board member who attended the cocktail party? She had two ways of presenting her new experience—one positive, one less so. It is important that everyone understand that their role in the entire enterprise is essential, and part of your team marketing effort.

❏ **FOR EXAMPLE:** During the late 1990 buildup to the Gulf War, Americans saw interviews with dozens of young military personnel. Often they were asked: "What are you doing here?" Regardless of their job—cook, truck driver, munitions handler, mechanic—they answered: "Driving Saddam Hussein out of Kuwait!" No matter how menial their task in the huge war machine, these soldiers, sailors, and airmen had been taught that their small component was critical. I remember hearing a dock worker who spent his 105-degree days offloading cargo at one of the ports saying, "Hey, no one eats, moves, or fights without supplies, and no supplies get to nobody [sic] without me. That means I'm winning the war!" And he meant it. You want to work on that type of ownership with your staff and the understanding that what they do *does* affect the whole, even if on the surface there is not a direct impact on your services or your funding.

In the discussion on staff management, I talked about the fact that the lowest-paid people in your organization are the most important: They are the ones who have the most direct contact with your clientele and the public and the most impact on your marketing potential, directly or indirectly. These people need to be involved in your marketing, in the planning and execution of your marketing plan. They need to understand their critical role in the marketing of, and therefore the future of, your organization.

B. MARKETING BASICS

Marketing is so often considered a "dirty" word in not-for-profits. It is unseemly, and after all, you are not in *sales*, right? Wrong. You need to attend to your markets (and there are more of those than you think), find out what they want, and give it to them within the limits of your resources.

Let's start by looking at the basic marketing flowchart shown in Exhibit 9-1. As you can see, the entire process starts not with developing a product or service and then trying to sell it, but instead with choosing

Exhibit 9-1   Marketing Flowchart

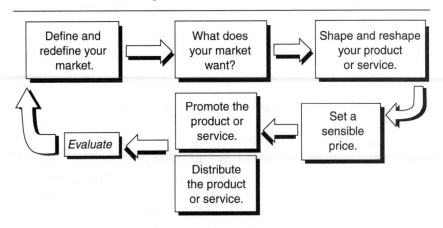

your target markets. Now, what do we do in our organizations? Usually, we say: "We're here to provide arts (medical, educational, etc.) services and we know how to provide them. So we'll let you know when we're open and y'all come!" This is known as *product-driven marketing:* We believe in our product (or service) and that it will sell itself. Let's go through these parts of the marketing diagram one box at a time.

1. IDENTIFYING YOUR TARGET MARKETS

Fact: The not-for-profit industry is the only industry in the world that regularly gets together in groups to berate and complain about its best customers. Think about it. Your best customer is the group or groups that send you the most money. For most readers, that is some branch of local, state, or the federal government. Do you see them as customers? If you are like 99% of not-for-profit managers, you see them as the *enemy.* This, to say the least, is a self-defeating viewpoint. You and your staff and board need to start thinking of your largest funders as your best customers, and then start treating them that way.

But, before we discuss how you can do that, I need to realign your thinking about who your markets really are. Stop and think for a minute. Who *are* your markets and how can you identify them? Look at Exhibit 9-2 for a start in breaking down the concept that the only market you have that counts is your clientele.

I have divided the not-for-profit marketing mix into three main categories:

1. *The payer markets.* These are the people who send you money. They may be the federal, state, or local government; donors; foundations; users; or others. Each of these should be considered a different market segment. For example, if you get money from three different

Exhibit 9-2   The Markets of Your Not-for-Profit

Internal	Service
• Board & Staff	Service A
Payer	Client Type 1
• Government	Client Type 2
• Foundation	Service B
• Membership	Client Type 1
• United Way	Client Type 2
• Donation	Referrers
• User Fees	

state programs, each program should be assessed as a different market segment. I also include in the payer markets a box for "referrers." These are the critical people who send other people your way. They might be mental health counselors, social workers, friends, physicians, or ministers, but without their referrals you would be in trouble. You need these people. Their referrals translate into income.

2. *The service markets.* These are the people that you serve. Think about how many different markets are represented here: each different program you provide multiplied by each different age, socioeconomic, and gender cohort you provide those services to. For example, if you provide family planning services, the way you provide them to married couples is a great deal different than how you would provide the same basic service to single teenage boys and girls. You have lots of different service markets.

3. *The internal markets.* These are two different markets: *staff* and *volunteers.* The brutal truth is that you need good, solid staff more than they need you. The same is true for your volunteers. They are, in the truest sense, essential markets, ones that you have to attend to if you want to do any mission at all.

Each of these markets warrants special attention. You need your payer markets: no money, no mission. If you accept the payer markets as your customer (whether you like it or not) then you need to figure out how to keep them as your customer. You need your service markets to be happy and satisfied, otherwise you are not doing good, high-quality mission. If you run out of service markets, you've just run out of a reason for existing. You need your board and staff as resources to plan and execute your mission. You are also *competing* for each and every one of these markets, just the way Ford competes with Toyota or Delta competes with United. The payers, the service recipients, and the staff and board all have choices, and those choices are only going to increase in the coming years. Without your paying constant attention to those markets, the choice they make may very well not have anything to do with your organization.

☞ **HANDS ON:** To get a handle on your organization's many markets, do this: Sit down with a chart that looks something like the one shown in Exhibit 9-3, and put all of your markets into it. The key here is to try to distinguish (segment) markets to ensure that you give each the attention that it deserves. Note that I have included only one or two

Exhibit 9-3   Market wants

Category	Market	Wants
Payers	Special education districts	Low cost, accountability
	State department of rehabilitation	Good bookkeeping, timely filing
	Private payers	Low cost, prompt billing
Staff	Speech therapists	Career growth
	Physical therapists	Varied patients
	Teachers	Continuing education
	Administrators	Stability, retirement
Service	Children 0–3 with perceived disabilities	Happy, loving staff
	Children 3–5 who need physical or cognitive testing	Happy, fun place
	Parents of children 0–3 in the above programs	Safe place that helps their child
Referral	Special education administrators	High-quality services
	Pediatricians and family practitioners	Highly educated staff
	Disability-specific parents' support groups	Inclusion

"wants" for each market. In reality, there will be many. You need to ask. Also, note that there are different wants for the special education *districts* (payers) and the special education *administrators* (referrers). This is not unusual. The paying side wants one thing and the program side another.

Before we go further, I want to give you one overriding caution about markets and market segmentation. Do not ever fall into what I call the "census" trap, saying that your main market is the 590,400 people that live in your county. It's not. Your market is never *everyone*.

It is the people between ages 12 and 90 who enjoy live classical music and have the ability to pay and attend concerts if you are a symphony orchestra; it is (primarily) women between 12 and 50 who are sexually active if you are a family planning organization; but it's *not* everyone. We were trained to think of our "markets" by the federal government in this style as a result of capitation funding, wherein an organization's government grant each year was based on the service area's population. This was poor training, but you can begin to relearn if you develop this chart. And, if you do this for your organization, I guarantee that you will be stunned as to how many markets and market segments you have. Don't panic. At least now you know who your markets *really* are, and now you can decide which merit the most immediate attention.

2. ASSESS THE MARKET WANTS

Note that I said "wants," not "needs." Professionals tell people what they need. People buy what they want.

❏ **FOR EXAMPLE:** Statistics tell us that one in eight American adults is in need of substance abuse treatment—mostly for alcohol, but some for harder drugs. If we assumed that a third of those people need inpatient care, that's still over 8.3 million adults in need of treatment. There are not one tenth that many treatment beds available in the country, and many of them are empty. Why? Because, as anyone who has an addiction will tell you, people will not seek services until they *want* it. Do they all need it? Sure, and we can prove it to them medically. But until they *want* treatment, there is no point in even trying. Here is a second example for anyone with small kids. How many of your children *need* additional toys? How much of your income do you spend per year at Toys R Us?

With this background, we now need to establish ways to find out what all of these markets we've identified *want*. There are a variety of ways to do this, and they all start with a basic discipline that has just three letters:

A-S-K

It's really very simple. You ask people what they want, why they came to you, what made them happy or not so happy about your services; whether they will return, and if so, why, if not why not; and how you can improve services to meet their wants. By developing a discipline of asking, by getting everyone in the organization in the habit of market research through asking, you will learn extremely important things, many of which will completely astound you.

How do you ask? You can ask formally, through surveys or focus groups. You can also ask informally every chance you get. You should, at the very least, establish some kind of baseline of employee and consumer satisfaction through a formal survey. You can then remeasure that satisfaction every 12 to 18 months. You should also ask everyone that seeks or utilizes your services in any way how they came to you: was it a referral from a friend, did they see the ad in the paper, did they hear about you from their doctor (or minister, or art teacher)? You need to know these things and evaluate trends over time.

There are a variety of ways of asking. Surveys and focus groups often sound very technical, complex, and expensive. Not always so. They are essential tools for you as you develop your asking skills, so let's look at them in some detail.

a. Surveys.

Many organizations wrongly assume that establishing baseline survey data is very expensive and the purview of only expensive marketing firms like Harris Polls or Gallup. And certainly, polls and surveys *can* be expensive, sometimes prohibitively so. But let's focus on the five important components of a good survey, and then you will need to decide whether you can provide or find the expertise in-house, locally, or from out of town.

1. Surveys need to be *focused* around a central theme. Don't ask a referral source the same things you would ask an employee, and also don't ask the employee 10 questions about job satisfaction if your main survey goal is to find out what the staff wants in terms of noncash compensation.

2. Your survey needs to *ask the right questions*—ones that will generate the information you need. In deciding what questions to ask, be frugal. What do you really want to know? Is it about customer satisfaction in general or their satisfaction with a particular program? Target your questions.

3. You need to *ask the questions right*. There is a great deal of difference in the responses you will get depending on how you ask the question. I can generate a huge difference in responses about a

particular program if I ask the question, "On a scale of 1 to 5, how much did you like the program?" as opposed to asking "Did the program appeal to you or not?"

4. Surveys need to be *short enough* to have people fill them in. As a rule, if it looks like it will take more than 5 minutes and the respondent is filling out the survey only out of kindness, it won't happen. (You can have longer surveys filled in if you are compensating them: giving them money, a lunch, a free coupon for a pizza, etc.)

5. To make the whole exercise worth it, you have to survey enough people to have a *representative sample*. If you are a church and you want to survey your congregation's attitude toward a new church building, asking three people out of a congregation of 600 will not tell you what you need to know. However, not making a move until you have surveyed the other 597 members is foolish.

As you can see, many of these issues are technical, and thus most organizations get some help in setting up their surveying. There are some excellent written resources on surveying. A second source is the marketing department of your local university, where you might get adopted as a student project. Also, the marketing professor might be willing to help you pro bono or for a much lower fee than a proprietary marketing firm.

Surveys are excellent information gathering tools, but get some help with your first one, and don't do just one. Do them regularly, and compare and analyze the data you receive.

b. Focus groups.

Focus groups are great. While they do not generate the kind of objective data that surveys do, the subjective information gathered on feelings, reactions, impressions, and opinions is invaluable. At their core, focus groups are sessions of 1 to 2 hours with a *focused* set of questions posed to 10 to 15 people who represent a market or homogenous group. A focus group is almost always run by an outside facilitator, and I urge you to find a local facilitator who is experienced with focus groups, because the quality of the facilitator makes or breaks these sessions. The great benefit of a focus group is that a talented facilitator can follow up on ideas and answers generated by the group, investigating leads that you could never expand on in a formal survey. For instance, a facilitator might ask: "What kind of service improvements could we make for kids?", and a participant might give an excellent idea. Right then and there, the facilitator can pose the new idea to the rest of the group, gathering on-the-spot reactions and modifications that can lead to earlier and ultimately more successful implementation. When looking for a facilitator, look for the talent in group facilitation first and the knowledge of your program second. Once you retain the facilitator, he or she needs to get up to speed on all aspects of the issues your focus group will be discussing, including jargon, and potentially controversial issues.

You also need to hold separate groups for separate issues, even though it is more time consuming and costly. Don't expect a group of lower-income service recipients to be as forthcoming if they are mixed in with affluent donors. You also need to focus your questions. You just can't ask everyone everything you might want to know. People wear down after about two hours, so don't wring them dry.

c. The discipline of asking and listening.

Asking people what they want is in itself an image enhancer for your organization. I have facilitated over 100 focus groups in the past 10 years, and our firm has surveyed at least 15,000 people. During those activities, one of the comments we hear most often is: "Thanks for asking! No one ever has before." By asking, you get valuable information *and* make people feel better about your organization, all in one action. What a deal!

However, there are a couple of other important points to keep in mind about asking. If you ask, you *must* listen. And you may not hear things that make you happy, especially at first. You will almost certainly hear criticisms of your programs, your management style, your philosophy of service. Take them as opportunities to improve, not as personal assaults on your capabilities and character. And, if you listen, you need to respond, both orally and in writing. Thank people for offering their insights, perhaps in a memo to all who participated in a survey or in a personal note to anyone who took the time to offer their reactions in a focus group. In that correspondence, close the loop with them and let them in on what you are doing with their ideas. You can put the main ideas that came out of the survey/focus groups into four categories as follows

1. Things that are suggested that you will be able to do right away
2. Things that you will have to work on over the near term
3. Things you will need to defer to future years
4. Suggestions that are inappropriate or impossible

Tell people all of those things. If the ideas are going into a strategic plan, say so. If they are being passed on to your main funding source, let that be known. If they are going to be used to plan a major capital campaign, a new program for a specific group, an additional site, or any tangible outcome, let people know. Be forthright—don't promise what you cannot deliver on, but *do* get back to people.

What can you learn by asking? Wonderful things.

❑ **FOR EXAMPLE:** A few years ago, our firm helped a rural primary care health center with a community perception survey and focus groups. We facilitated a number of focus groups: two of current patients, one of former patients, and one of community officials. We found several common complaints/suggestions during these sessions. These are listed below, with the actions that the health center took to respond.

- *"Your center looks run down, inside and out."* The center found that the grounds maintenance service was not doing the job. Over time, the appearance of the facility had declined and the staff had not noticed. But the patients, who only came in once or twice a year, noticed the difference. The clinic changed maintenance contractors with an emphasis on trash removal and neatness. Inside, a new coat of paint and more staff emphasis on picking up and neat work spaces resulted in a much higher satisfaction rating in this area the following year: Total cost: $500 in painting.

- *"Your receptionist is rude."* This feeling was prevalent among *former* patients, but a fact that the administrator had never noticed, because when he was treated, he didn't enter through the normal patient reception lines. The receptionist was given sensitivity training. That didn't help much, so she was transferred to a different clerical job. Total cost: $100 for the training.

- *"Your toys are dirty—I worry about the kids catching a "bug" when they play with them."* In fact, the toys were cleaned every night, they were just old. The center bought new toys each year and had the staff clean them in front of the patients every day. Total Cost: $200 per year.

After these items and a few others were resolved, the center got back to all those interviewed, with particular emphasis on the former patients, noting the changes—new toys, new receptionist, better maintenance—that had resulted from the information gathered at the focus groups. *Every single former patient returned* within the next six months for an office visit. The patients liked the practitioners, and the practitioners hadn't thought that they cared about these nonmedical, but still important issues. The center never would have known why patients were leaving if they hadn't asked.

Ask, listen, act, respond! It works.

3. DEVELOP AND REDEVELOPING THE PRODUCT OR SERVICE

Only now that you know who your markets are and what your markets want, can you, to varying extents, modify your service array or develop a new service. Some readers will be hamstrung by service definitions dictated by their funding source: "You must provide inpatient 28-day residential rehabilitation," or "You must have each child tested in an approved setting every 18 months," or whatever guideline you must follow. But you need to try to match your services to your markets and their wants as closely as possible, noting that those wants will change over time.

This is an excellent place to note the conflict represented in the preceding paragraph: The funder wants you to provide a service in a particular way, whether or not the recipient wants it that way. Look carefully at what is going on—to meet a payer's want (service provided within specific guidelines), you may have to give the service market's want a lower priority. This is an excellent example of the conflicts that you need to try to resolve and the balance that you need to try to achieve. It's tough, and no one should misunderstand that. Often, a program that is wildly successful in one community catches the eye of a funder who wants to have it replicated elsewhere. Too often, the success was a result of a confluence of events in that initial community—a key staff person or volunteer, a community event that precipitated demand for the program—and not because of the fundamental attractiveness of the program itself. In his book, *Reinventing Government,* Addison, Wesley Publishers, 1992, David Osborne recounts the story of a woman in the Bronx who organized a tenants' group to run their low-income housing unit and turned it around. The group worked out all sorts of ideas and methods to reduce crime, increase occupancy, and improve tenants' lives. But Osborne, who advocates similar empowerment programs elsewhere in the country, also found that without the key leader, all of the other items, no matter how admirable, were not used.

In marketing terms, if people didn't *want* it to happen enough to *work* for it, it won't happen, and in many cases your organization will take funds to try to replicate a program before there is a demand for the program. That is very hard work. In these cases, you also need to ask, and ask regularly, to see if you can refit the program to meet the wants that exist in your community now, rather than in some other community three years ago.

You must also make sure that you have *listened*, and that *all* of the staff is on board and prepared for the changes the market wants.

❏ **FOR EXAMPLE:** A few years ago, my firm was asked to assist a number of community substance abuse rehabilitation providers with assistance in broadening their markets. In discussing this project with the providers, it was clear that they wanted to move beyond the Medicaid-eligible client to, as they put it,"serve the executive covered by Blue Cross." The reasons for this market shift were understandable and valid: The providers could recoup $120 per day from Blue Cross for a service for which they were then getting $65 per day from Medicaid. But were they ready to provide the services? They said they were, and many had in fact upgraded their physical plant markedly.

I asked them if their staff were also ready to serve this different clientele, noting that business executives, even ones with substance abuse problems, have significantly different expectations than their traditional clientele: those eligible for Medicaid. I was assured that the staffs were ready for this change. I doubted it.

So we checked. We had a woman on our staff call each of the agencies in question and ask for help for her husband, who was portrayed as an alcoholic who worked for a large firm and had Blue Cross coverage. She also called the community hospitals that had competing substance abuse programs in each community. In every single case, the community rehab center staff blew it. The receptionist didn't have any knowledge of Blue Cross. She referred the "patient" to a staff person who was either equally limited in knowledge or never called back. There was never any follow-up to the call in writing or by phone. Conversely, every single hospital had its act together. The caller talked with a knowledgeable and sympathetic nurse immediately in each case. The nurse followed up by phone and with solid marketing material in the mail.

I returned to a meeting of the community providers armed with this information, and they, frankly, didn't accept it as valid. So I asked them to exchange business cards with another provider, take a break, and go call in pretending to be a person seeking care. They returned 15 minutes later and reported their experiences, which were uniformly awful.

They and their staff were not yet ready to serve the market that they had targeted. They were not ready to meet the market wants, because they had not asked the market what they wanted: They had *assumed* that they knew, and in marketing, assuming that you know what the market wants is not only egotistical and arrogant, it is suicide.

Ask, but *listen* to the answers.

4. PRICE THE SERVICE

There are so many variables in pricing, most of which you don't control, that I won't take a lot of space discussing pricing here. Also, there are many excellent resources in pricing strategy. Suffice it to say that most not-for-profits underprice their services through either the training you have gotten from funders throughout your career (funders don't want to reimburse all of your costs) or naivete, or both. However, learning how to price, to say nothing of what providing an individual unit of service *actually costs* to provide, is a critical skill to develop in any organization. Knowing what your costs are and which programs are making money, which are losing money, and which are breaking even is a key component of any plan for financial empowerment (see Chapters 11 and 12).

I do, however, at least need to cover these key points. Pricing is both an art and a science. Price development is fluid, not static. It exists in a world where there are many dynamics occurring. Pricing is comprised of four components:

a. Fixed costs.

These are the costs that you normally think of as "overhead." Technically, they are the costs that are fixed whether "sales" rise or fall. So, for example, in a school, the administrative costs and building and maintenance are fixed costs, because they won't change if the enrollment (the sales) goes from 70 to 90 (or 70 to 50). The crux of charging a fixed-cost component is the issue of how quickly you want to recover these costs: over how many sales. For example, if you tried to recover the entire fixed cost of a Chrysler factory in one auto, the price would be a little steep. Chrysler tries to recover that cost over millions of cars. But if they add too low a charge for the fixed-cost component in each car's price, and don't sell enough, they lose money on their fixed costs.

b. Variable costs.

These are the costs that vary as the sales vary. In manufacturing, they include the raw materials for the product, the unit costs of labor, and the energy to produce the product. In my school example, they would be the costs directly associated with each student: food, supplies, linens, and differing energy costs (for a residential school). As the enrollment increases, these costs increase.

c. Profit.

Yes this is OK. A not-for-profit can have a profit, and nowhere in any regulation or law does it say that you can't. It is just your funding sources that say you shouldn't. The profit you make will help you pay off debt and put money aside. This critical issue will be discussed further in the financial empowerment chapter, but for our purposes here, let's just note that you need a profit, and the component of price attributable to the profit will depend on how quickly you want to recover your initial investment and how much the market will bear. The profit margin will usually be some small percentage (probably 3 to 8%) of the price.

d. Competition and market conditions.

The competition has much to do with what your price is. If you price out your item (e.g., tuition at our hypothetical school) and find, in comparing your tuition to the competition's, that yours is 20% higher, what will that mean? It may mean that you will lose students to the lower-priced school. Conversely, it may mean that you will gain students who want to go to only the "elite" (read: expensive) school.

Obviously, this is a very fluid situation. In the case of the school, let's imagine a teacher's union arriving, and a contract signed guaranteeing increases in salary for the next five years. What just happened to fixed costs? They went up. What if three graduates get full scholarships to Harvard, or if the test scores for seniors are tops in the state, or if the football team is nationally ranked? Demand for enrollment will increase. In one case, your price (tuition) *needs* to go up due to cost increases, in the other the price (and the profit) *can* go up due to market conditions.

Don't fall into the trap of assuming that you can just underprice everyone and that that will make people come to your organization. First, it's just plain dumb (which is not to say that people don't do it all the time). If you just keep cutting prices, and have prices less than your costs, you will soon be out of business unless you have very deep pockets and can outlast your competition. All one has to do is look at the suicidal price wars that the major airlines have engaged in over the past decade to see that. A second good example is auto rebates. They do encourage sales, but at a loss to the automakers. I can think of a dozen examples of our not-for-profit clients in business development coming to us and saying that they planned to compete on price without knowing whether or not they could do so and still make money. As noted earlier, there are a number of good resources on pricing, and your auditor may also have ideas on this.

5. PROMOTE THE SERVICE

There are dozens of ways to promote your services: word of mouth, referrals, advertising, personal contact, presentations to community groups, flyers put under windshield wipers, and, of course, the classic two-fold six-panel brochure. How you promote your service will depend on your budget, your service, and the people you are trying to inform that you are there. But no matter what your status, think about this: With all of the different *payer* markets and all of the different *referral* markets you have, to say nothing of all of the different *service* markets you are trying to attract and retain, does one brochure with a short history of your organization and a picture of your building really get your point across? Of course it doesn't. Yet that is what most not-for-profits have: a brochure that talks about the organization's genesis; lists its services, often in jargon; and sometimes doesn't even include a phone number.

My question is: Who really cares about a picture of your building? No one but the architect and the builder. Who cares about your history? Hardly anyone, except those who were there at the time. Can one short brochure really attract people with all sorts of different wants to your organization? Can it really explain how your organization can meet the wants of funders, donors, referrers, or service recipients? Of course not.

Promotion, whether in person or written, must *never sell the program.* Rather, it must *attempt to solve the customer's problem.* If I am the parent of a developmentally disabled child, do I care how long you've been in business? No. I want good evaluation and educational opportunities for my son or daughter. I want you to recognize me as a customer. I want to feel that you are sympathetic to my feelings and that you will provide only the best services on the planet to my child. I want to know how much it is going to cost me. So your marketing material must say those things, clearly and in straightforward prose. Show me the benefit that I will receive by sending my child to your organization.

Remember the number 1 rule of sales: *Don't sell the product—solve the customer's problem.* You need to let the potential users of your service, the potential funders, staff, and board (in other words, all of your many markets) know what benefit they will gain from using your services or donating you money. Don't just tell them who you are, or what you do;

make the connection between what you do and how it will help them. Wording such as "XYZ agency provides substance abuse rehabilitation services" is much less compelling than: "If you or a loved one have a problem with substance abuse, the staff at XYZ can help put them on the road to a more productive, less dependent life." The first talks about services (in jargon), whereas the second promises benefits.

The other major flaw in most not-for-profits' promotion comes from falling into the "census trap" discussed earlier in the chapter. Organizations that wrongly assume that their market is the entire population often also assume that the entire population needs to know about their organization and waste a great deal of time and money trying to achieve that goal.

❑ **FOR EXAMPLE:** A client of mine, a rehabilitation facility specializing in head injury patients, recently bemoaned the fact that they had done a public awareness survey and only 6% of the area's population recognized the organization's name and knew what general services were provided. Both the executive director and the board were adamant about spending money (a great deal of money) on a public awareness campaign that would, in their words, "solve this problem."

"*What problem?*" I asked.

"Not enough people know about us!" was their startled answer.

"*So? Do patients self refer?*"

"No," they replied.

"*Do you get 5% or more of your money in small donations from the general public?*"

"No" they replied.

"*Where do your referrals come from?*"

"From area neurologists and surgeons," they said.

"*What percentage of those physicians know about your programs in detail?*" "We don't know," was their answer.

"*Find out, and forget about the public. They don't need to know about you (nor do they want to, for that matter). You need to focus your efforts on your referral sources.*"

This example is a classic one of misunderstanding the target market, as well as the market wants.

6. PROVIDE (DISTRIBUTE) THE SERVICE

Once you have developed the service, you need to provide it. Here you have lots of choices, and are probably doing an excellent job in being flexible, but let's review the options. Just like solving a mystery, writing a story, or preparing a book report, the key parameters of service provision to meet a market wants are who, what, when, where, and why.

- *Who provides the service.* You can't just have someone who is knowledgeable in the service area, you need someone who can "connect" with the service recipient. Someone who doesn't speak Spanish is not going to be an optimal provider in a largely Hispanic neighborhood. Someone who acts very "square" probably will not be the best with kids in a youth ministry.

- *What service is provided.* You've already established this through the previous steps.

- *Where the service is provided.* Your clientele need easy access to the extent possible. Is the place you provide service convenient? Is there adequate parking, sufficient security? In the past few years, more and more hospitals are providing off-site radiology and therapy sites that are closer to where their patients live. This helps the patients avoid having to come to the central hospital where parking is often difficult; security is sometimes inadequate, especially after dark; and patients must walk long distances from their car to their service site.

- *When the service is provided.* A family planning seminar for teenagers is pointless if held at your office on weekdays: The kids should be in school. The flexible *when* is a key component of market sensitivity in today's predominantly two-income and or single-parent families. People seek services at odd hours, and value time-saving convenience over many other considerations. Thus Domino's Pizza thrives, Toys R Us is experimenting with around-the-clock stores during the pre-Christmas period, and 24-hour convenience stores are solid franchise investments. Be convenient and you will increase both market share and market satisfaction.

- *Why. Don't forget the why. Why is this particular service being provided?* To educate, to prevent, to entertain, to cure, to soothe, to enlighten? The *why* becomes a key component of the provision mix, and should always be close at hand.

7. EVALUATE THE MARKETING EFFORT

As mentioned earlier, you need to know how you are doing. Getting baseline information is a good start, but steady and consistent asking is essential. Are your staff happier than they were last year? Are you getting better quorums than you were two years ago? Is attendance or occupancy up or down? Are more people responding to advertising or to referrals? You need to ask, regularly and consistently.

Also, be cognizant of the fact that the wants and needs of the markets are constantly changing. Thus, you may need to change with them. The only way to accurately assess the changes is by asking and tracking the answers over time.

C. ASKING DOES MAKE A DIFFERENCE

I am often asked to speak to annual meetings of statewide or national not-for-profit trade associations, and I regularly point out to them that their best customers are their biggest funders. There is usually uncomfortable silence. I then ask them: "When was the last time any of you went to your state (federal, county) project officer and asked, 'How can I make your job easier?' " There is either silence or laughter. I then point out that this is basic marketing. After these sessions, I am often asked: "What difference will it make if we ask bureaucrats how we can make their life easier? They have no control over our money."

This is an understandable question, and in response I want to offer two examples of what a difference such a simple, no-cost technique *can* make.

❏ FOR EXAMPLE: As I told you in the first chapters, in the early 1980s I was the executive director of a health systems agency, a not-for-profit formed as a result of federal law, and almost 100% federally funded. We did health care planning and regulation for a specific geographic area. Our federal contacts were in Chicago, at the Federal Regional Office Building.

Shortly after I became executive director, I had to go to Chicago for a meeting, and I made it a point to meet not only with my federal program officer, who was nominally my key contact, but also with the woman who was our grants administration officer, the person who processed our budget, vouchers, and grant checks. This woman, whose name was Betty, worked in a windowless office in the midst of a vast, drab, government building, but she was warm, personable, and obviously pleased to have been visited. "I rarely get to meet the people at the agencies," she said. "In fact, I think it's been three years since I got face-to-face with someone from the field." I said that I was glad to meet her, and that I hoped that our staff would process all of the forms for her correctly, but if we messed up, I wanted her to call me right away. Betty responded appreciatively, noting that everyone usually denies filling in the forms wrong, or complains about their length, instead of offering to cooperate. I told her I just would think of her as my best customer. She laughed and we parted friends. The next time I was in Chicago, and the next and the next, I stuck my head in Betty's office and said hello. That was the total extent of my "marketing" with her.

Two years later, 10 days before our 200-page grant application for federal funds was due, our financial manager quit on three days' notice and left the financial part of the application incomplete. I did my best to fill it out and get it in on time, and beat the deadline by 12 hours.

Three weeks later, I found out that I had not done a very good job. Betty called me at work on a Thursday afternoon to let me know that a number of figures were wrong, and that she could not submit our application to Washington the next day at 5:00 unless they were redone. My heart went through my shoes. How could I rework all those figures and still get them in to her in 24 hours? Betty said, "Stay cool. Just put me on hold, pull out pages 23 through 27 of the financial section, go make a copy of them, and get back on the phone." I obediently did so. Betty said, "Okay, see line 27c, column 2? You have $356,798 there now. Change it to $398,558." And so it went. Betty had done my work for me. She had spent the previous evening redoing over 100 calculations and essentially saved my organization. I filled out a new form and overnighted it (this was the era before faxes) to Chicago. We got the grant.

I have always believed that because I treated Betty like a friend and a customer rather than as a bureaucratic enemy, she went the extra mile for me. There was no serious cost to this, it was just good marketing.

❑ FOR EXAMPLE: A few years ago we did a number of focus groups for a residential school that worked with behavior-disordered teens. One of the groups was with a primary referral source: juvenile delinquent officers (JDOs). The session was spent assessing what the school was doing well, not so well, and what it could do better. At the end of the session, I posed the question: "What can the school do to make your job easier?" After a long silence, one JDO said, "Interesting question, and one I've never heard before. But one thing does come to mind. You know the admission verification form (J-345A) that you need to fill out after you admit a child that we refer to you? Well, my supervisor is all over me to get those in, because then we get our federal match.

Your people are getting those to me in 45 to 60 days, and they're only one page long. Could you get them to us in 21 days, maybe?" The other five JDOs in that session concurred with the need for these forms to be turned in sooner.

I said, "How would seven days be?" "*Terrific!*" they replied, "Oh, and thanks for asking." "Keep letting us know what we can do," I said.

I returned to the school to report on the session and brought up the request. "No problem," said the staff, "we didn't realize they needed the form in a hurry. We'll get them out the same day, as part of the admission protocol. They started implementing the change that day.

The next year, the referrals from those six JDOs were up 15%, and at this writing, seven years later, they continue to climb, and those six people constitute the highest referral group for the school.

The lesson here is twofold. First, by asking, we made a very positive impression. By responding, we made an even bigger one. It was a small thing—a minor question, a no-cost response—but it paid huge long-term rewards.

Don't assume that people who work in a bureaucracy are necessarily mired in it. Choices have to be made: where pilot money goes, or lapse funds, or the most interesting research is run, and on and on. If you meet the wants of the funders, the funders will help you meet yours.

RECAP

Marketing is an excellent example of the topic that was broached in Chapter 1: that the business world has a lot to offer the not-for-profit world in terms of techniques and expertise. As a mission-based manager, you want to tap that experience in surveying, market identification, promotion, and pricing, all in an effort to do more mission, more efficiently and effectively.

You market every day. Your staff need to understand this and that they are a critical part of the marketing team. If you don't market aggressively, if you don't work to keep your market share, you may have none in 10 years.

In this chapter, we have covered several issues that are central to the improvement of your organization:

- The fact that everything you do every day is marketing
- The fact that your markets are much more numerous and diverse than you may have previously thought

- The real process of marketing
- The ways to ask what your markets want
- The ways to develop a discipline of asking
- The methods to ensure that your marketing efforts are on track
- Examples of organizations that have profited by asking and by giving even their governmental funders what they want

Hopefully, you have found ideas that you can incorporate into your organization as you go about building a culture of marketing, a tradition of asking, and an organizational appreciation for your markets, their diversity, and their changing demands.

The importance of continuing marketing cannot be overstressed. It needs to become part of your culture, and should also become an integral component of your staff training and continuing education program—for everyone in the organization.*

Questions for Discussion

1. Who are our markets? Within those, who are our target markets?
2. What do our markets want? How do we know? How often should we ask our target markets? In surveys, focus groups?
3. How do we ramp up our informal asking? Should we look at staff training in this area?
4. What about customer service/satisfaction training for staff? Can we instill the idea that everyone (even our funders) are customers, and that everyone is on the marketing team?

*For much, much more on this subject, see my book *Mission-Based Marketing*, also published by John Wiley & Sons.

10

Financial Empowerment

OVERVIEW

There is a rule that I like to use whenever I am confronted with a staff or board member who wants to provide a new service, or an expanded one, and is taking the attitude: "We're here to provide the service; if we do that the money will take care of itself." When I hear this, I say:

NO MONEY, NO MISSION.

Mission *is* important, but so is money. This does not mean to suggest that money is paramount. You are not a *for-profit*, so you should always be *most* concerned about mission. But being most concerned about one thing does not mean that you should be unconcerned about everything else. You must factor into your zeal to provide more and better mission the reality that there is only so much money to work with. The fact that your organization is a not-for-profit does not mean that the rules of economics are suspended. You still need working capital to grow, still need to make money to have the money to innovate, still pay back debt from profits, just like any other organization.

Chapter 8 focused on using the business model to provide more services while making money to provide even more services. The purpose of this chapter is to show you how to keep more of that hard-earned money so that you can do more mission, and most importantly, more mission that you want to do, not the mission that your traditional funders limit you to.

Imagine having funds that you can both depend on and that you can spend without approval from anyone other than your own board of directors. Imagine having a great idea or noting a terrible problem in your community and being able to attack it head on, this year, this *month,* without having to go to your state capitol or to Washington, D.C., for a lengthy review and then denial. Sound great? You bet. This is the reality for many not-for-profits today, the ones that have worked toward financial empowerment, and away from the traditional dependency (and thus subservience) model discussed at length in Chapter 2. Successful not-for-profits, those that will flourish in the twenty-first century rather than wither, will be those who are financially empowered.

Here's the hard truth, if you want to be around doing good service in 10 years: You had better work toward financially empowering your organization, starting today.

Here's the good news: You don't have to be big to do this; small not-for-profits can be just as empowered as large ones, and often remain more flexible, a key ability of a social entrepreneur. Also, you don't have to have been around since 1932—many start-ups are positioning themselves for financial empowerment from day one.

Here's the bad news: If you are like the vast majority of not-for-profits, you are anything but empowered; you are regularly teetering on the brink of financial disaster, you have little or no operating reserves, your cash flow is too often a trickle in and a river out. For you (and this includes most not-for-profit managers) the road to financial empowerment will not be short or smooth. But, you *can* do it; in fact, you must if you are to do your job at all.

In this chapter, we will cover the issues that will allow you to start your plan toward becoming a financially empowered organization. For those who are already working in an organization that is financially stable, these discussions hopefully will reinforce your good habits, and perhaps provide an insight or two to help you improve further. In the following pages, you'll learn about the eight characteristics that exist in financially empowered organizations. You'll learn which of the many numbers you can review mean something important, how to communicate about finances inside your organization, and how to estimate the capital needs that you will have from expansion in the next decade.

Then we'll concentrate on how to keep what you've earned, how to find and work with a lender, and how to use your empowerment to benefit your mission, your clientele, and your community. By the time you finish this chapter, you will know what you need to do to become and remain financially empowered.

A. WHAT MAKES A FINANCIALLY EMPOWERED NOT-FOR-PROFIT

I define a financially empowered not-for-profit organization by the following eight characteristics, which I break out further into three subgroups: *Measurable* (having quantified outcomes), *Management* (requiring some change in policy or attitude), and *Mission* (things that directly impact or enhance your ability to do mission. Let's look at the eight in a little bit of detail.

Measurable

1. *The organization has more revenue than expenses in at least 7 out of 10 years.* Nowhere in any state or federal law or regulation does it say that just because you are a not-for-profit, you must lose money. Remember, you are formed for purposes that are primarily charitable, and thus "not for-profit." No one in Congress ever said you had to lose money or just break even to qualify for your 501(c)(3). In fact, the Internal Revenue Service (IRS) Code says "that the profits of the [501(c)] organization shall not inure to the benefit of . . ." proving that profits are legal in the IRS's eyes.

On a practical level, we all know that an organization that loses money each year will eventually fold—it's just a question of how long it will take. I contend, however, that each of you should evaluate having a goal of making money nearly every year to allow you to continue to provide high-quality services in the years to come. Why? For many of the reasons we discussed in Chapter 2: little real new government funding, coupled with higher demand for services at the same time that there is more competition for everything. You need a profit-yes a profit-to give you some maneuvering room.

2. *The organization has a cash operating reserve of at least 90 days.* So many not-for-profits go from financial crisis to crisis, and I see organization after organization struggling to make rent and payroll every month. Why? The most common answer is that "we just never seem to be able to get ahead." Trust me, "getting ahead" never just happens. It is planned. It is the result of careful discipline. A comfort reserve is not only stress reducing on senior management, it is also a turnover reducer, a morale booster for both staff and board. As you become financially empowered, you should strive to have funds in an accessible interest-bearing account equal to at least 90 days'

operations. Some funders do not allow you to keep more, but we'll get to how to circumvent that a bit later.

3. *The organization gets at least 5% of its annual operating income from its endowment.* Endowment? Yes, endowment. They are not just for the big organizations, the ones that have been around for decades. I have a client organization that is only five years old, grosses only $250,000 a year, but annually gets between $10,000 and $13,000 from its $125,000 restricted fund. Endowments for not-for-profits are the best way you can get and maintain a source of income that is steady and inviolate. You cannot, like a for-profit, sell stock or even usually issue debt (although that is changing). You can, however, use your 501(c)(3) designation to secure long-term funds in a restricted account or subsidiary corporation (more about this later).

4. *The organization has sources of revenue from nontraditional, nongovernmental funds: It has business income.* More and more not-for-profits are developing a business that supports its mission without drawing its revenues from traditional sources. This means risk. We will discuss business development at length in the next chapter, but suffice it to say that organizations who meet this test have done one of the things we need to do: expanded their universe of income streams. Don't assume for a moment that these entrepreneurial organizations are swimming in cash and now independent of their traditional funders; they aren't and never will be. But they do have a source of funds that is no longer dependent on bureaucratic or political whims, and that is a strength in and of itself.

Management

5. *The organization shares its financial information widely and practices bottom-up budgeting.* John Chambers, of Cisco Systems (the people who build the stuff that run the Internet) says this about his huge organization: "No one of us is as smart as all of us." This wisdom requires him to share information about the company with all of his staff. For you, the empowerment benefit comes from training all your staff how to read financials, and then how to read your financials, and then to see them regularly. You need to get staff more involved in budgeting and spending those budgets. This is, by far, the most threatening criterion of empowerment for most

organizations, and we'll spend considerable time later in the chapter on these techniques.

6. *The organization is appropriately leveraged.* Leverage, which is defined as borrowing against an asset, allows many not-for-profits to do more mission sooner. It is not for every organization, however, and certainly not for every situation. The ironclad rule is: **Never borrow unless you are making money, or plan to shortly.** Thus, borrowing is a way to do more mission, not a way to bail out past poor management decisions. And, as odd as it may seem, your organization can have *too little* debt! We will discuss more on borrowing later in this chapter.

Mission

7. *The organization supports its mission directly by establishing and using a rapid response mission reserve.* More reserves, you ask? Where does all this extra money come from? First, it is not extra. You need all your money, but putting aside a mission reserve allows you the ability to respond to local needs as they occur, not when someone far away with control of the dollars finally recognizes the problem. This is the ultimate result of financial empowerment.

☞ **HANDS ON:** Empower staff to do what you need done here. The absolute best way to use this is to decide on your amount of reserves (you can start today with $500 or $1,000), and then solicit ideas from staff to spend that amount (or some part of it) on *direct service*. Once all the ideas are in, convene a group of line staff members and let them decide which idea(s) should be funded. The key here is to let your line staff make the decision, not you. You get much more motivation and ownership if you let them spend the money.

8. *The organization is financially flexible enough to accommodate changes in the service delivery patterns.* Far too many not-for-profits have all of their limited assets in their buildings, and none in cash. Thus, when an opportunity arises, they cannot take advantage of it. And their mission capability suffers. Financial flexibility may mean having access to cash quickly through a line of credit, or it may mean looking at more leasing and less owning. Or, it may mean a larger than 90 day cash reserve. Whatever it takes, if you are going

to be a social entrepreneur, you have to let your finances empower you to do so.

As we move through the rest of the chapter, we'll examine some techniques to become empowered, some of which are basic good financial management, and some of which are a bit more entrepreneurial.

Something should be emphasized here and now. Becoming empowered is not easy, and it is not the result of a single action in a single year. It is a long-term commitment that combines a commitment to financial well-being by all members of the board and staff, a setting of reasonable goals in each year, savings, reexamining the budgeting process, fund raising, and usually some corporate restructuring. It is a multiyear (and in some cases decade-long) task. But it can happen in almost any organization with the will to make it happen. So let's get started.

B. NUMBERS THAT MEAN SOMETHING (AND THOSE THAT DON'T)

While it is important to have more and more diverse income, and to spend less through bottoms-up budgeting, it is also a staff responsibility to manage what you have well. This means knowing where your money comes from, where it goes, what causes income and expenses to go up or down, and in general to understand the finances of the organization. Many managers think they know their organization when they really don't. For example, I know of 10 large organizations in which the executive wants to know the cash flow, cash in over cash out for the day, but never asks to see a cash projection. So what if cash flow is positive or negative today? For a senior manager, it's the *trend,* the projection into the future, the analysis of a long period of the past that is important, not so much the present. These execs think that they are in control because they know how much money is in their organization's wallet. They aren't.

On the other hand, Robert Crandall, the former CEO of American Airlines, ran a multibillion dollar corporation with hundreds of thousands of employees, billions in assets, and operations in 40 countries. Was it possible for him to know what was going on everywhere? Of course not. But Crandall did need to know what was important, the numbers that did mean something, and every day, seven days a week for the nearly 15 years he was CEO, he got a sheet with 10 numbers on it: the 10 key numbers that helped him run the airline. What were they? He never told, but in an interview with him, he noted that the 10 numbers changed over the years as the priorities of the airline changed. Why just 10 numbers and not 12 or 20? Crandall noted that that is all anyone can handle and use, and that he set the number as a discipline for himself. If there was something off from the goal or standard in a particular number, he investigated, pursued, prodded and demanded answers. If not, he left it alone.

A number of points should be noted here. First, Crandall, who was a very successful leader, realized that his job was too complex to spend all his time with a calculator, but that didn't mean he should *ignore the numbers.* Ignoring the numbers is a key mistake that managers who were not initially trained in business (which includes nearly every reader of this book) make: "I'll leave those to others who really like to deal with numbers." This is a big mistake, and one that can be fatal. Remember, while the subject of the chapter is financial empowerment, the point of the exercise is *mission.* If you, as a mission-based manager, do not take the time to learn how to most effectively use your financial resources, you are short-changing your organization and your clientele. Second, Crandall realized that he would lose the big picture if he drowned in detail (pardon the mixed metaphor). Therefore, he limited his daily (and I assume weekly and monthly) numbers to a critical few.

Crandall made his own job easier by setting benchmarks and goals. If the number he got was fine in relation to the benchmark, he moved on; if not, he asked questions. This is called putting your numbers in context. This is a critical tool of the successful manager, and will make your job a lot easier. Instead of just getting a report with a bunch of numbers, whether it be a budget, an expense report, a report on occupancy, or new donors, always put it in the context of the past and the goal. So what if you had $450,453.67 in income last year? Was the budget (the context) that you should have had $440,000 in income or $500,000? If your occupancy is 78%, is that good or bad? It depends on the context, which could both be a goal, and also the trend from the past three months. Here's the rule: Numbers by themselves can be interesting. Numbers in context are *useful.*

So, what numbers do you need to know? The choice will, obviously, depend on your organization. Most, if not all, readers will be in organizations that cannot produce daily numbers of any great accuracy. But that does not mean that they cannot produce numbers at all, or on a more regular basis than just monthly. Again, what you need to know depends on your organization, but let me at least propose some general areas that you need to have information on. You will see that most of these numbers are either trends or numbers weighed against a goal or an industry norm. This is important to give you perspective. Also, later in the chapter, we will discuss internal reporting, and there will be some actual sample forms for you to consider.

1. CASH

Cash is like blood or water to an organization—you die without it. You need to have reasonably accurate cash flow projections for six months in advance, and you need to see these every two weeks (have them updated after each payroll). This can be done most efficiently on a computer spreadsheet such as Lotus 1-2-3 or Microsoft Excel, and it is essential to your organizational well-being that you know when you will be cash rich and when cash poor. Daily cash in and out is fine, but it is the trends and future projections that you need to focus on most.

2. INCOME

If you have income-sensitive numbers that you can see, read them regularly. For example, if you are a museum and your income is heavily dependent on the number of people through the turnstiles each day or week, take a look at that number and compare it to a month ago, a year ago, and any goals that you may have. If you are a school and get reimbursed on a student day, what was your attendance last week? If you are a hospital and in the new managed care environment, you probably want to know your inpatient occupancy, and hope, unlike five years ago, that your beds are *empty*, not full. If you are a church, what was your count of parishioners this week, and what was in the collection plate?

3. PAYABLES

Payables is the amount that you owe people in the short term. Particularly if you don't write the checks yourself, you need to know the trend in this area. What is the amount of payables that you have (usually recorded monthly), versus a month ago or compared to average monthly expenditures. For example, if your average expenditures per month are $100,000 and your payables are $150,000, you are not paying your bills in 30 days. Worse, if that payables number is climbing while your expenditures are staying the same, you are falling further and further behind, something you *really* want to avoid. Keep on top of your payables, and ask questions about making sure you are keeping current and not incurring late fees. You should also see, with your monthly reports, a listing of any and all accounts that are late: usually 30 days past due. Find out why these are late and do your best to get them paid. If they are going to be very late, call the person you owe and explain why.

4. RECEIVABLES

This is the other side of the coin. Particularly in organizations in which primary customers (government, foundations, insurance) often play such a huge part in your income stream, you need to stay on top of what you are owed. It is very easy for organizations to pay you late if you let them. You need to be on top of the system, know how it works, and be a pleasant bug in their ear to get paid sooner rather than later. You need to know how "old" your receivables are, and have a policy of when you personally get involved to get a late check cut. Again, if your income is $100,000 per month and your receivables are $140,000 month after month, or are growing in relation to income, you are getting paid late and it's getting later. Watch this number as a trend and take action as needed.

5. EXPENSES

Usually, expenses are recorded and fully accounted for once a month in a monthly statement. I assume that you see the statement the minute it comes out, but do not be content with just the overall statement. You should see the income and expense statement compared to your budget for the month, and your year-to-date statement compared with the budget for the year to date. Only by having these comparisons can you ask reasonable questions about expenditures, make staff justify any changes in the budget, and generally stay on top of this key area. Again, this is a once-a-month set of numbers, but many managers just look at the bottom line and don't examine the statement against their previous goal as embodied in the budget.

It should also be noted that your highest expense, unless you are very unusual, is your payroll. You want to keep a handle on how much your people are costing, because cutting people is the most painful thing you will ever have to do as a manager.

6. BALANCE SHEET AND RATIOS

Balance sheets are snapshots of your organization at the end of each month (assuming that you generate them monthly). They show your assets (what you own or what you are owed), your liabilities (what you owe or are obligated to over the short and long term), and your fund balance (assets minus liabilities). For many nonfinancial managers, balance sheets are often confusing. However, balance sheets can be used to generate important numbers that help you manage: financial ratios. Like so many other tools, ratios are often misused, and too often misunderstood.

A financial ratio is a comparison of two factors in your balance sheet (or in your balance sheet and your income and expense statement) that allow you to get a common denominator viewpoint on your organization's financial position.

There are literally hundreds of such ratios, but you do not need to deal with more than a few key ones. Like everything else, which ratios you need will depend on your organization: Talk to your CPA or financial expert on your board about which ones are most important to you and how to use them. Examples include:

- *Profit margin.* Net revenue divided by total income. Is the percentage of profit high enough?

- *Current ratio.* Current assets divided by current liabilities: This is a measure of how much liquidity you have—can you pay off your current obligations with cash and current receivables? The number should always be higher than 1.0 and probably your goal should be between 1.5 and 3.0 (not including your endowment). Much higher means that you are probably sitting on too much cash.

- *Debt-to-fund balance.* The total debt divided by your fund balance. This number measures the ability of your organization to take on more debt if you need to and monitors your debt against your net worth. You don't want this too high or you will get overleveraged and interest costs will begin to eat you up.

As I noted, there are lots more of these than bear discussion here, since the specific ones that will help you may be very obscure. See your CPA and your banker. Talk with them about which ratios will give you the best help in monitoring your finances.

7. NONFINANCIAL INDICATORS

Not all of the numbers you need to see have to do with money. There are other items that bear regular scrutiny that are indicative of whether or not you are succeeding with your mission, your people and your stewardship. For example, the number of units of service provided per FTE staff person, the number of people on waiting lists for service, the average turnover of staff per quarter or per year, the number of people seeking service for the first time, or the number of people who return repeatedly all could be important to you. Now that you understand that even a nonfinancial manager needs to pay attention to the numbers, don't limit those numbers to the ones with dollar signs in front of them.

8. PROFIT AND LOSS

You need to know what you are earning and losing, and this is so important an area that I've broken it out separately.

C. KNOWING WHAT YOU EARN (AND LOSE)

As you have read repeatedly in this book, it's okay for a not-for-profit to make money. Not just that, it is essential that you make money 7 out of 10 years to maintain and improve your ability to help your community. To do that, you have to know what programs and what parts of your organization make money and what parts lose money and, in both cases, how much money is involved. It is fine to have some programs that are subsidized by others: There are things that not-for-profits do that will never be fully reimbursed. But, you *have* to balance those programs with profitable ones or you will be out of business.

The problem for most not-for-profits, especially those who get government reimbursement, is that they are trained to fudge the numbers, and this training leads them to take shortcuts in actual accounting so that they don't know their real costs of operation for anything.

❏ **FOR EXAMPLE:** A not-for-profit mental health agency in the South received federal funds for one of its programs. For the past five years, this particular program has allowed for a 15% overhead charge (for all administrative support) in addition to rent, utilities, and actual documentable costs. Whether the actual time spent on the project by the administration was 9% or 19%, the "charge" was 15%, the allowable maximum. If it was higher, the administrator would just say, "That's the most we can get reimbursed." If the actual administrative cost was lower, the administrator would rationalize, "We can get the reimbursement, and we need it to cover underpayments elsewhere." In truth, probably no one in the agency ever checked their real costs of administration by watching them for a three- or six-month period. Thus, they never really knew the real costs. As time went by, they began an internal accounting method that charged each program for administrative time. The percentage: 15% of the amount that they had all gotten used to as their overhead cost. But was it really 15%? Almost certainly not, and definitely not on every program.

You need to know your real costs of doing business. If you are like most organizations, you probably are pretty good at recording income by program and in doing estimating and accounting of direct costs for an individual program: the costs of the people, supplies, transportation, and equipment used each day, week, or month. But it is in overhead, administration, rent, depreciation, and utilities that many organizations grossly under- or overestimate their expenses.

☞ **HANDS ON:** Time sheets are a start in teaching your staff where their time is *really* spent. I admit that they are no fun, particularly when staff have never used them before. To make a point with administrative staff about how important accurate accounting is, try this. Ask your administrative team to estimate how many hours in the coming week they will spend on different tasks. You should ask them to break their roles out by program where possible, and then by administrative task: budgeting, marketing, evaluation, fund raising, and so on. Develop categories that make sense for your organization and then let staff fill in their hour estimates in advance.

Now collect their estimates, and have them do it for real, in 15-minute intervals for that week. Have them carry their time sheet with them all day and stop intermittently (at least at lunch and at the end of the day.) If your staff are like most of us, they will find serious differences between their estimates and reality. Use this to underscore the fact that a standard organization-wide percentage is not the best way to account for overhead and administrative costs.

Once you know your real administrative costs, you can really begin to examine which programs are profitable and which are not. Why? Are you going to simply cut out the "losers" and keep the "winners"? Of course not. There will always be programs that you need to provide that will lose money, and it is naive to think otherwise. But knowing which programs are making money and which are losing (and how much each year) is part of both the management and policy-setting mix. If, for example, a program that is a high priority in your needs assessment or strategic plan is losing money, you will probably be more willing to subsidize a large amount than with a program that has outlived its mission-based usefulness. Alternatively, decisions about where to put your marketing dollars will be a mix on where the most net income can be generated (to subsidize other programs) and how much mission will be accomplished. Thus, the profitability of a program is not, and never should be, the only issue. But it *is* an issue, and one that your management team needs to consider.

D. SPENDING LESS THROUGH BOTTOMS-UP BUDGETING

I will start with the assumption that you have an organizational budget. If you don't, STOP READING AND GO DEVELOP ONE. Now that you are back, let's discuss why bottoms-up budgeting saves money, because, if it is appropriately implemented, it *always* does, even in the best-run organizations.

The term bottoms-up budgeting comes from the idea that people at the bottom of the organizational chart (those nearest the provision of service) make the best decisions about resource needs and use. In my ideal organization, these people would be nearest the top of the chart, just below the recipients of service. But, no matter, the people that need to develop and then monitor your budget are the people who are as close to the provision of service as possible. These people know more than you ever can about what their real needs are, how to spend money most effectively, and how to monitor outcomes best. Why? Because it affects their lives on an hour-to-hour basis.

1. THE COMPONENTS OF BOTTOMS-UP BUDGETING

You cannot just make a major change in your budgeting process by going to your line managers and staff and saying, "Here, write the budget," and expect it to work. You have to do the whole process, and that includes some things you may not care much for. Bottoms-up budgeting has some important components:

• *Training and orientation.* Many of the staff that will be included in the budgeting process will have never seen the budget, much less understand how it is generated. You need to walk them through the budget and help them to understand where your income comes from and its limitations, as well as the history of your expense numbers and how they have been developed in the past.

• *Delegating both budget responsibility and authority.* In using this process of budgeting, the entire point is to pass the responsibility and authority for the budget development and implementation to other than senior staff. But note that I said responsibility *and* authority. If you just ask your staff to help you develop the budget but then micromanage its implementation, you are no better off (and arguably worse) than you are now. What you want is for staff to have ownership and input into the budget development process. Once the budget is reviewed by senior staff and adopted by the board, the line items in the budget should, within programs, be authorized and approved by the line managers within those programs. Thus, if your board has authorized a $5,000 line item for supplies for one of your programs, you as an executive should have no real oversight into what supplies are bought, or when or from whom, as long as the program meets any bidding requirements and stays within its $5,000 per year. For some readers, this will require changes in procedure for check writing approval, and in rethinking their control systems. That is probably overdue for many organizations, and this is a good time to look at these areas. Remember, it's key to give authority with responsibility.

• *Risk taking and risk reward.* This system will not work without the added component of risk and reward. Staff who are monitoring budgets must be at risk for their implementation. Thus, their evaluation should, in part, incorporate their budget management skills. More importantly, if staff come in under budget on the expense side or over budget on the income side (for those programs that can impact on their income statements), they should be rewarded. My recommendation is that, when a program beats its budget, it should get to keep half of the "net." In other words, if you are a private school and your preschool staff cut their expenses by $40,000 under budget, they get to keep $20,000 (at no penalty on next year's budget) to do with as they see fit: buy extra equipment, fund training, allocate funds for a part-time aide, and so on. This reward system is absolutely essential—otherwise, the staff don't have the incentive to look for bargains or cut their costs. Any less than half of the savings and your incentive levels really start to drop. Don't be greedy as an administrator. Remember, you just got some "free" savings. Share the wealth and there will be more. Get greedy now and the source of those savings will dry up.

• *Regular feedback and reporting.* The only way that your staff can monitor how they are doing is by regular reporting back to them from your accounting people. The best format is to have a monthly statement that shows actual income and expenses versus budgeted for the current month and year to date. These should be done for each program, and the administrator in charge of overseeing that program should go over the statement with the line staff and manager but only question lines in which there are large discrepancies— perhaps 10% in a monthly line and 5% in a year-to-date line. This communications flow will help everyone be more comfortable with the delegation of responsibilities and ensure that no program area staff have concerns or questions that are not answered.

If you do this kind of budgeting, you will see results, 10 to 15% savings in nonpersonnel lines, and even personnel cuts in some cases. I would not, however, suggest that you implement this wholesale if you have had a traditional top-down approach. Try this next year in the one or two programs with the highest likelihood of success, orient all staff to the new approach, and at the end of the year publicize the results and expand the program.

Don't expect all staff to welcome this idea. Again, here, we have change on the march. Perhaps your biggest surprise will be that those staff who always gripe about not having enough say will resist having control over their budget.

❑ **FOR EXAMPLE:** A few years ago, a good friend of mine took the job of headmaster at a large residential school on the East Coast. His predecessor had been at the school for 20 years and had been the penultimate autocrat. For the first full year my friend was there, he listened to staff griping about management making ridiculous decisions, and how the allocation of resources was just plain stupid. In his second year at the school (the first in which he was on hand for budget planning) my friend called all the program heads into his office and told them that they were going to make the allocations of resources based on the budget mark (amount) that had been received from their state funders. He told them that the first year they would only have to allocate the purchases of equipment, books, and classroom supplies. This meant that the managers, who had previously been given these allocations and could just sit back and gripe about not getting enough, now had to come to a consensus on how to divvy up the school's entire allocation for each line item.

They hated the job and found it was much tougher than they had ever imagined. Four days later, they came back to the headmaster and asked that he do the job. He refused, saying that it was crucial for them to have the ownership and understanding of the budget dilemma and the allocation of resources.

Resistance to change aside, this process works. If you can come in under budget for the next three years, and have enough discipline to then set the funds aside, you are well on your way to a culture of financial empowerment.

E. REPORTING INSIDE THE ORGANIZATION

One of the key areas where empowered organizations excel is in the area of internal reporting. In external financial reporting, what you do is dictated by your funders, by your auditor, and in some cases by tradition. But internally, you can be much more flexible and creative.

Internal reporting means getting the right numbers to the staff and board. All organizations are different, and what you report and who you report it to will vary with your management style, your organizational policies, your organizational history, your size, and whether or not you have a collective bargaining unit (a union), but no matter what your shape and size, there is one key tenet of internal financial reporting:

**GIVE PEOPLE THE INFORMATION THEY NEED IN
THE WAY THAT THEY WANT TO SEE IT
AS OFTEN AS THEY NEED IT.**

Why should you be flexible in your reporting? Why not just give everyone the monthly profit and loss statements and perhaps a cash flow projection. Let's look at the different groups you need to report to. As you review this list, ask yourself: Do all these people need the same information on the same schedule?

- **BOARD—All**
- **BOARD—Finance committee**
- **BOARD—Treasurer and chairperson**
- **STAFF—CEO**
- **STAFF—Senior management**
- **STAFF—Mid-management**
- **STAFF—Service providers**

Of course, they need different numbers in different forms at different times. And with today's accounting and reporting software, giving each of these groups what they need in the way they want as often as they need it is neither time consuming nor expensive.

In the next few pages we will review some sample ideas of the kinds of information these different groups might want in your organization, as well as look at some sample formats that transmit this information the most efficiently. Understand that these lists are starting points for you, not all inclusive—because they can't be. You will need to find the mix of reports and the types of formats that work best for your organization, and to do that you need to return to our high-tech marketing technique: Ask!

Ask the people in these groups what information they need, how often they need it, and why they need it. Ask whether they want their reports in numerical form, on a spreadsheet, in graphs, or interpreted in writing. Or do they want some combination of these? Once you have established what people want and how much they need, remember to ask them regularly if the information is working. If it is, great. If it is not, amend it. Remember, this kind of information targeting is cheap in both time and money, particularly if it gets the information that people need in their hands promptly. If you gave each of 20 people a half hour a month by saving them from wading through unnecessary data, that's 120 person hours per year or *three weeks* of staff time saved. This is not an unusual savings obtained by targeting your information.

There is, however, information that is *off limits*, information that should not be generally shared. Briefly, this information includes salaries, perks, retirement, and medical information as well as information on individual contracts and contractors. Additionally, you should never send out inaccurate, indecipherable, or misleading numbers, reports, charts, or graphs. For excellent examples of just such inaccurate or misleading information, look at charts and graphs included in many advertisements and much of the press.

With all of that as background, let's examine when you do send information and who gets what. Let's start with some premises:

1. *The more your people really understand how your organization's finances run, the better.* If your organization is like most, few if any of your staff outside of your central management team understand how your finances work. Most of your staff assume that the money comes from the state (feds, city, foundation), that you have lots of it, and you are just stingy in giving it out. They probably have no real understanding of how long it takes you to get paid, the reporting requirements that you have to go through, or the true nature of your balance sheet. In truth, most of them have probably never seen a balance sheet and wouldn't know how to read one if they saw it— through no fault of their own.

If you are going to include staff in budgeting, give them responsibility for their areas of budgeting, value them as individuals: Let them see the numbers that help them do their job. I work with dozens of organizations in which no staff but the executive director and comptroller/financial manager ever see the budget or the monthly profit-and-loss statements or know how much over or under their budget line they are. They don't know where they are in relation to their budget—how much they have left to spend in any line item.

But, consistently in these organizations, the exec will tell me that his staff are involved in the budget process and have spending authority. How can they when they haven't a clue about where the money came from, is, or will be going?

2. *The more people participate in the budget development process and are held accountable for its implementation, the better.* We've already discussed how you save money by including staff in the budgeting process. Letting line staff develop and be responsible for the budget in their area saves money. But for staff members at any level to be involved meaningfully in the budget development and budget implementation process, they have to have the information they need at the time they need it in a format that they can understand and use.

3. *A little knowledge—especially in the financial area—is a very dangerous thing.* Imagine (and this may not be too much of a stretch for those readers who have had this very thing happen in their organization) a staff member who makes $25,000 per year being given a copy of your organization's balance sheet and reading things like "Total Assets $1,450,000" or "Cash and Securities $767,560." To a person unfamiliar with financial terminology, that could sound as if you have bags of money hidden in your office somewhere. Without the context (that perhaps 90% of your total assets are fixed [buildings] or that most of the cash and securities are in restricted funds), this person will be justifiably upset with the fact that the staff got only a 2% raise last year or that needed programs have been cut.

The moral? If you are going to hand out financial information, *train* your people in how to use it and what it means. If possible, have an outsider (who will be seen as neutral) come in and go over what a balance sheet is and explain an asset, a liability, a fund balance, a restricted account, a fixed versus liquid asset, and how your cash flow really works. Have the trainer explain how your income streams are set up, how staff can influence them, how growth may actually mean less cash in the organization's hands instead of more, and how an organization should configure itself for financial strength. This training is not only important for the development of the staff involved, but it is a key preventative against a general uprising over resources.

Now let's look at who needs what.

1. STAFF

a. CEO.

The CEO of your organization will need a variety of information. Again, what the CEO wants is a decision he or she will have to make, but at the least, the CEO should see the following:

- *Cash flow projection.* The cash flow projection should be for the coming six months shown by payroll or by the 1st and 15th of each month. It should have a rolling net cash line to show the total cash situation. This is a key piece of information that too few people have.

- *Monthly/annual statements versus budget—overall and by department area.* This statement should show the actual income and expense in the previous month and for the fiscal year to date versus the budget for the same period. Problem discrepancies should be investigated.

- *Working capital projections.* How much is the expansion of the organization going to cost? How much should we set aside for a new program? These numbers tell that. We will go over how to project these key pieces of information later in the chapter.

- *Receivables (aging).* How long has it been since your major funder paid you? How much are you owed now versus a month ago and a year ago? This item is important for the CEO to know as he or she interacts with your funders.

- *Occupancy/utilization.* If you have a "capacity" number or a census, show it versus a month or a year ago. For example, if you have residential beds, what is the percentage of occupancy in each program. If you have a capacity of ticket sales, what percentage were sold? Or, what is your count of patrons last week, or the number of students or parishioners? Trends here are key.

- *Cost of capital.* How much is the cost of the capital you have? For most, this will be a calculation of the overall cost of any debt reduced by your cash invested and adjusted for your working capital "losses." Talk to your CPA about how to calculate this, but watch the number carefully from quarter to quarter. You don't want it to rise too steeply.

How often and in what format should you provide this information? Look at the samples of a CEO Data Sheet (Exhibit 10-1), a Statement of Income and Expenses (Exhibit 10-2), and a Cash Flow Projection (Exhibit 10-3). Note the simplicity of the executive director's sheet, the combination of numbers and charts. Some people like their information this way. If so, give it to them!

b. Senior managers.

What senior managers want and need depends on the areas that they supervise. They will need at least:

- Organizational cash flow
- Overall agency statements of income and expense versus budget
- Similar statements for each department they supervise
- Budgeting information
- Occupancy/utilization figures for the areas they supervise

c. Service staff.

Service provision staff need information too. If you agree with my philosophy of information being a good thing and of staff becoming involved in the budgeting process, then they need at least:

- Organizational cash flow
- Statements of income and expense versus budget for their area of work

2. BOARD OF DIRECTORS

Does the board of directors need the same information as the staff? No, most of the board should focus on policy and have no need to see the nitty gritty. They are, however, fiduciaries, and responsible for supervising the appropriate utilization of your financial resources. The board needs:

- Information that they can use efficiently
- Information that makes sense
- Information without jargon
- Information that is not out of date

Exhibit 10-1   CEO Data Sheet

	Current Month	Last Month	Last Year	Budget or Goal
Revenue	144,533	142,456	132,677	144,000
Occupancy (unit 1)	87.0%	88.0%	90.0%	95.0%
Number of hours billable (outpatient)	2,435	2,490	2,680	2,750
Staff turnover (12 months)	24.0%	26.0%	45.0%	12.0%
Receivables (in days)	43.5	45.0	55.0	40.0
Payables (in days)	32.1	32.0	34.1	30.0
Current ratio	0.50	0.56	0.76	0.45
Cash reserve (in days)	47.6	45.6	32.1	90.0

Cash Flow Summary

	Month 1	Month 2	Month 3	Month 4	Month 5	Month 6
Total receipts	144,000	144,150	149,400	134,080	120,575	265,625
Total disbursements	133,271	132,831	134,861	180,541	133,371	216,611
Net cash flow	10,729	11,319	14,539	(46,461)	(12,796)	49,014
Ending cash balance	34,289	45,608	60,147	13,686	890	49,904

Exhibit 10-2 Statement of Income and Expenses

Line Item	Monthly Actual	Monthly Budget	Monthly Variance	% of Budget	YTD Actual	YTD Budget	YTD Variance	% of Budget
Income								
State program	55,400	53,000	2,400	4.5%	310,045	321,000	(10,955)	-3.4%
Medicaid	65,443	61,000	4,443	7.3%	422,449	415,000	7,449	1.8%
United Way	5,000	10,000	(5,000)	-50.0%	30,000	60,000	(30,000)	-50.0%
Fees	18,440	19,500	(1,060)	-5.4%	114,598	124,600	(10,002)	-8.0%
Donations	250	500	(250)	-50.0%	10,500	3,000	7,500	250.0%
Total Income	144,533	144,000	533	0.4%	887,592	(887,592)	(36,008)	4.1%
Expenses								
Salaries	105,800	107,900	(2,100)	-1.9%	623,980	602,300	21,680	3.6%
Fringes	9,522	9,711	(189)	-1.9%	56,158	54,207	1,951	3.6%
Occupancy	2,500	2,500	0	0.0%	15,000	15,000	0	0.0%
Insurance	8,000	8,000	0	0.0%	8,000	8,000	0	0.0%
Utilities	1,244	1,200	44	3.7%	7,698	7,400	298	4.0%
Telephone	857	900	(33)	-3.7%	4,680	5,400	(720)	-13.3%
Depreciation	6,588	6,588	0	0.0%	39,528	39,528	0	0.0%
Supplies	2,240	2,500	(260)	-10.4%	12,679	15,000	(2,321)	-15.5%
Travel	1,243	1,500	(257)	-17.1%	11,340	9,000	2,340	26.0%
Total Expense	138,004	140,799	(2,795)	-2.0%	779,063	755,835	23,228	3.1%
Net:	6,529	3,201	3,328		108,529	(1,643,427)	(59,236)	

Exhibit 10-3 Cash Flow Projection

	Month 1	Month 2	Month 3	Month 4	Month 5	Month 6
Receipts						
State program	53,000	53,000	53,000	53,000	53,000	53,000
Medicaid	61,000	61,000	61,000	0	0	183,000
United Way	10,000	10,000	10,000	10,000	10,000	10,000
Fees	19,500	19,500	24,500	18,500	17,450	19,500
Debt received	0	0	0	40,000	40,000	0
Donations	500	650	900	12,580	125	125
Total Receipts:	**144,000**	**144,150**	**149,400**	**134,080**	**120,575**	**265,625**
Disbursements						
Salaries	107,900	107,900	107,900	107,900	107,900	107,900
Fringes	9,711	9,711	9,711	9,711	9,711	9,711
Occupancy	2,500	2,500	2,500	2,500	2,500	2,500
Insurance	0	0	0	48,000	0	0
Utilities	1,200	800	850	950	1,450	1,650
Telephone	900	900	900	900	900	900
Debt service paid	7,960	7,960	7,960	7,960	7,960	88,000
Supplies	2,500	2,500	2,500	2,500	2,500	2,500
Travel	600	560	2,540	120	450	3,450
Total Disbursements	**133,271**	**132,831**	**134,861**	**180,541**	**133,371**	**216,611**
Net Cash Flow	**10,729**	**11,319**	**14,539**	**(46,461)**	**(12,796)**	**49,014**
Ending Cash Balance	34,289	45,608	60,147	13,686	890	49,904
Starting Cash	23,560					

Let's look at the differing needs of different parts of the board, from the people that need to most and the most detailed information to those that need just the overviews.

a. Board (Treasurer and chairperson).

These two people need to *understand* how the money flows in your organization—how it is earned and how it is spent. They need to be able to articulately advocate for your financial needs in front of a funder, as well as to give the other board members some peace of mind that someone understands your arcane finances. Thus, they need to see at least:

- Organizational cash flows
- Statements of income and expense versus budget
- Critical information about new or crisis programs
- To be involved early in the budget development process
- Early information on major changes in funding streams (a rate change, a foundation award)

b. Board (Finance committee).

The finance committee is the key oversight group of the board, and should have at least:

- Organizational cash flows
- Occupancy/utilization figures
- Statements of income and expense versus budget each month
- Budget projections
- Working capital projections
- Close involvement in budgeting prior to the budget's going to the board

c. Board (General).

These people need to be the least involved in the financial oversight, if there is a strong finance committee, and if the treasurer really understands how the numbers run. They need:

- Summary information on cash and income and expenses
- Audited statements from your CPA
- Management letter from your CPA
- Organizational cash flows

See Exhibit 10-4 for an example of a Board of Directors Summary Report.

Again, the key to all of this is to give people what they want in the format they can best use, and to train, train, train in the information's use and meaning. Good information is critical to financial empowerment in your organization. Don't force fit your people's needs to one format. Scrimping of the time and software to make flexible reports will only cost you big time in both the near and long term.

Finally, remember to ask at least annually whether the information is still working. People's needs and wants change, as does the key information the organization produces. For example, a particular program that was running in the black last year may be a loss center this year and need more senior-level attention. Or you may have received some kind of accreditation and need to monitor a new data set. Ask and amend as necessary, but no less than once a year.

F. PLANNING FOR YOUR FUTURE CASH AND CAPITAL NEEDS

One last part of constructing a financially empowered organization: planning for your future cash and capital needs. This is an area in which many organizations (for-profit and not-for-profit) fall flat on their faces, because they forget that growth costs money. You need cash for new programs and cash for growth. Unfortunately, it is not just the cash that you will spend on equipment or on a new building or on people. It is the cash that will be lost in the mail: working capital.

Working capital is the money you need to operate on between the time you manufacture a product or provide a service and the time you get paid. The more business you do, the more working capital you need. The longer it takes people to pay you, the more working capital you need. A simple example is this: If one of your programs is currently reimbursed at cost for $120,000 per year, and if the funder of that program pays you in 60 days, you need two months' working capital ($20,000) just to carry your receivable for that program. Now suppose the program doubles in size—presto—you need $40,000. Or perhaps the funder now decides to pay in 90 days—your working capital needs just went up by 50%. This is why so many rapidly growing organizations are starved for cash—it all gets sucked up into their working capital. Exhibit 10-5 is a working capital needs worksheet.

You will see a format for estimating your working capital needs that I recommend you use every year. The first column shows the current income per year, the second column shows the projected income, and the

Exhibit 10-4 Board of Directors Summary Report

Income and Expense

Line Item	Monthly Actual	Monthly Budget	Monthly Variance	% of Budget	YTD Actual	YTD Budget
Total income	144,533	144,000	533	0.4%	887,592	923,600
Total expense	138,004	140,799	(2,795)	–2.0%	779,063	755,835
Net	6,529	3,201	3,328		108,529	167,765

Cash Flow Summary

	Month 1	Month 2	Month 3	Month 4	Month 5	Month 6
Total receipts	144,000	144,150	149,400	134,080	120,575	265,625
Total disbursements	133,271	132,831	134,861	180,541	133,371	216,611
Net cash flow	10,729	11,319	14,539	(46,461)	(12,796)	49,014
Ending cash balance	34,289	45,608	60,147	13,686	890	49,904

	Current Month	Last Month	Last Year	Budget or Goal
Revenue	144,533	142,456	132,677	144,000
Occupancy (unit 1)	87.0%	88.0%	90.0%	95.0%
Number of hours billable (outpatient)	2,435	2,490	2,680	2,750
Staff turnover (12 months)	24.0%	26.0%	45.0%	12.0%
Receivables (in days)	43.5	45.0	55.0	40.0
Payables (in days)	32.1	32.0	34.1	30.0
Current ratio	0.50	0.56	0.76	0.45

Exhibit 10-5 Working Capital Needs Worksheet

Programs	Start Up Costs	Current Budget	Next Yr Budget	Days Payable Currently	Days Payable Next Year	Cash Need
Residential	0	440,000	480,000	95	100	10,959
Day	0	327,500	410,000	56	56	12,658
Outreach	0	457,000	395,000	55	55	(9,342)
Hot lunch	0	110,000	115,000	45	45	616
Prevention (new)	45,000	0	197,000	0	65	80,082
					Total New Cash Needed:	$94,973

third column shows the days to get paid. If you subtract the projected income from the current income and multiply that times the days to get paid and then divide by 365, you'll get the new cash needed next year for the growth in that program. If, as in this example, you do it for all your programs, you'll get a better idea of your working capital needs for the entire organization. If the number is very large, you may need to start working with your banker to borrow funds to cover the cash shortfall.

The second part of the format has to do with the new program working capital needs. Here you have the development costs (the "up-front" costs) and the working capital costs, which are the income per year times the days to payment divided by 365. Here you see the agency needs 80,082 just to open the new program that will only bring in 197,000 per year!

Do these calculations. They are part of your better understanding of how your organization works, how the cash really flows, and how to do business in an enlightened and empowered manner.

G. KEEPING WHAT YOU EARN

I wish I had a magic potion to give you to avoid what is still a major problem for many not-for-profits in this country: being punished for being financially responsible. However, many funders, from the government to foundations to the United Way, still have the feeling that if you don't use up what you said you were going to spend on a project or a service, they deserve the money back. Worse, some funders still feel that if you have any money, you don't need theirs.

So, if you do become empowered, and you have reserves for mission, or for simple financial stability, how do you keep it? How can you do what I suggest and make money 7 out of 10 years and not get punished? There are a number of ways, and these work solely or in some combination for most of our clients. However, I must caution you: In some states, the government is extremely aggressive about coming after "excess funds." They have an overdose of what I see as "what is yours is ours" (discussed in Chapter 2). Thus, for some readers, there may be little protection today. You may need to start now to lobby for some commonsense regulation that allows you to set aside your earnings in the future.

Here are some techniques that have worked.

1. *Avoid "use it or lose it": contract rather than grant.* When negotiating with a funder, contract for a specific set of services rather than accepting a cash grant. Negotiate into the contract wording that says that you will provide X services for $Y dollars at Z level of

quality, and that any excess is yours to keep, not theirs to recapture. Please understand that this means that if you don't keep your budget under control and you spend more than $Y, you eat the losses: You can't go back to the funder to ask for an increased contract unless they change the scope of services that they want.

2. *Put income-producing ventures and/or property into separate corporations.* In Chapter 8, we discussed earned income ventures. If you start having large enough net revenue from these ventures, it may be beneficial to place them in a new not-for-profit subsidiary to harbor their assets. Many not-for-profits have their property (buildings, vehicles, equipment) in just such a second corporation and lease it at fair market rates to the primary corporation since the funders will reimburse rent but not depreciation or interest on debts. Please understand that corporate restructuring is a tool, not a panacea. You will probably have to have a related uncontrolled corporation hold your assets to qualify for reimbursement and thus, technically, will lose control of your assets. Check your funder's regulations on related-party transactions before setting up a second corporation to house assets (other than a foundation).

3. *Have restricted accounts.* Set up accounts that are restricted in use for specific items (e.g., a depreciation account, a capital fund account, etc.). Funders are more likely to attempt to go after general revenue than targeted, restricted funds. Have a board resolution to restrict the funds, and have your accountant show them that way in the audit.

4. *Set up a foundation.* Later in the chapter, we will examine the need for an endowment. The most common method to house this money is in a second 501(c)(3) that people loosely term a foundation. (*Note:* You do *not* want to be a foundation in the technical sense with the IRS. If you file your own paperwork for your new 501(c)(3), do not check the line that says "Private Foundation".) A foundation corporation will allow you to keep the money that you raise "off the books" of your current 501(c)(3) and will be a marketing tool for donors, some of whom will be concerned that their donation will just get eaten up in operating expenses.

5. *Work with your funders.* Try to work with your funders to help them see the cost of growth (in working capital), the cost of future capital expenditures, and the need for financial stability and a quick

reaction fund for your mission. Explain to them that you aren't just hoarding the money; you are managing your resources to the best mission outcome possible.

You can't be financially empowered if you lose everything you have gained. Try these ideas to retain your earnings.

H. DOES YOUR BOARD PROHIBIT DEBT?

As I work with not-for-profit organizations around the country, I regularly see organizations that have board-generated policies prohibiting the organization from taking on any debt. Often, these policies are many years old and may have resulted from abuses by former staff, from former board members' concerns about major funding cuts in the early 1980s, or from a feeling that this policy reduces the board's risk and exposure.

When I ask each organization's board about the policy, the conversation usually goes something like this:

Board: We cannot take on debt because our funding is only approved annually. If our funding were cut, we would be unable to pay a loan back.

Peter: How many of you have lifetime guarantees of employment? (No hands go up.) How many of you live in a house that you paid cash for? (No hands go up.) Okay, so you took on a debt, a risk, even though your major source of income (your salary) may be ended at any time?

Board: But that's different. We are individuals. Our board job entails responsibility for an entire organization, and we must be prudent.

True. But not-for-profit organizations are also business, and business is risk. The real issue here is how much risk your organization is willing to take on behalf of your clientele. Understand that I am not talking about highly leveraging, pyramiding craziness. This is not the "Real Estate with No Money Down" commercial you see on your cable channel.

What is important to understand is that, in some instances, taking on debt to expand a service, build a building, or purchase equipment may be a *good* risk to take on behalf of your clientele. Each organization is different, as is each situation, but I strongly recommend that you consider *all* your options in planning your future; and carrying a prudent amount of debt is one avenue many highly successful businesses (both for-profit and not-for profit) use to grow and serve their customers better.

I. WORKING WITH LENDERS

As a CEO or CFO (chief financial officer), you may think that your most important working relationship is with your board president, with your key governmental or foundation funding source, or with another key staff person. But, sooner or later, your most key business relationship is going to be with your banker. The problem is that, if you are like most not-for-profit staff, you have little or no relationship with a bank, other than having a checking account and perhaps a certificate of deposit (CD) or money market account.

Why is this a problem? There are a number of reasons, the most important of which are:

- At some point, if you become a social entrepreneur, you will need to borrow.
- The lending decision process excludes you.
- Most bankers don't understand not-for-profit finances, and all bankers fear what they don't understand.

Let's look at each of these in more detail.

1. *You will need to borrow.* Sooner or later, you will almost certainly need a loan, either to cover cash flow (when your major governmental funding check is late and you have to make payroll) or to cover the advance costs on a new contract.

Nearly all organizations need some form of debt at some point, and your credit rating (how the local lenders look at you) is influenced in no small part by how well those lenders know you and how promptly you have repaid any past debt. But commercial banking is, oddly enough, a personal business, and your personal relationship with a single person in a single bank will go a long way toward improving your "creditworthiness."

Nothing, of course, can help you like a solid balance sheet and profitable (net revenue over expenses) operations, but you will find that even with good numbers, no one will want to take a risk on your organization until they know you and understand your organization (more on this later).

2. *The borrowing process excludes you.* Second, when you go in for that debt, you will (let us hope) have prepared your numbers, showing the need for the debt, the term (length) of the loan you need, and how you plan to pay it back (where the funds will come from, over and above your normal day-to-day expenses). You will give this information to your banker, and the banker will ask you a number of questions and then say, "Thanks for coming. I'll get you the answer in a week."

What happens now? The banker prepares whatever forms and applications are necessary and takes the application before a loan committee, made up of people who probably don't know you, who have only a superficial understanding of your organization, and whose job it is to minimize the bank's risk (in other words, figure out all the reasons they can to turn your loan down).

Your only advocate, aside from the material you prepared, is your banker. If you have not kept your banker up to date on your organization, your activities, and your plans, the odds are that the bank (particularly in the current environment) will not take a risk on you, and your loan may be reduced, be made very expensive (a high interest rate or loan fee), or denied altogether. So, you need your banker solidly in your corner, and later I will show you how to do so.

3. *Banks don't understand not-for-profits.* The third issue is one that makes the first and second tougher to resolve: Banks don't understand how not for-profits work. To a banker, not knowing about something is risky, and risk to a banker is like acid rain to an industrialist—something they'd rather avoid thinking about, thank you very much.

Look at it from the banker's point of view:

You get most of your money from one source—government—and everyone "knows" that this source is, at best, unpredictable and, in any event, only guaranteed for one year at a time. You (the executive director) are probably not a trained manager, and your organization prides itself on giving services away and doesn't collect very well from those who are supposed to pay. You are overseen by a citizens' committee of well-wishers and do-gooders, staffed by a bunch of program zealots. Who's watching the store, and why should I lend my bank's money? I mean, you are a NOT-for-profit, and loans are only repaid from profits!

Sound exaggerated? It's not. I have heard every single one of these arguments from well-educated, well-meaning bankers, referring to not-for-profit organizations that were (despite the banker's prejudice) very well run. The problem is one of education as much as it is internal operations, but you do have an uphill battle with most lending institutions, no matter how much they love what you do and no matter how much they have given you in donations or staff time in the past.

There are a number of things that you can do to beat these problems and to develop or improve your relationships with your lenders. Here are the steps to take:

1. *Fix up your finances.* First, get your internal house in order. No business, for-profit or not-for-profit, is going to be given a loan if its financial house is out of whack. Make sure your internal act is together before you go the bank. Regular statements, an annual audit, and good cash and receivable controls are all essential. So are many of the things we've talked about in this chapter: making money, knowing which programs makes money and which lose, tracking your productivity, being aware of trends in your field. In short, be businesslike while pursuing your mission.

2. *Seek a banker, get to know him or her.* Once your house is cleaned up, if you don't already have one, go down and meet a real commercial banker. As noted earlier, banking is, at its heart, a personal business. The banker will want to know lots of information about your organization and will also be keenly interested in *you*—your background, your attitude, your management skills.

Meet with this person regularly, every six months (one good time to go in is just after your annual audit comes back, then on a six-month basis). Talk business—your industry, your past six months of operations, your high and low points. Let the banker see that you know your organization from a business point of view.

3. *Give the banker lots of information.* Give your banker lots of information. As we said before, what people don't understand, they fear. This information should include at least the following: your monthly statements; your audit; your newsletter; copies of all major grant awards, certifications, and so on; and all news releases and newspaper articles on your organization *and* your field. Keep your name regularly on your banker's desk. The more they know, the better off you are.

Invite the banker to visit your program site(s) once a year. If you have multiple programs at many locations, pick a different one each time. Invite the banker to a board meeting, particularly the one that includes discussion of your budget. Let them see you in action. If you have an open house, or ribbon cutting, or press conference, send the banker an invitation.

When you are developing your strategic plan, invite your banker to sit in on the financial parts of the discussion or at least review the numbers. The same for a business plan, a capital spending plan, and so on. Such a consultation will have lots of benefits. First, you will receive excellent advice and ideas. Second, you'll know what to expect from your banker if any part of the plan requires debt. Equally important, your banker will be similarly forewarned about your requests, and you will give the banker more "ownership" in your organization.

The idea is to develop a long-term relationship that benefits your organization and the bank. It is an ongoing process, a discipline, but one that will pay off enormously when you need it most. Remember, the banks want "good" business. You want to be a good business that does good things. By working together, you can both accomplish your goals.

J. FINDING THE RIGHT BANK

Now you know why a good relationship with a banker is so important to your organization. But there's more to it than that. The banker with whom you work will only rarely be the owner. Bankers are employees of the bank and must abide by its policies, processes, priorities, and, of course, its prejudices. These may very well affect your banker's ability to meet your needs and thus may preclude your wanting to invest a lot of time fostering a relationship that, as far as you are concerned, is a one-way street running the wrong way.

So what should you do? Well, first, let's get our perspectives straight. You are the *customer*. I know that's hard to believe, given the way some banks treat you, but it's the truth. Remember, the bank is *selling* you money. In fact, the bank is almost certainly selling *your* money (your checking deposits) to *other* people for short periods of time. Unfortunately, some bankers tend to forget this with small businesses or with not-for-profits, and it is up to you to remind them politely of the fact.

Still, you want to find the bank with the best set of services and the best possible attitude toward your organization. Just as with anything you buy, it is prudent to shop around for a bank, even if you have been using one to your satisfaction for some time (some would say, *particularly* if you have been with one bank for a long time). But what is the best way to compare? Here are the steps to take.

1. *Start at the top.* Find someone who knows the CEO of each of the three or four (or more) banks that you wish to check out. Have that person (let's call him Mike) phone the CEO (let's call her Jan) and inform her of your interest (let's call you Joe). Have Mike say, "Jan? This is Mike. I heard that Joe's organization is looking around for a new bank, and I thought you might want to give him a call, since I know you're always looking for some new customers. He's got an annual budget of around $1.5 million. Just thought you'd like to know."

Now what has Mike done? He's done his friend Jan a favor, and he has not taken any risk by declaring you a good risk. Proving that is your job.

Now you wait and see how far down the organizational chart you dribble. If Jan or her first vice president calls you back and invites you to lunch at the bank to explain their services, you know the bank is interested and will probably treat you pretty well (assuming their prices are competitive). If, on the other hand, you are never called back, or your call is returned by a junior loan officer with $2,500 in personal loan approval authorization, then you have a good idea about what that bank thinks of not-for-profits in general, and of yours in particular.

2. *Remember that you are the customer.* For the banks that call back, you need to take the next step: shop prices and services. Always ask what services are available for a commercial account. Are there checking fees? What minimum balance waives such fees? Do balances in checking over a minimum earn interest? How much? Are investment services (CDs, money market accounts) available? What types of loans does the bank make? What collateral do they want? Who makes the decisions?

Also ask for comparative interest rates and terms on lines of credit, equipment loans, and receivable loans.

☞ **HANDS ON:** Banks will often tell you that your loan is "two over prime." The question to ask is, "Whose prime, and what is it today?" Some banks use New York prime, and some use their own (often inflated over New York by one or two percent). You need to know the rate so that you can make a valid comparison.

Ask the bank for small-business references, as well as references on other social service clients. (Be prepared for a shocked look. Bankers are rarely asked to give references.) Then check out the references. Ask the reference person at least the following questions:

- Who is your contact in the bank? How is your relationship with that person? Do you think your contact person values your business with the bank?

- How long have you been a customer? Why did you choose this bank? What services of the bank do you use? Are they of high quality? Were loans easy to apply for or a major hassle?

- If there were periods during which you had a downturn, did the bank stand by you or get nervous? How did your banker act toward you in hard times?

- Do you feel that your banker understands your business? What has your banker done to show interest in your organization?

- (Explain a little about your organization.) Would you recommend your bank (and banker) to me? Any advice on how to deal with your banker?

Weigh the financial information along with the reference checking and then make your move. If you are bringing a major account to the bank (over $1 million in payroll in most towns, less with smaller banks), negotiate for the waiving of fees. Then stick with your bank. You should build a long-term business relationship with the bank and the banker. Jumping from bank to bank is bad business, unless you are poorly treated over a period of time.

Note, however, that many banks are being bought and sold these days. If your bank is acquired by a new owner, this should lead to a reevaluation on your part of whether the bank still sees you as a priority customer. You should also reevaluate whenever you are assigned to a new loan officer.

Finding a good bank, one that values you for your economic contribution to the community as well as for your mission, is one of the best management moves you can make. It takes some time, but you will reap the benefits over and over in the coming months and years.

K. CREATING AN ENDOWMENT

Wouldn't it be nice to have a cash machine, one that churns out money every year—whether or not the government funds you or donors give to you, one that you could depend on, not have to advocate or beg for? There is such a cash machine: It's called an endowment, and lots of your peer organizations have one—even organizations that are very new and very small.

My rule for endowments is this: You need a large enough endowment to have *at least* 5% of your total annual income come from the endowment's earnings. That means if your endowment earns 5% return each year, it needs to be the same size as your annual budget. If it earns 10%, it needs to be half the size of your annual budget.

Why do you need to do this? For a number of reasons. First, it's good fund-raising marketing: You need a steady source of income, and sophisticated donors know this. If you just ask for money with no endowment, you can ask only for operating or special funds. If you create an endowment (usually in a separate 501(c)(3) foundation), you can attract larger funds from people who know that their gift will keep on giving. Second, you need the steady income, income that is free of the need to lobby, the need to beg. And don't stop at 5%. That's the *minimum.* If you can have 20% of your income per year from the endowment, great! Just think of all the additional things you can do. Third, you have the resource of your 501(c)(3) status, which allows you to take financial contributions. Use it, and not just for current operations. Show some long-term vision and save for the future.

I am not an expert in development and fund raising. Thus, I will not even attempt to tell you how to go about this. I would merely lead you astray. There are, however, a number of excellent texts on the subject. Make it part of your long-term planning to put aside funds in a restricted fund or in a foundation established so that you get the income, but do not touch the principal. This is the toughest part: the discipline of not touching sources of funds when you have done without for so long. Learn how, and your organization will really benefit.

L. USING YOUR EMPOWERMENT

Getting to the point where you feel you are financially empowered will continue to be a tough, long-haul job. So why do it? Why raise the expectations of your staff, board, and yes, yourself to do this work now for the benefit of others in 5, 10, or even 15 years? For a number of reasons. First, it's your job. You are not just a senior staff person for this year's work, you also are building a better organization for the long term, at least you are supposed to be. I hope you buy property for the long haul, with an eye to minimal maintenance and hopefully to appreciated resale value. I hope that you buy computers and software with the capability to upgrade easily and inexpensively, and that you buy vehicles based on utilization and on repair and resale records. If you are doing this, you are investing in the future. When you spend money and time on a strategic plan, you are investing in the future. And, when you train staff, or start a marketing plan, you are counting on a future reward for your investment.

Imagine if you or your predecessor had started financial empowerment planning for the organization 10 years ago. Just think what you could do with that money now! The second reason to become financially empowered is that it is good mission. Only by becoming less dependent on your key funders will you and your organization be able to meet the needs of your community quickly and with the skill and knowledge that you alone possess. Your ability to do good mission and thus the value that your community places on your organization will both rise. If the mission is the reason for your existence, financially empowering your organization is a key component, and one that you need to start on—today.

One other caution: It is key in empowerment planning that you bring all the staff, board, and funders in on the plans early, if possible. You need to educate your staff and funders to the fact that having money is okay, and the fact that you have some funds now and are putting other funds aside is not an indication that you have given up on the mission and are hoarding. You need to let them know that these funds that you are setting aside are targeted for mission, for long-term income, and for financial stability. As noted above when we discussed keeping what you earn, work with your funders and staff on the front end to let them have input, and it will pay off here.

RECAP

If only doing all of these things could be included in your next one year plan! But there is much to be done, and some of it takes a great deal of time, no matter how good your intentions or how great your financial or service needs. But by reading this chapter, you've made a start on the long road.

We have covered a lot of ground in this chapter, and have started you on the road to empowering your organization financially. Now you know the five characteristics of financial empowerment, you know how to use numbers to your benefit, and how to pick those numbers that mean something to you and those that don't. You have been exposed to methods of using financial and nonfinancial indicators to tell how your organization is doing, and how to give different people in your organization the numbers that they want and need to do their job.

Finally, I have shown you some ways to predict future financial needs so that you can plan well in advance and not get caught short.

Again, no money, no mission. Financial empowerment will take your organization from being a creature of the 1970s to being a thriving, contributing member of your community in the twenty-first century.*

Questions for Discussion

1. What parts of this chapter apply to us?
2. How do we do in relation to Peter's eight characteristics of empowerment? Where can we do better?
3. What can we do to improve our internal reporting? What information do people need to see when? Can our software accommodate different reports?
4. How do we feel about spending the time and money training our staff to understand our financials? Do we want to share them? Why or why not?
5. How do we get started on an endowment? How soon can we get something in place?

---

*For much more on this subject, see my book *Financial Empowerment, More Money for More Mission,* also published by John Wiley & Sons.

11

A Vision for the Future

OVERVIEW

Organizations that succeed, organizations that thrive, organizations that are going to be providers of services in the next century all know where they are going. A vision for what you want your organization to be, and a road map of how you want to get from here to there, is absolutely essential if you are to be a good steward of your organization's resources. This chapter will give you some hands-on ideas of how to plan, and how to use both the planning process and the plan itself as a tool for the benefit of the organization.

In this chapter, you will read about the nine distinct phases of the planning process, and I will provide some detailed ideas on how to use that process to your best benefit. We'll review the four reasons why you should develop and maintain a plan, examine some varying philosophies of planning, and I will offer recommendations on how often you should plan, how inclusive the planning process should be, and how to go about evaluating the planning process and the plan's implementation status.

After that, we will look at various types of plans, define some important terms in the planning process, and look at outcomes that you can expect from a good planning process and plan. I will also describe a variety of uses for your plan once you have it completed. We will look at some barriers to planning, and I will include an outline for your plan to help you get started.

By the time you finish with this chapter, you should have a better understanding of the task you need to tackle. If you are new to planning, reading this chapter will help you get acquainted with the need for planning and how to do it. If you are an experienced planner, you will probably pick up a nugget or two for how to do your next plan even better.

A. THE PHASES OF PLANNING

Good planning comes in several phases. The following phase list is fairly complete, and we will review each phase in some detail. However, I want to make several points about the list as a whole. First, the sequence listed is just that: a sequence. While it allows for a great deal of flexibility in how you actually do the planning, I urge you to do your planning in this order. Since 1982, I have helped well over 50 organizations of all types and sizes develop their planning processes and their plans, and this sequence has been tried and tested: It works. While there may be a certain overlap, for example, with Data Gathering starting about the same time as the Retreat and extending into the time of Drafting Goals and Objectives, the basic sequence should be preserved.

The phases of planning that I suggest are:

1. Preparedness
2. The Retreat
3. Data Gathering
4. Drafting Goals and Objectives
5. Outside Comment
6. Final Draft and Adoption
7. Implementation
8. Evaluation
9. Go to one.

We will go through each phase in some detail, but first we need to discuss some philosophies, decide on which type of plan you intend to develop, provide some definitions, and look at the outcomes of planning that you can expect.

B. WHY PLAN?

Too few organizations that I consult with have a strategic plan. The excuses are many, and we will discuss them in more detail near the end of this chapter, but the most prevalent concern is "with rapidly changing circumstances I don't want to be stuck with some plan that is totally out of date." I agree. But the planning horizons that we will talk about are not overly long (3 to 5 years), and the key to strategic planning is one of strategy, not of tactics. The issues that you should be considering in a strategic plan need to be planned for and should not be greatly changed within the planning cycle. Also, your planning process should be ongoing, so that if some major change is initiated in your field, you can adapt the plan to it. I would also argue that few, if any, major changes in service delivery or funding patterns show up for work at 8 A.M. one morning unannounced. Usually, major changes are researched, discussed, rumored, and debated for months or even years before they are enacted. Thus, in the part of the planning process during which you look at the environment, you will be able to predict most of these changes in advance.

Good plans actually help you remain flexible, because, like good marketing, they keep you and your organization focused on what is important. They assist you in not wasting resources and not getting tied down in fruitless or out-of-date services, and keep your staff and board up to date on the realities of the world in which you are working. Also, the well-run planning process is often a wake-up call for board and staff members who still think they are working in 1980, and this enlightenment makes later change less difficult for them.

With that in mind, let's examine the four reasons that you should expend the time, money, energy and political capital to develop a plan.

1. WITHOUT A PLAN, THE ONLY WAY YOU GET WHERE YOU ARE GOING IS BY ACCIDENT: WHAT YOUR ORGANIZATION DOES IS TOO IMPORTANT TO OCCUR BY ACCIDENT

Yogi Berra said it even better: "If you don't know where you are going, you will wind up somewhere else."

❏ FOR EXAMPLE: Let's look at the planning process through the metaphor of a family vacation. If you and your family are getting ready to go on vacation, once you know you have the time off and want to go together (Preparedness) you will certainly get together as a family and decide where you are going (the Retreat). Let's assume that you decide to drive to San Francisco and stay for a week. You have to first set the long-term goal of getting there. Your strategy is to go by car. To achieve your goal, you buy a road map, check your money and the condition of your car (Data Gathering), and plan your route and your itinerary (Set Goals and Objectives). You will check the conditions en route and in San Francisco—things like the weather, roads, tolls, and fuel and hotel costs (assess the environment)—and probably call some friends who have been to San Francisco recently for ideas and feedback (gather outside comment). You then finalize your plans, get packed and leave (implement). If between home and San Francisco, you find that a road is under construction or that there is a place you had not heard about that you want to see, you may vary either or both of your route or your timetable.

Congratulations. You have just done strategic planning. The important thing to remember here, however, is what you didn't do. You didn't just pack up, drive to the first corner, and say "Where are we going?", and then go to the next intersection and say "Which way?" and the next and the next. But in your organization, when you do not have a plan, when you act only in reaction to events, when you go from only one funded program to the next or one community need to the next, you wind up in some very strange and sometimes dangerous places, just the way you would on your vacation if you chose each turn at random. Planning allows you to see where you are going and to transmit that information to the people who are going with you: your staff, board, funders, community, and most important, your clientele.

2. A STRATEGIC PLAN ALLOWS ALL OTHER PLANNING (BUDGETS, STAFFING, FUND RAISING) TO BE COORDINATED

When you have a good, current strategic plan, you can coordinate the activities of your organization better by using the strategic plan and its overall goals as a backstop for decisions. You can discuss management, program, and policy choices in light of the priority goals of your plan. You can ask questions about whether a particular item in the budget supports the long-range plan. For example, if in your strategic plan you have a 5-year goal to build a new building and you need to have 30% of the cost of the building put aside, you probably need to show that set-aside in this year's financial plan. And if, as part of that building program, you intend to have 40% of the cost paid for by a capital fund drive starting in two years, your marketing and development staff had better be laying the groundwork for that fund drive this year. Without your strategic plan, you cannot accomplish this type of coordination.

3. PLANS ALLOW YOU TO DELEGATE MORE EFFECTIVELY

Successful managers know how to delegate well and how to push the line staff to make as many decisions as possible. Giving up responsibility and authority is very difficult for some people, and having the framework of the strategic plan can make that action easier: The manager who is delegating has a work plan based on the strategic plan for the subordinate to work with. Also, if the subordinate was involved in the planning process, his or her understanding and ownership will be much higher, and the likelihood of effective delegation will increase.

4. PLANS ARE GOOD BUSINESS—AND GOOD STEWARDSHIP

By now you know that I consider your not-for-profit a mission-oriented business. Good businesses of all types know where they are going. They know their markets and their resources, and they have a plan of how to use the second to please the first. They may differ in their products or services, and often differ in their internal philosophies, but they all have one thing: a strategic plan that frames the rest of their activities and provides a benchmark for evaluating their success or failure.

C. PLANNING OPTIONS

There are a variety of ways to do planning. These options include how often plans should be updated, how inclusive the planning process should be, and whether to regularly evaluate the implementation of the plan. I have summarized these choices below to point out some of the advantages and disadvantages of each. I then provide my recommendation for each area.

1. FREQUENCY

While there are an infinite number of permutations of the combination of planning horizon (how long the plan is to be in effect) and planning update (how soon should the plan be redone), the following options are the most common.

- *A five-year plan updated every five years.* This is obviously the long-term view, and the advantage is that you only have to think about the plan twice each decade. The problem is that it assumes that everything will go as planned, both inside the organization and outside it, for the full five years, and that is naive, to say the least. Imagine a five-year plan written in 1979. It could not have foreseen the Reagan Revolution and the huge effects that it would have on the nation's not-for-profits. Now imagine a five-year plan written in 1991 that assumed that George Bush would win reelection and that there would be no such thing as national health care reform. You get the point. The second problem with this approach is that as you get to the end of five years, you lose the momentum from the planning process. People (on both the board and the staff) will have left, and there may be only a few of the core planning team remaining. Thus, the lessons learned and the ownership gained will be lost.

- *A one-year plan updated each year.* This sounds and acts an awful lot like an annual budget and work plan document. It is the most capable of reacting swiftly to changing circumstances, but you lose the big picture and tend to be shaped by events rather than shaping them. We criticize the government (at all levels) for not thinking beyond the current fiscal year. Don't fall into the same trap. Strategic planning needs to be that: strategic.

- *A five-year plan with one-year components.* This is a combination on the first two, but one that works fairly well. It allows for the long-term strategic vision to guide the flexible annual plan developed each year. The problem with this is that the overall big document is not done often enough, at least in my experience.

- *Recommendation (five-year plan redone every three years, with annual plans).* I believe that the best way to approach the strategic planning cycle is on the basis of a five-year plan, redone completely every three years, but with annual work plans done every year. Let me explain. A five-year horizon forces the staff and board that create the goals and objectives of the plan to step back from the day-to-day concerns of the organization and do some big-picture thinking. This is essential. By reworking the full plan every three years, you accomplish three important things: You keep the planning process fresh in the organization, you can react to environmental changes, and you can have each board member take part in the creation of a strategic plan once in each of his or her three-year terms, which is the term that I recommend in Chapter 5. By having an annual plan of actions that support the strategic plan, you have the staff pull out the highest-priority items for each year's work plan, and the board is kept apprised of the implementation status of the plan.

2. PROCESS

Once you decide what planning horizon and update schedule you will use, you then need to decide what process of planning you will have. Here, you have what I think is a golden opportunity to maximize the use of the planning process itself as a tool for organizational growth, improving staff and board morale and marketing your organization. However, your realization of that goal is dependent on the type of process you choose. Some choices are:

- *Keep it small.* The idea here is to have the fewest possible number of people involved in the planning process so that you get it done quickly. Thus, staff and board might go on a short retreat to set the goals and priorities, then the senior staff (or just the executive director) would draft the plan and bring it to the board for review and approval—short and sweet, and in the implementation stage soon. The problem with this idea is that it short-circuits one of the best parts of planning: bringing people in for their ideas and their ownership.

- *Highly inclusive.* Speaking of ideas and ownership, that is what the inclusive process is all about. Inclusion in the planning process is designed to get input from all of your staff, board, funders, community representatives, clientele or their families or representatives, and any other group that you may need or want such as referral sources or alumni. You do not need to put all of these people on one giant planning committee. They can be brought in in three ways: having a planning committee that is more broadly representative than just board members; asking a large number of people for input through surveys and focus groups during the data-gathering phase; and encouraging a broad review and comment on the draft plan during that phase. In this way, you offer the opportunity to have input to a much larger group, they in turn now have a feeling of pride in being asked and ownership in the final product that would not have been possible in the "keep it small" philosophy. Inclusion obviously takes longer and is somewhat more expensive, but I am a strong advocate for using this method.

- *Planning committee generated.* This model has the board appoint a strong planning committee, made up of all board members or board and staff combined, who generate the plan on their own and bring it to the board for review and comment. Although not exclusive of the inclusion method noted above, this type of process usually does not include a data-gathering phase that looks at more than hard data such as demographics and almost never includes outside review and comment before the board sees it. It is a variant of "keep it small," but the one that organizations with strong committee structures (which I also advocate for) tend to fall into. Again here, this process is fast and controlled, but it loses the opportunity for inclusion. It also does not include the entire board in the retreat setting, which is a mistake.

• *Staff generated/board reviewed.* In a strong staff model of organization, there is the tendency to allow the staff to lead the board, and this sometimes includes the development of the long-range plan. Here, a group of senior staff would develop a draft plan and have it reviewed (and usually adopted with few changes) by the board. This model leaves the board—an essential resource—out of the loop, and also usually forgoes the inclusion that we have been discussing. It is fast and it is controllable, but I feel that it has more drawbacks than benefits.

• *Recommendation (inclusive as possible).* My recommendations are easy to predict here: include as many people as time and money will allow. Start with a retreat of all board and senior staff. Then give the primary responsibility for coming up with a draft plan to a planning committee made up of board, senior staff, line staff, clientele, and community members. Ask lots of people for their input. Circulate the draft plan and listen to the comments. Publish and distribute the plan widely. This method is a lot of work, but it is the best method of maximizing the value of the planning process in addition to getting the best plan.

3. EVALUATION

Unfortunately, most people don't evaluate their plan at all, or hold off doing the evaluation until it is time to do the next plan. If you are going to use the plan as a management tool, you need to constantly be reviewing where you are in relation to where you wanted to be (your deadlines for your goals and objectives).

You need to review your progress toward your goals regularly. Otherwise, you will get to the end of the planning cycle (3 to 5 years), look back, and discover that you have achieved only 15% of your goals because you got distracted.

• *Recommendation.* Use the plan as a management tool. Once a month, review it in senior staff meetings, asking the question: "Are we on schedule for this goal?" If not, why not? Have conditions changed, are the resources that we thought would be available not there? The same holds for board meetings, but this should only be done quarterly.

Also, when the plan is complete, your planning committee needs to make written recommendations to the board about how to do the planning better the next time. These can be used by the next planning committee. If you don't write it down now, you will forget, and the experience of this committee will not benefit the next one.

D. TYPES OF PLANS

There are several categories that I put plans into. I have seen literally hundreds of strategic plans and I think that these categories are relatively fair. All of the plans that fit into these categories are intended to be strategic plans, and every one of the people who wrote them intended them to be useful and flexible. But something happened along the way, and the results are:

1. TOMES

These are documents that rival a New York City phone directory in size, take a professional football lineman to lift and that nobody reads. They include everything you ever wanted to know plus a lot more, and are too imposing and all-encompassing to be flexible and useful.

2. WORK PLANS

These are just work assignments for the staff, often put together to submit to a major government funder. They cover the "what" in minute detail, but don't relate it at all to the all-important "why"—the mission. They also ignore the larger strategic issues such as overall strategies of service.

3. PUBLIC RELATIONS DOCUMENTS

These documents purport to be plans but spend most of their time selling the organization. They focus on the need for the organization in the community and the wonderful things it has done in the past. This leads to a lack of objectivity and an inability to see the organization "warts and all," which is crucial to good planning. Also, a strategic plan is not an appropriate place for you to do your marketing. It is not supposed to be a sales brochure or a "feel-good" document.

4. HISTORY TEXT

These plans make up for their lack of forward thinking with a heavy emphasis on past accomplishments and how your organization was formed and grew. They are often produced by organizations that have grown rapidly and are so caught up in looking back at how far they have come that they forget to look ahead and see where they are going. This kind of plan is a great document for a student of your discipline who wants to know your history, but it usually only pays superficial attention to the changes in your community and where you want to be in five years.

5. DOCTORAL DISSERTATION

This is a highly technical document, full of jargon and acronyms. These types of papers are written by staff people who use the technical veil to hide a lack of understanding of some of the fundamental issues such as "What is our mission?" They cannot see the forest for the technical trees, and such a document is useless to nonprofessionals in your field such as your board, some staff, the community, and the people you serve.

6. WORKING DOCUMENT

This is a document that provides strategic vision, but also practical application. A document that attends to the mission. A document that is written in lay language. One that is true to the wants of your clientele and expresses the best of what your board and staff have to offer.

- *Recommendation.* I want you to do your best to get a working document as the product of your planning process. I'm sure you do too, but be wary of the traps that others have fallen into and try to avoid the other types of plans listed above.

E. PLANNING DEFINITIONS

Now it is time to define what I mean in the planning process. There are lots of different definitions and ten times that many misuses of the terms listed here. But, for purposes of our discussion, here are my definitions:

- *Strategic plan.* A working document that discusses the organization's mission, the environment that it will work in over the planning period (3 to 5 years), and the goals and objectives to realize the mission over that period. This is not a work plan, but it should be written with enough specificity that it is usable on a monthly basis by staff.

• *Goal.* A statement of desired long-term outcome. A goal may or may not be *quantified*, but usually does have a *deadline*.

• *Objective.* A much more specific statement that supports the goal. All objectives must have a *deadline*, be *quantified*, and have an *assigned responsible agent*—the person, group, or organization that is responsible for implementing the objective on time. There can be many objectives to implement a goal. Sometimes they will be sequential, sometimes simultaneous.

• *Action statement.* The most specific item on the list, action statements support the implementation of an objective. They too need to be *quantified* and have a *deadline* and an *assignment of responsibility*. For most organizations, these statements will be included only for high-priority goals or in the one-year plan that flows out of the five-year plan.

F. OUTCOMES OF PLANNING

What can you expect from the planning process? If you use my recommendations and renew your plan every three years, use an inclusive model, and evaluate the plan regularly, you can expect at least the following benefits:

• *Better and more effective services.* By evaluating during the plan development process what is needed and wanted and what is not; by asking people instead of assuming you know; by bringing customers, clients, patients, students, or parishioners into the planning loop, your plan will result in better and more effective services. You may find that you need to reduce or eliminate services that no longer make sense in terms of mission or in terms of markets, and you may find that services that you are sure are needed are not wanted and that certain services that you never even considered are in high demand. You will also hear a lot about current services: what works, what doesn't, small ways to make big improvements, practical (and sometimes impractical) methods of being more effective. The planning process helps you focus your resources on what is important, and that means better and more effective services.

• *Higher ownership and morale.* If you follow the inclusive model recommended here, you will have a higher overall morale of staff, board, funders, community, and clientele. Just asking people their opinion, just including them in the loop flatters them. If you then follow through and actually use some of their suggestions, and get back to them and let them know that they were listened to, all of those who participated now have a stake in what you do and who you are. Additionally, if you are like most organizations who do not either (a) have an organizational strategic plan or (b) have developed it a long time ago with only a few people, most of your staff as well as many of your board may never have been given the opportunity to see the big picture, to step back and look at the organization as a whole. Being part of an inclusive strategic planning effort allows that to happen.

• *Lower levels of conflict.* Planning and the planning process I recommend facilitate a forum for healthy debate over resources, discussions over direction, and airing disagreements over policy and the shape of the organization in the future. By providing a positive structure for healthy conflict to emerge, and for unhealthy conflict to be vented, you allow those who harbor a grudge, have not had their say in the past, have felt "muzzled," to get their soapbox and have that say. While not a preventative for all conflict in the organization around policies and resource allocation, planning does provide the forum and it does also let people have a clearer view, in writing, of what the organization stands for. This will confront some board, some staff, and perhaps some funders with the choice of staying or leaving, but the clarity of purpose and the focus on the future shape of the organization does make future actions more predictable, and it is often when people are surprised by actions that they are most upset. You will hear much less "nobody told me we were going to . . ." than before you developed and then published your plan, at least on major issues.

G. THE PLANNING PROCESS

Now for the planning process itself. As I said earlier, I hope that you will adopt a process that meets your own organization's needs and capabilities but still holds to this basic sequence. There is a lot of room for customization in this outline. For example, there is the time set aside for each activity. You may want the entire process to take three months (which is very, very fast) or allow it to take 18 months. You may want to do focus groups only in your Data Gathering phase, and not to do primary research or surveys. You may decide to have the planning committee meet monthly, or just three times during the process. You may decide to minimize the Preparedness phase or take three months to have everyone in the organization trained in goal setting.

All of these variations are fine, as long as you don't skip any of the phases altogether. I know it is tempting to go straight to the fun part— the drafting of goals and objectives—but if you do, you miss a once in three-to-five year opportunity for your organization. Take the time to do this right.

1. PREPAREDNESS

There is no point in starting this until you are ready. To get prepared, make sure that a number of things are in place. First, ensure that your senior staff and key board members agree that planning is important and that they are willing to commit the time and the money necessary to see the process through. Second, develop a planning process and get your board to agree to it. Third, using the draft planning process, develop a planning budget, both of time and cash, that will be committed to the plan. Cash costs could include a retreat facility, meals and travel, data-gathering costs such as surveys, focus groups, and possibly a consultant. I always recommend that organizations get a facilitator for their retreats, and, if this is the first time you have planned, you may also want to hire a planning consultant to help you lay out the process and advise you around the potholes. Never hire a consultant to write the plan. That is your job.

2. THE RETREAT

The best way to get started is by getting away. I strongly suggest that all board members and senior staff go away for a day to cover at least the following things: a review of your mission, an agreement on the planning process itself, a discussion of the environmental conditions under which you will be operating, the development of preliminary goals, a prioritization of those goals and an appointment of a planning committee. Have such a retreat at the start of each revision of the plan (every three years in my model).

☞ **HANDS ON:** Having facilitated over 60 retreats, I strongly prefer the evening–morning model over any other. Get your group together for dinner, let them review your planning process, review the mission, and consider what kind of world they will be operating in in the evening. Then quit and socialize. In the morning, the retreat participants will return fresh and ready to set goals and put them into a priority order for you. This model produces better results because it gives people a break and also allows the staff present to socialize with the board—a key extra benefit.

At the retreat, you need to do at least the following:

- Review and agree to the planning process.

- Review and update your mission statement as necessary.

- Discuss your predictions for the world in which your plan will be implemented. What trends or activities are going to affect you and how? Walk through a SWOT analysis at this time as well (SWOT stands for strengths, weaknesses, opportunities, and threats).

- Set preliminary long-term goals.

- Discuss the goals and do an initial prioritization.

3. DATA GATHERING

Once you have the key goals, you can begin the job of data gathering. You can do this through hard data research and gathering from your internal data or at the library. Additionally, you can run focus groups and surveys of such people as staff, clientele, funders, alumni, and the like. For more information on surveys and focus groups, see the section on them in Chapter 9.

The data that you gather now will be used to help the planning committee and its subcommittees make the most knowledgeable decisions about the issues that confront you. Some data gathering will go on throughout the planning process, and you do not need to wait to begin drafting fuller goals and objectives until all the data is in.

4. DRAFTING GOALS AND OBJECTIVES

Now comes the fun part: the examination of the goals and the setting of objectives to support them. You can use one of two methods for this. The first is to have your planning committee do all of this work for all of the goals set at the retreat. The second, used by most of the organizations that I assist in planning, is to have specialty subcommittees that examine certain areas in depth. For example, you might have a subcommittee on Administration, one on Finance, one on Programs, one on Marketing, and so on. The breakout of the groups will depend on your organization. A school might break the issues out by primary, middle, and secondary programs. A church might have subcommittees on Finance, Church-Based Programs, Outreach Ministries, and Buildings and Grounds.

The benefits of using the subcommittee model are that each subcommittee can go into their subject in great detail, and you can add people to the planning subcommittees who are experts in this area. More inclusion.

Whoever is setting the goals and objectives needs to look first at the goals that came out of the retreat. Can they be consolidated? Improved? Are there important issues that were overlooked in a one-day retreat? Once the goals are established, then each goal in turn should have objectives added to it. This will happen before, during, and after the data are gathered. In fact, the setting of preliminary objectives will help you identify additional data that you need to go after.

Remember that the goals are long-term statements of desired outcomes, but the objectives need to have a deadline, be quantified, and have someone or some organization responsible for their implementation.

5. OUTSIDE COMMENT

This is really the most important step for the organization as a whole. Once the goals and objectives have been fully drafted, it is time to get outside opinion. Let as many people as you have time for offer their comments. I usually suggest that major funders, your banker, key referrers, community leaders, representatives of your clientele, and all of your staff get a chance to review and comment with a deadline for getting their comments to you of about two weeks. Bring all of the comments to the planning committee. Many organizations resist this step—and do so to their detriment. By asking outsiders, you get great ideas, develop relationships, and foster ownership. Don't skip this step!

6. FINAL DRAFT AND ADOPTION

When the planning committee has reviewed the comments and any late arriving data, the final draft can be written. At this time, a second prioritization should be done, and the highest priority goals should be tackled in the one-year plan for the first year of the planning cycle.

This one-year plan should be developed by staff and should include action steps to accomplish high-priority goals and objectives. The staff should run the one-year plan by the planning committee, but it really needs only a cursory review. The one-year plan is really a work plan for staff and board, and is the plan that needs the most careful monitoring.

Once the board adopts the plan, get it printed and distribute it widely.

7. IMPLEMENTATION

As noted earlier, the plan should be a working, useful document. Its use as a tool will be discussed in a page or two, but the point of the product is to do what the plan says. You have invested a great deal of time and effort getting the plan together, and, while the process has been useful, you still need to do what you've committed to. Implement!

8. EVALUATION

I have already told you how I think you should evaluate the plan's implementation, but you also need to evaluate the planning process. Write down any things you would change or improve and file them away for the benefit of the next planning committee to benefit from.

9. GO TO ONE

In three years, start again. By then, you will have had three one-year plans, conditions will have changed, you will have accomplished a great deal, but probably not all of your goals, and it will be time to develop a new five-year plan.

H. USING THE PLAN AS A TOOL

Once you have the plan completed, printed, and distributed, you now need to use it. There are a number of uses for your plan, some of which people neglect or never even consider.

1. A MANAGEMENT TOOL

It should go without saying that the plan should be written in a format that allows you to use it as a management tool. Too few organizations do, however. The plan tends to collect dust until it is time to update it, and then there is no interest in doing the update.

The progress in achieving the goals, objectives and action statements in the *one-year plan* should be reviewed at least monthly in staff meetings, and, in some cases, every two weeks to make sure that you are still on track, that situations have not changed or resources have not been reduced to make it more difficult to implement the plan. The senior staff as well as the line staff need to stay on top of anticipated deadlines and work toward meeting them.

The *strategic plan* implementation should be reviewed monthly at staff meetings, and quarterly at board meetings as a formal part of the session. Either staff or the planning committee can report on progress.

As new issues develop during the year, staff and board need to consider their impact on the plan. How will this affect our ability to complete the goals and objectives? If it will interfere, is this a higher priority? Which is more in line with our mission and our strategies? Use the plan as a guide, but don't be constrained by it.

2. A MARKETING TOOL

An organization that has a plan has a marketing tool. I know that I said that marketing and sales material belong in a marketing or sales piece, and that is still my position: The plan should be written as a plan, not as a sales brochure. But the very fact of your having a plan puts you ahead of many organizations, for-profit and not-for-profit. It is like having a mission statement: It helps people to know who you are and where you are going. For certain people—funders, potential donors, elected officials—it lets them see who you are and where you intend to go. This is excellent marketing in and of itself.

3. A POLICY TOOL

A plan will help you do good policy, because the strategies included will remind you, and help new staff and board who join you to see what the belief of the organization is. For example, if you are a school for hearing-impaired children, your organization may have adopted a communications policy that calls for the use of ASL (American Sign Language— the language preferred by most deaf people as opposed to signed English) on the campus. This policy will be reflected in your goals ("Within two years the school will have 100% of faculty and 90% of nonteaching staff fluent in ASL") and objectives ("The Director of Instruction will provide four ASL courses each year for staff," "The Director of Instruction will offer three off-campus ASL courses for parents per year," "The Director of Instruction will offer ASL to the general community three times next year"). All of these push the communications policy further and actualize it with a speed that would have only happened haphazardly otherwise. If you don't agree with the policy of ASL implementation, the plan tells you right up front, and if you are an ASL advocate, you also know that the school is in agreement immediately upon reading the plan.

4. A RECRUITMENT TOOL

As with the use of the plan as a marketing tool, the plan becomes an excellent recruitment tool to attract the board and staff that you want. You can show people the plan, and they will know before they decide to come what kind of organization you are and where you are going. If they like what they see, they are more likely to stay. Also, the better potential candidates (both staff and board) will be impressed with the simple fact that you have a plan and are more likely to choose your organization over a competitor for their time or services.

I hope that you recognize that your plan is valuable in a number of ways beyond the process and the document. You have spent a lot of time, effort, and money to develop the plan. Now, as a good steward, it is your responsibility to use this new resource as fully as possible.

I. SAMPLE PLAN FORMATS

I have included some outlines of plans to get you started, or to help you revise and update your plans if you already have them. These are templates, ideas that you can use and improve on. Do not be wedded to them if they don't work for your organization. Rather, use them as a starting point.

For each type of plan, I have included my suggestions on the purpose, horizon (how long the plan should look out), and cycle (how regularly the plan should be rewritten), as well as a definition of what the plan should support. Note that the horizon is often longer than the planning cycle. That is intentional. I want you to think long but rewrite regularly enough to keep abreast of current events.

1. STRATEGIC PLAN

Purpose: *To guide the organization as a whole toward the realization of its mission.*

The Plan Supports: *The mission*

Planning Horizon: *Five years*

Planning Cycle: *Develop a strategic plan every 3 years, with annual components written every 12 months.*

Strategic Plan Outline

1. **Executive Summary:** key areas of action, priority goals

2. **Introduction to the plan:** Why you developed the plan, how it will be used

3. **The planning process:** Who was included, what the process itself entailed

4. **The history of your organization:** No more than two pages on your organizational heritage

5. **The organization today:** A 3- to 5-page description of your services, clientele, and funders

6. **The world we will work in:** A listing of assumptions about the future environment, and how they will affect your organization

7. **Goals and objectives**

8. **One-year plan:** The priority goals and their objective and action steps for the first year

9. **Time line:** A visual representation of the goals, objectives, and action steps. Usually called a Gantt or PERT chart

10. **Evaluate and update methodology:** How and when you will evaluate progress toward implementation, and when you will revise the plan

11. **Appendices:** Minimal supporting information for the plan

2. MARKETING PLAN

Purpose: *To guide the organization as a whole toward the realization of its mission*

The Plan Supports: *The mission*

Planning Horizon: *Five years*

Planning Cycle: *Develop a strategic plan every 3 years, with annual components written every 12 months*

Marketing Plan Outline

1. **Your mission statement**

2. **Executive summary:** A brief summary of the marketing plan including a list of your target markets, your core competencies, and how they match up with the wants of the markets.

3. **Introduction and purpose of the plan:** A rationale for the uses of the plan. This section can also include a brief recitation of the planning process and its level of inclusion.

4. **Description of the markets:** A full description of your major markets, their wants, their numbers, and projected growth or reduction in demand from these markets

5. **Description of the services:** A description of each of your services, including number of people served, service area or criteria for service, and any accreditation that these services may have earned

6. **Analysis of market wants:** A review of the surveys, interviews, or focus groups that you do to prepare the plan. The wants of the markets and how they match up to your core competencies should be included here.

7. **Target markets and rationale:** Out of all your potential markets, you will choose a few priority targets. Describe them here in more detail along with your reasoning for their prioritization

8. **Marketing goals and objectives:** The goals, objectives, and (for annual plans) action steps that will get your marketing strategies implemented

9. **Appendices:** Minimal supporting information for the plan

3. BUSINESS PLAN

Purpose: *To guide the organization as a whole toward the realization of its mission*

The Plan Supports: *The mission*

Planning Horizon: *Five years*

Planning Cycle: *Develop a strategic plan every 3 years, with annual components written every 12 months*

Business Plan Outline

1. **Title page identifying the business plan as the property of your organization:** This cover letter includes your name, address, and telephone number and the month and the year that the plan is written or revised. One paragraph states in simple terms who the business plan belongs to and the limitations on its distribution.

2. **Table of contents**

3. **Summary of the plan:** A brief paragraph about your organization; a four-line description of the product or service; a four-line description of the market; a brief paragraph on production and one on distribution, if needed; and a short paragraph on the financing requirements

4. **Description of your organization and its business with the following subheadings:**

   - The organization
   - The product or service
   - The target consumer
   - The consumer's want for the product or service
   - The sales strategy

5. **Description of the market:** For your product or service, including information on the competition and cost price comparisons between competitors and your organization

6. **Marketing plan that includes information on:**

   - The markets
   - Customers
   - Competitors
   - The macro-environment
   - How each of these areas affects the marketing and selling of your product or service
   - Evaluation of potential pitfalls

7. **Financial plan with sources and applications of cash and capital and**:

- An equipment list
- A balance sheet
- Break-even analysis
- Cash flow estimates by month for the first year, by the quarter for the second and third years
- Projected income and expenses for the first three years, and notes of explanation for each of the estimates

8. **Goals and objectives with a timeline**

9. **Minimal appendix with:**

- Management resumes
- Survey or focus group data from customers
- Other pertinent material about your organization and its work

RECAP

In the first pages of this chapter, I said that without a plan, the only way you get anywhere is by accident and what you do is much too important to be accidental. Too many people depend on your organization and its services to let your management and policy setting be one long ad lib. You need to have a plan to focus you, to help you set priorities, and to guide you in the most stressful times that you will face.

In this chapter, we have covered the key parts of planning, the five reasons why it is critical, both in the process and the product, for your organization to have a consensus on where it is going. I have urged you to use an inclusive process, which will help your implementation of the plan and improve the ownership in your organization, the morale of your staff, and the positive impression of your funders. We have seen a planning process that has worked well for many of my consulting clients, and finally I have reviewed for you the outcomes and uses of planning, how to get the most out of the document that you have put so much into.

Planning is good management, and thus good mission. It is a way to get everyone involved in having your organization meet its mission commitments more efficiently and effectively. You have the time to plan. All you need to do is choose to.

Questions for Discussion

1. What parts of this chapter apply to us?
2. Should we consider developing a strategic plan in the next year?
3. How can we integrate more long-range planning into our culture? Who should be involved?
4. What kind of plan should we start with?

12

The Controls That
Set You Free

OVERVIEW

All managers—for profit or not-for-profit—worry. They worry about things going wrong, people messing up, accidents happening, checks not clearing, wrong items being ordered, low-quality services being provided, supervisors not following disciplinary procedure, and the thousand little and big things that can occur without warning.

Over and over in my work, managers and executive directors tell me that they worry about not being on site all the time because "people won't know what to do if something goes wrong, and I'm liable if they screw up." This, of course, chains the executive director to his or her desk, because it assumes that the staff people are incompetent and unable to handle all but the most ordinary and routine situations.

If you agree with my suggestions and theories on delegation that were laid out in Chapter 6, you know that you cannot reach your potential as a manager nor as an organization until you delegate well, at all levels of the organization. But how can you do that and still sleep at night? You can with good controls in place, good training on how to use those controls, and accountability to make sure that those controls are used each and every time.

Let's first define controls: Controls are sets of policy and procedure that both standardize actions in your organization and clearly lay out accountability and responsibility in key areas of the organization. You want controls that protect you, but do not overly hamper your flexibility and creativity, and admittedly that is a balance. Too much controlling and people have no room for personal creativity and contribution; too little control and people lose the guidance and checks and balances that come from well-written, balanced policies and procedures.

This chapter will help you sleep better. Why? Because having good controls is the best sleep medicine I know. In this chapter, I will give you my insights on how to write good, solid management control documents, ones that guide your organization, reduce risk and waste, and let you manage rather than administrate. We'll first look at how to develop controls, and then review the following types of controls.

- Bylaws
- Conflict-of-interest policies
- Financial controls
- Personnel policies
- Media policies
- Volunteer policies
- Quality assurance policies
- Program policies
- Disaster policies

Finally, we'll examine how to train and enforce the standards and controls that you have set.

A. THE CONTROL DEVELOPMENT PROCESS

The process for control development and management is daunting if your organization has none in place, but can be broken down into segments and taken one step at a time. The process that is suggested below will be inclusive, bottoms up, and as relatively painless as possible. I would suggest looking at the list of policies that you need and putting them into priority order for development. Try to develop the policies that you need within the next year to 18 months. If you already have some or all of the controls that I will discuss, you can review your current policies and consider the items that I suggest for inclusion.

- *Get examples from other organizations.* There is no point in reinventing the wheel. Ask your trade association or other not-for-profits in your community for copies of their policies. Note the strengths and weaknesses, but do not automatically adopt their system; it may not be the best for your organization.

- *Write the policy in draft.* You have to start somewhere. Write the policy in draft for your organization, or have a staff person do it.

Then review it with a board/staff committee, and, in the case of certain policies, such as financial or personnel, with a specialist such as your banker, certified public accountant (CPA), or a board member who is also a professional human resource specialist. Make sure that someone on the committee is a person who will actually use the policy day to day. For example, if it is a disciplinary policy, include a line supervisor, mid manager, and senior manager on the policy development team.

• *Float the policy for comment.* Let *everyone* who may have to work with the policy have a chance to comment. This means letting your funders see quality assurance policies; your entire board review conflict-of-interest and media policies; your bank, CPA, and funding auditors look at your cash controls; and your staff see discipline, reward, and compensation policies.

• *Implement the policy.* Start by printing the new policy and then hold orientation and training sessions for all staff and/or board who are affected by the policy to make sure that everyone understands why the policy is there, how and when it is to be used, and their responsibilities and authority under the policy. Repeat these sessions until everyone has been trained, and then repeat a refresher course, particularly for conflict of interest, interviewing, hiring, discipline, and firing at least once a year.

• *Review the policy regularly.* Each policy should be formally reviewed at least every two years. Dating the copy of the policy on file will help remind you to update it.

☞ **Hands On:** In many of your policies and procedures, you will have forms: evaluation, cash receipts, travel reimbursement, time sheets, and the like. Make sure that in every case you include a sample of the form *filled in* as an example. I have yet to see a form and instructions, no matter how clearly written, that were not misinterpreted by someone. Having a filled-in form as an example, in addition to blank ones for immediate use, allows the potential user to have a clear idea of how to use the form. It will reduce frustration and save a great deal of time.

• *Enforce the policy.* There is no point in doing this if you are not going to enforce your expectations that people follow them. State clearly in the policies that failure to follow them will be cause for discipline for staff and for removal for board and volunteers. Put similar wording in the personnel policies and board and volunteer manuals, and make the following of policy a criterion in your evaluation process.

The development of good policies may seem to you to be tedious and bureaucratic. Tedious, yes; bureaucratic, no. This is good management—excellent stewardship. Why should you take the time to do control and policy development when you have so many other pressing things to do? Because having good controls will free you up to do good mission. Good controls emancipate managers from constant worry about people making avoidable mistakes, they allow you to delegate fully, and to use your time, energy, and talents on *managing* the organization rather than *administering* it. This is a crucial difference.

In *In Search of Excellence,* Peters and Waterman noted that those organizations that had good controls could free their managers to be the visionary leaders that were necessary to achieve and maintain excellence—the "simultaneous loose–tight" organization. Waterman later expanded on this characteristic in his book *The Renewal Factor.* Other management gurus have noted the same correlation: If you are sitting around worrying about cash controls, personnel management, or discrimination suits, you are wasting time. Those things can be (for the most part) controlled by having and enforcing good policies.

Again, this is not bureaucracy or a waste of time putting things on paper: This is good, solid management. It can turn into bureaucracy at its worst—a constricting, top-down, controlling, initiative-limiting mess—but it shouldn't. You need to work with your people to design the controls, and do it with an attitude that "these will help us do our job better, will take a lot of the questions out of routine procedure, and will free us up to be creative to do more of our mission."

B. TYPES OF CONTROLS

There are numerous sets of policies and controls that you can develop. The following list is not intended to be all inclusive, but it is extensive. It covers the types of policies I have seen organizations develop poorly, or sometimes not at all. Sometimes the latter is better than the former, because poorly written controls can be very dangerous. At the very least, you need:

- Bylaws
- Conflict-of-interest policies (usually in your bylaws)
- Financial controls
- Personnel policies
- Media policies
- Volunteer policies
- Quality assurance
- Program policies
- Disaster policies

Each of these areas will be discussed in some detail in the following pages. Note, however, that I am *not* contending to be an expert in each of the areas noted. Many are highly technical and have to do with your compliance with state and/or federal law. You will need to consult professionals in your community to ensure that you are in line with local, state, and federal laws as well as with your funders' regulations and your contractual obligations. What I will try to do is to point out key items that people forget to put in, and to point out places where we have observed flaws in policies at many organizations.

☞ **HANDS ON:** Policy development is one of the areas where my technique of recruiting a "professional volunteer" works best. The purpose of the recruitment is to get a real expert to look at your problem—in this case, your policy—without requiring him or her to a long-term commitment as a board member. What you do, taking your personnel policies as an example, is go to the chief executive officer (CEO) of your bank or of another large company that has supported you in the past, and say "We're reviewing our personnel policies this year and wondered if you had a staff person who could provide us with his or her expertise in personnel issues for three or four two-hour meetings over the next three months? Then the CEO gives you the name and feels like he or she has made a "donation"; the expert gives his or her time, but doesn't feel saddled with a long-term commitment; you get your expertise for free; and the expert may, in fact, become enamored of your organization and agree to help again, serve in another capacity, or donate to your organization! Try this, it works.

C. BYLAWS

Bylaws are required by statute in all 50 states for a not-for-profit, and by IRS regulations. You have them, but how recently did you and your board review them? Here are some things you should check for:

- *Mission statement:* You should review this every two years. You should file any substantive changes in your mission statement with the IRS and with the appropriate state official in your state (usually the Attorney General or Secretary of State). (For more on missions, see Chapter 4.)

- *Board selection and term.* Have the board turn over. My suggestion is that each board term be no more than three years, with two consecutive terms before a member has to go off. Perpetual boards tend to perpetuate past policy—long after it is out of date. The selection of the board can be from the membership, by the membership or by the board itself, depending on your state and funding streams' requirements. (For more on boards, see Chapter 5.)

- *Quorum.* Don't box yourself in by saying that you need eight members for a quorum (on a 15-member board). What if, due to unforeseen but reasonable circumstances, four board members resign, and you have no one to replace them with for six months? Suddenly you need 73% (8 of 11) rather than 53% (8 of 15) to do business at a board meeting. You need to say: "A quorum of the board shall be constituted by more than 50% of the board members serving as of the date of the meeting."

- *Dissolution clause.* Make sure you have a clause detailing what happens in case your organization closes. You need to state that you will pay off your liabilities and that the remaining assets will then be distributed to one or more 501(c)(3) corporations. You can specify the corporation if you wish.

- *Standing committees.* I urge people to name the standing committees and their responsibilities. (For more on Committees, see Chapter 5.)

- *Intentions and restrictions:* Without being too wordy, you should state particular intentions and restrictions. If, for example, there is a second signature requirement on checks over $5,000, say it here. If, as I hope you do, it is the intent of the board that the committees will have a great deal of authority, say so here. If it is the intent of the board to delegate certain authority to the executive director, say so here.

D. CONFLICT-OF-INTEREST POLICIES

While conflict-of-interest policies are usually included in your by-laws, they are more than important enough to discuss as a separate item. Remember in the first chapter, I briefly discussed my prediction that you will operate under more and more scrutiny during the next 10 years—scrutiny from the public, the press, your funders, and your donors. One of the areas where not-for-profits are most vulnerable is in the writing and interpretation of their conflict-of-interest policies. Don't forget: It is not the facts that count if you wind up in the local paper as having had board members who benefitted financially from their board position, it is the *appearance of impropriety* that will sink you. You want to design your policy to prevent the appearance of impropriety, to prevent actual abuse, and to be enforceable should someone try to self-aggrandize.

There are three schools of thought on these policies, at least as far as I have observed in my consulting experience. They can be categorized as follows:

1. OVERKILL

In an effort to prevent any and all appearances of impropriety, the policy says that no board or committee member can provide any service to the organization for compensation, and if a relative of theirs is under consideration for such a service contract that they not only cannot vote on the issue, but that they have to actually leave the meeting until the discussion is concluded.

This is a bit much. If you live in a small town like I do, there are only so many qualified people around, and automatically excluding them from providing services to you will not only prohibit you from using some valuable resources, it will also almost certainly be a disincentive to serve on the board.

2. UNDERKILL

The policy says that the board shall not personally profit from its relationship to the organization, but has no clear guidelines as to what that means, how to assess it or how to enforce a violation. In essence, it trusts the board members to do what is right. This is living in la-la land. Board members are like all the rest of us: 97% honest, 3% not so ethical. You need to use common sense, and have policies that prevent abuse, while at the same time not insulting the 97% of the board that are honest and upstanding.

❏ **FOR EXAMPLE:** A number of years ago, I was on the board of a social services provider, and became vice chairman of the board, and thus by default the chairman of the finance committee. This organization was then 20 years old, and had only had one executive director, who had run the organization from its infancy through the stage of having well over 100 employees. When I arrived, the board was a loose confederation of original board members, titular members (local state representatives, aldermen, etc.) and family members of persons served by the organization.

At the time I became finance committee chair, I was also the newly hired executive director of a health-planning not-for-profit, and in my new job had undertaken a complete overhaul of the financial controls, board policies, and other internal procedures. I had researched the issues thoroughly and tried to also use this fresh knowledge in my board and finance committee work. Our finance committee examined the financial policies and made many changes, including requiring at least two bids on contracts over $1,000, and reviewing insurance purchases every three years.

About two months into my term as chair, our comprehensive insurance package came up for renewal, and the executive director called to tell me that I needed to sign off on the contract. I asked her if we had bid the insurance out, as called for in our newly rewritten financial policies. Her shocked reply was: "No, of course not. George (a board member for 10 years) gives us a great rate on the premiums, so we always go with him. We're *not* going to bid this." I informed her that I differed with her, and that if we were going to have policies, they needed to be followed for everyone, every time. Besides, if George were giving us such a great rate, he'd certainly retain the business. The Exec was very uncomfortable with this idea, noting how dedicated George had been to the organization, how his daughter was one of our first clients, and in general setting George up for immediate canonization by the Pope. So, I added, "I know you and George go back a long way, and that he has been a great help to us. Let's blame this on me, and I'll even be the one to tell George in person, okay?" Fine, she said, still not very happy. We set the meeting with George for the next day.

George arrived at our meeting, assuming it was merely a formality and that I was there just to sign off on his contract and to pass him a check for the first month's premium. After the initial formalities, he slid the papers across the table to me, and I slid them back, saying: "George, this is *absolutely* no reflection on you, but as you know, we now have a financial policy that requires us to bid out all contracts over $1,000. Since this premium is over $35,000, we need to bid it out. You are very familiar with our insurance needs and may have put everything we need in the material you have today. So, I can either take the papers that you have as your bid, and hold them until we get two competing bids, or you can rework them into a more 'bid-like' form. I have a request for proposal [RFP] here for you to look at if you would like. We have been very happy with your service and hope that you will bid for the work, but I'm sure that you understand our need to get the best price we can."

George looked at me for a moment, then smiled slightly, but didn't say a word. He simply crossed out the premium amount on the contract, *reduced it by 20%,* and slid it back across the table! I could hear the executive director gasp and saw her flush red as I tried to keep from getting angry. The best response I could muster was: "Should I take that as your bid?" "Nope," he said, "I've provided good service here for 10 years. I don't do bids. This is a one-time offer. Take it or leave it." "We'll take it!" said the exec. "Wrong. We'll leave it," I said. I handed George the RFP and walked out of the room.

The point? Good old George—the board member, the parent, the supporter of our organization—had been *stealing* from us for years by inflating the premium way over the market price. He got away with it because the organization never bothered to check, and he knew about our lax policy. Once we had reasonable checks and balances, he was forced to play fair. Oh, and the executive director never forgave me for *embarrassing* her in front of George!

3. A BALANCED APPROACH

You need to attempt to reach a balance between overkill and under-kill. I suggest the following components of a conflict-of-interest policy:

- *Bid out contractual work.* Set a threshold, and get bids on things over that amount: contracting, equipment, supplies, food, anything. You'll need to learn how to write out your needs in an RFP, and once you learn how, and get in the habit of doing it, you will not only save money, but you will avoid anyone's saying that a board member got a "no bid" contract.

- *If a board member bids on a contract, he or she should get it only if it is the lowest bid.* This is somewhat restrictive, but again avoids potential bad publicity. And, the board member must follow the policy to the letter. You have to play by the rules 100%, 100%

of the time. The other person who loses the bid is just waiting to go to the press (or your funder) to accuse you of favoritism, or to the IRS to accuse you of "inurement of benefit," which is illegal. Play by the rules you set.

• *In discussions wherein a board member has or feels he or she may have a conflict, the board member should disclose that conflict or potential conflict immediately.* After such disclosure, the board member should be able to participate in discussion, but should recuse him- or herself from voting. The board member's participation in the discussion may bring important insights to the table, and, as long as everyone is aware of the conflict, should not be inappropriate.

• *Include your staff in your conflict policies.* We always focus on board members and forget our staff. What if the husband of your vice president of finance owns a computer firm and you need computers. Can he bid or not? You should specify. Can staff work on their own after hours? Can they consult with other agencies? You should spell it out.

You may need to be more stringent if you have had a bad experience with your board or if there has been a scandal at another organization in your community, but try to attain a reasonable balance. Put your policy in your bylaws, and have a training session with your board and staff about what it means. Repeat that training annually.

E. FINANCIAL CONTROLS

Good financial controls can be very technical and certainly should be designed to meet your organization's unique needs. Thus, you will need to rely on your CPA and your funding source for help on these controls. I will, however, highlight the major areas that need your attention. The key to financial policies is to have good oversight in reporting, good theft prevention by reducing temptation, and good records to allow for easy auditing and analysis.

1. CASH CONTROLS

You should already have cash controls in place, wherein one person logs in checks and cash, another deposits, and a third reconciles the bank statement. Even if there are only three staff, this is possible. Try to achieve it. *Note:* Everyone who handles any cash or checks should be bonded. It's cheap.

2. RECEIVABLES CONTROLS

The person who signs for the receivables and checks them in should not be the person who writes the check to the vendor. This will help prevent collusion and overpayment.

3. DEBT POLICY

You need to spell out your policy on taking debt. Can the Exec add to the line of credit without board approval? Can the executive committee approve a payroll loan without board approval? Be specific here. In Chapter 8, we discussed social entrepreneuring and why prudent debt can be a good thing and not a bad one. Whatever you decide on this issue, you want a policy and you want it to be specific.

4. CHECK SIGNATURE

Most boards let the staff write checks within the budget, but sometimes it takes two signatures above a certain threshold, such as $1,000 or $10,000. Some organizations make payroll exempt from this provision. How high or low your threshold is, and how many signatures you need will in some part depend on your organization's history, the community practices on the issue, and the requirements of your funders.

❏ **FOR EXAMPLE:** A few years ago, my consulting firm received a check from a small town in Alabama for a subscription to our six-issues-per-year newsletter. The check was for one year's subscription—$12. It had five (that's right, *five*) signatures: the mayor, the town treasurer, the town deputy mayor, the town clerk, and the police chief. After all of us had stopped laughing, I asked our staff: "The question is, in this town, who stole how much and how recently?"

We never found out the answer to the question, but the point is that you need to be reasonable. That town spent probably $50 in someone's time running that $12 check all over the courthouse getting five signatures. If you have had a bad experience with a former staff person, do take extra precautions, but not absurd ones.

5. REPORTING

Your policies should note who gets which reports how often. For example, your board may get quarterly financial statements, but your executive committee and financial committee get monthly income and expense statements, cash flows, and an aging payables and receivables. You need to have reporting requirements and formats that meet the needs of the people reading the reports to do their jobs. That means that different groups will get different reports. How do you know what they want and need? Be a good marketer. Ask them. (For more on this, see Chapter 9.)

6. CONFIDENTIALITY

A lot of people forget about confidentiality, but your financials are your business. You need a statement that specifies that this information is not to be shared outside the agency except with auditors, funders, and others and only with the express written approval of the board. You don't want your numbers floating all over town.

F. PERSONNEL POLICIES

I know that this will seem like a cursory discussion of an all-too-important issue, but it is intentional. Personnel policies, and not following them, are in my view the biggest single liability you have. Angry staff sue their employers more and more. We are, after all, a litigious society. We as not-for-profits also don't pay our staff enough, and probably never will. The one major area where angry, underpaid staff can sue us is in personnel: discriminatory hiring, sexual harassment, unjust termination, the list goes on and on. You simply have to have policies that meet the current law and regulation and are followed to the letter every single time.

Additionally, there have been some major changes in civil rights law in the past 10 years, not the least of which is the Americans with Disabilities Act. Getting your personnel policies right is a job for a professional, and someone on your staff or board should be or become such a professional. Invest in training for these people: Send them to seminars, buy them manuals; help them to get it right and keep it that way. Also, train your supervisory staff on your discipline process at least annually.

I intentionally did not include even a brief checklist here for fear that some reader would think that it was all inclusive and get into trouble. I think of personnel issues as management neurosurgery. Just as with that very technical specialty, you should get help and not try to do it yourself. Please talk to an expert.

G. MEDIA POLICIES

The media love to sell papers, magazines, and air time—that's their business. You want to avoid being part of that sales effort by not becoming a negative story in the scandal sheets. The public's and thus the press's zest for scandal is one of the reasons that you need to develop such detailed policies in all areas of the agency: It helps avoid the things that the media love to run on the front page or the evening news, for example, "Board Members Get Sweetheart Contract," "Staff of Agency File Discrimination Suit," "Executive Director Had Vacation on Agency Funds." *No one* wants to wake up to see or hear those stories about the organization that they work for.

But what if you do? What does one do when the reporter calls for information on a story, good or bad? Your media policies should tell you. I strongly suggest that your policies include at least the following:

1. EXTERNAL FLOW CONTROL

You need to have one person designated as the spokesperson for the agency. Usually, this will be the chief staff person, but, if you are large enough, it could also be the public information officer. In some cases, your board president should be the spokesperson. But the rule is: Limit the voices talking to the press. You want one message and one only. This rule is particularly important to impress on your board members, because they can be easily contacted and are often susceptible to press badgering as they are only volunteers and may not know the whole issue.

2. INTERNAL INFORMATION FLOW

Keep people informed: staff, board, the people you serve, funders, and donors. Get your side of the issue to them and quickly—before the papers hit the stands, if possible. Keep your staff fully informed of what is happening, and how it will affect them and their programs. Use these opportunities to remind them *not* to talk to the press on their own.

While we are on the subject, remember these rules of dealing with the media, in good times and bad:

- *State facts only, not assumptions.* For example, if a reporter asks: Doesn't your new program provide services in a discriminatory manner?", don't answer yes *or* no. An appropriate factual response (if true) would be, "Our board has a long standing nondiscrimination policy in all aspects of service provision, hiring, and employment. That policy includes our new program."

- *Don't be afraid to say "I don't know, but I'll get back to you," and then do.* It is better to check your facts and call back, but always do call back. Also, always get back to reporters by *their* deadline, even if it is inconvenient. They will run the story anyway, and put their slant on it, so return their calls, and try to get your two cents worth into the story.

- *State and restate your concern for the people you serve,* your prior awards and positive press, and how this issue, whatever it may be, will not affect the long-term program(s).

- *Don't try to be a "spin doctor."* Most reporters are pros and know spin when they hear it.

H. VOLUNTEER POLICIES

Volunteer policies do not need to be tedious or long, but at the very least they need to cover orientation, with an explanation of your mission and a description of all of your services, job descriptions, descriptions of responsibility and liability, and a list of staff positions that the volunteers relate/report to. These policies can then be distributed to staff and volunteers, and all can better understand the role volunteers play in your organization and how each individual participates as well.

I. QUALITY ASSURANCE

Quality is Job One, or so goes the advertisement. However, it is true that a passion for quality is not only good mission, it is also good marketing. No matter what service you are in, you need a quality assurance (QA) program. The recent interest in total quality management (TQM) has provided a whole new generation of references on quality and a great number of very qualified consultants in the area as well.

In some areas of service, there are quality boards that certify the quality of the organization. Programs like the Joint Commission on the Accreditation of Hospitals (JCAH) and the Commission on the Accreditation of Rehabilitation Facilities (CARF) are two good examples of such organizations, and there may be equivalents in your field. Additionally, you may have a trade organization that has developed standards of excellence for your field. For example, the National Society of Fund Raising Executives (NSFRE) has standards for its members that they publish. Your trade association may do the same.

At the very least, you want to set some standards for yourself to try to meet and exceed. These are not just goals and objectives in the planning sense, but standards of quality. For example, if you were a mental health assessment facility, you might have a standard that says that all new patients in crisis will see a counselor for initial assessment within 3 hours of a call 24 hours a day. If you were a church, you might have a standard that one or more of your ministerial staff will attend every church activity to facilitate counseling and fellowship. If you were a museum, you might not display any new works that have not passed a rigorous peer review of experts.

Your goal should be to do what you do better and better. You want to earn a reputation as a quality program, and that reputation is both tough to earn and tougher to keep. Setting standards in writing will help you, your management team, and your staff and volunteers achieve those standards.

J. PROGRAM POLICIES

Program policies are essential tools for you to convey your mission and your values to your staff, volunteers, funders, and service recipients. They may be short and general or long and detailed, but they should outline both the steps involved in any and all service provision and the philosophy of that provision. For example, an arts association may have a set of hands-on art exploration programs for young children. The association would need to put down their philosophy of "having children explore various creative media in a wholesome, safe environment" as well as such finite details as the need to register children, have emergency phone numbers if the children are dropped off, and perhaps (in this sad day and age of fear of child abuse) always having two adults in the room with the children. They might also put into their protocols to have the child's name added to their mailing list for future announcements of similar classes.

A second example is a health clinic, which might have very specific health care protocols for admission, screening, lab work, information gathering, insurance billing, and the like. These go a long way to ensure that staff understand each and every facet of what they need to do with each and every patient.

☞ **HANDS ON:** Don't assume that *anything* is too minute or too obvious to write down! That is why it is so critical to develop these with a group of line staff as well as with managers. I once saw a set of program policies for a health clinic that had such items as the information required on check-in, directions on how to offer coffee or tea in the waiting room in English and Spanish, what to do with blood tests, and so on, but forgot to direct the nurses to take the temperature and blood pressure of the patient! When a new nurse came on board, she was trained in the policies, and it wasn't until the patient charts were reviewed a week or two later that people noticed that these key items were not being assessed. When asked why not, she said, "You have great procedures, and I was just following them. It didn't make a whole lot of sense, but I'm new and didn't want to make trouble."

Don't fall into this trap. Let your staff know that policies are not substitutes for common sense.

J. DISASTER POLICIES

The bumper sticker says (paraphrased) "Stuff Happens." Fires, earthquakes, tornadoes, floods, power outages, and hurricanes all do occur, and regularly. I know that you have fire evacuation procedures for all of your buildings, and I hope that you have fire drills for any residential facilities you may run. But do you have disaster procedures? Perhaps not, and you need them. Make sure that your policies have at least these parts:

- *Disaster preparedness.* What is in here will depend on where you live and work. Are you in a hurricane-prone area? One that is regularly visited by tornadoes or earthquakes? If so, consult your local disaster preparedness agency and get up-to-date advice on being as prepared as possible. This may mean something as simple as laying in a supply of water, food, flashlights, and batteries, or as complex as reinforcing your structures.

- *Postdisaster planning:* What will you do *after* a disaster? If you lose a building to a fire or a flood, how do you get back up and running in as short a time as possible? With a good plan that has a checklist of things that need to be attended to, people to contact, and alternate sites for provision of services outlined.

❏ **FOR EXAMPLE:** During the writing of the first edition of *Mission-Based Management*, a fire at the school where my wife teaches destroyed about 15% of the school, with extensive smoke and water damage to the rest. The fire occurred on Friday night, ending about 4 A.M. on Saturday. By Sunday evening, with a superhuman effort on behalf of the administration and school district maintenance staff, the following had occurred: The entire school (a large school, with 450 students) had been cleaned, and most areas repainted; all the carpeting had been removed, cleaned, and replaced; all the affected areas of the school had been rewired; transportation for 100 students and alternate sites for classes had been secured; a gym site for the entire student body had been found; medical forms had been prepared to let students and faculty know what cleaning materials had been used in case of allergic reactions; insurance had been extended to the new sites; press conferences had been held; and every student in the school had been called. By Monday evening when an open house was held at both sites, all the lost student materials had been replaced, the new classrooms (at the different site) were set up, every book in the library (which was smoke damaged) had been cleaned and reshelved, and all the computers and audiovisual equipment in the school had been cleaned and returned. Classes resumed on Tuesday, 76 hours after the fire was out.

There were 1,000 other things that these people did that I have not recounted, but the key for them was that they had a plan for what to do in case there was severe damage to a school. The plan was not all inclusive, and they had to ad lib a lot, but it kept them on track and made sure that their efforts were focused and directed. You need disaster policies, and not just for fire drills.

L. TRAINING AND ENFORCEMENT

While policies can be a great management tool, they are a lot of work to create and to keep up to date. As I have noted repeatedly, they are also worthless without training staff and board people in their use. Again, you need to have in-services on every policy with all staff when it is first in place and then with affected staff each year. Only by repeated exposure to the policies will staff people get it right; and at the same time, ways to improve the policies will be found.

Policies must also be enforced. There is no point in spending the time and money to develop these guidelines if you are not going to discipline staff and board when they don't follow the policies. Make it

13

A National Agenda: Empowering Our Not-for-Profits

OVERVIEW

In this book, we have covered the key components of how to operationalize success at your not-for-profit. You have read suggestions and applications of how to deal with your mission, your board, your staff, your markets, your money, and your long-range goals. Hopefully, by applying the ideas encompassed in the previous pages, you can change your organization for the better, become more mission oriented, more market sensitive, and a better financial manager. But one key component remains: how your funders and the community at large view and treat your organization. These two groups can help you in your quest toward becoming and remaining a mission-based organization. Or they can impede or even negate your progress toward that goal.

This chapter will address three outdated theories of how funders look at you, look at three new ways that our nation needs to view its not-for-profits, and provide a specific list of action items for government, United Ways, and foundations to use as they consider how to assist not-for-profits (or at least get out of the way) in the new century.

A. THREE OUTDATED THEORIES

In chapter 2, I recounted how not-for-profits came to the state that confronts us today. I related to you the three big driving principles of

clear at the outset (at the training) that a wide array of staff and boar
were involved in development and testing of the policies, and that wit
that involvement from all levels in development, you now expect thes
to be followed. Then note clearly that failure to follow the policies wi
lead to disciplinary action. And when someone does violate them know
ingly (and someone *always* does, just to see what will happen), disciplin
them. You will be amazed at how few violations you will have in the future

RECAP

Don't miss the opportunity to have and use good controls. Bu
remember that while controls are great, they should not discourage innova
tion, experimentation, and the taking of risk. Staff should know tha
policies are not excuses for total brain shutdown, and that common sens
is still expected.

In this chapter, we've reviewed why it is critical to your succes
and your ability to manage to have good, well-written and up-to-dat
policies and procedures. We have reviewed the essential kinds of policie
and gone over the key things that I have seen many organizations forge
to include. Remember, good controls are a key to good management an
mission success. Without them, you will almost surely have staff o
volunteers do something, major or minor, that distracts you from you
job: managing the organization. With controls, there will be less of that
although even the best controls are valueless if people ignore them. Tha
is why we went over the issue of regular training as a key to implementatioi
of your policies, and enforcement as a way to ensure that they are used

Good controls set you free from administration—they allow you t
be a manager. The time and money spent to develop and update then
will be returned to you tenfold. Without them, your organization is a
multitude of accidents waiting to happen.

Questions for Discussion

1. What parts of this chapter apply to us?
2. Let's examine each of the policies and look at this issues that are
   identified for each of them. We can list what needs to be updated, by
   whom, and by when.
3. What resources can we commit to training our staff to use these policies?
4. How can we more fairly enforce our expectations of our policies?

most funders' views of how not-for-profits really run. To recount briefly, these principles (from the funders' point of view) were:

- *What we (the funders) say goes.* Whether or not it makes any sense in your community, or with your mission, since we are paying the piper, we call the tune—much more invasively and comprehensively than any for-profit customer would ever dream of doing.

- *You can't do well doing good.* You are suspected of stealing if you are not threadbare, scrutinized well beyond the cost–benefit curve, and in general must take a vow of poverty to get our (the funders') money.

- *What is yours is ours.* If you take our money (even if it is just a portion of your overall income), we have the right to come and strip you naked and judge you at our whim. Additionally, anything that you buy with "our" money is ours, not yours.

As I said earlier, it is my absolute belief, based on being part of and working for and around not-for-profits for over 20 years, that these policies are not only outdated but are counterproductive social policy, short-sighted fiscal policy, and just plain egocentric at their core. They assume that the funder knows best, whether that funder is a government, foundation, United Way, or other source of revenue; that the not-for-profit is an inept, if not felonious, manager of public funds; and that the not-for-profit should be poor to prove their honesty. They also forget that at the center, the relationship among government and funder and agency is really one of purchasing services. It is not parenthood. Neither is it indentured servitude.

These policies and views must change, and there are five groups of people who must change them: governments, foundations, United Ways, the public, and you—the staff members of the nation's not-for-profits. Without fundamental change in the ways that these five groups view your not-for-profit and the 950,000 others in the United States, there are limits to what you can achieve. For example, if your funders demand that you have no fund balance, and will go to extraordinary lengths to recover funds from you, you can never be financially empowered, never help the community without running back to the funder for more funds, which come with all strings attached.

This concern with the way government contracts and treats its providers of service is not, of course, unique to me. Not only have the trade associations been harping on the issue for years, our centers of academic research have been looking at the issue as well. Such notables as Brian O'Connell at the Independent Sector in a series of publications, and David Osborne, in his excellent book *Reinventing Government,* have both called for a reexamination of the ways that government funds and supervises its contractual obligations. Osborne, in particular, developed a large number of examples of ways to make government more efficient and effective. Many, including the call for the end to "use it or lose it" and competitive bidding, parallel the ideas that I lay out below.

But, having criticized just about everyone in the power positions, what can each group do to fix the problem? It would be unfair just to take potshots without offering solutions, so here are mine. These are not, as you will see, fine-tuning or adjustments. They are radical realignments of our national views of our private not-for-profit sector. They will at some level threaten just about everyone, as they are not designed to be slow and cautious in their approach. I don't think we have the time to be slow and cautious. America's social, educational, arts, scientific, and religious needs are obvious to all but the most callous or out-of-touch observer. Even in our excellent new economy, there remain needs that are unmet. We cannot wait. Let's start now.

B. OVERALL PHILOSOPHY CHANGES THAT ARE NECESSARY

In chapter 1, I started the discussion of my three umbrella theories of not-for-profits. Those three philosophies have appeared in many forms throughout the book. But how do they apply to funders? I think that they do, and they bear another examination here.

The general philosophies below need to be adopted and practiced at all levels. As noted above, they require a radical rethinking of the role of not-for-profits by many of us. Those not-for-profit funders whose grantees and contractors are succeeding have already adopted many if not all of these tenets.

1. NOT-FOR-PROFITS ARE BUSINESSES

First and foremost, we have to stop thinking of not-for-profits as *charities.* They are businesses, albeit ones whose primary motivation is mission and not profit. In pursuit of that mission, a not-for-profit must act as much like a business as possible without sacrificing its mission. This means adopting many of the skills taught earlier in this book: a bias for marketing, watching the bottom line, building up equity and financial flexibility, growing and retaining a strong staff, having a long-range vision, and understanding that profit is *not* a dirty word.

We also have to realize that our not-for-profits contribute to our communities economically as well as in arts, human services, education, and theology. Not-for-profits contribute over 11% of our gross national product, and employ 13.5% of the workforce—and that is more people than the domestic auto industry and its immediate suppliers. In many rural communities, not-for-profits are major employers; in every community, they contribute to the local payroll in a significant way. Thus, a healthy, growing, and stable not-for-profit network can stimulate job growth just as much as small businesses, which get so much good press on the issue of economic stimulus.

I have never said, and never wish to be quoted as saying, that this business mentality should come at the expense of doing good mission. It does not mean that watching your cash flow equates with cutting all of your unprofitable programs. Doing some things that lose money is part and parcel of the service array that not-for-profits should continue to provide. But, using good, sound businesslike practices at the staff and board level can make all the difference: *It means getting more mission for your money, not having more money and doing less mission.*

2. NO ONE GIVES A NOT-FOR-PROFIT A DIME

Whoa, say the governments, we *give* them billions. Hold on, say the United Ways. We *give* them millions. Wait a second, say the foundations, what about our millions? And don't forget us, say the millions of Americans who dip into their wallets and purses each year to contribute to the nation's not-for-profits.

To all of you who fund America's not-for-profits, I say this: You're still focusing on not-for-profits as *charities*, not as the mission-oriented businesses that they are. Let's look at the transactions that *really* take place when you make a donation:

❑ For Example:

- The local art museum comes to you for a $100 donation. They describe their programs, explain their funding patterns, and ask for your help in meeting their program goals. You write them a check for $100.

- The statewide drug prevention hotline calls you for a $50 monthly donation to allow them to keep taking toll-free calls from people who need drug rehabilitation services and are in crisis. You sign up for a monthly contribution.

• The county shelter for the homeless is taking contributions to pay for a holiday dinner for the residents. You chip in $20.

Here is the crux of the issue: In each of these cases, what did you do? Did you *give* the museum, hotline, or shelter anything? Most people would say "yes, I *gave* them money." No, what you did was *buy services on behalf of someone else.* For the museum, that money might go to a new display of impressionist paintings that all can see; for the hotline, it might help pay for the toll-free 800 service; for the shelter, it literally will put food in someone's mouth. Thus, you purchased something, perhaps not as precisely as you would purchase food from the grocery store or a repair service from your plumber, but at its core, the transaction is the same.

There is still the other side of the equation yet to be mentioned, the side that is even more important than realizing that you (and all of the other funders, the governments, foundations, and United Ways) are buying something, rather than just giving money away. It goes like this:

Not-for-profits *earn* every cent that they get.

Step back and think about it. The government doesn't give money away for nothing (although I will be the first to contend that they regularly don't get their money's worth). The government wants something for its money: it *buys* services, whether they be scientific research, outreach to teenage moms, public broadcasting, or breakfasts for poor children. If it buys something, then the relationship is one of purchaser (the government) and seller (the not-for-profit). Thus the not-for-profit has to do something to *earn* the money, which usually means providing a service or array of services. The same is true for other funders.

The understanding that not-for-profits are earning their money rather than accepting a handout is, obviously, a critical part of the philosophy change. If not-for-profits are businesses and have economic worth in the society beyond their social, educational, or religious worth, then they also can and should stand up and stop being treated like a poor cousin.

3. NOT-FOR-PROFIT DOES NOT EQUAL NONPROFIT

Here's the most important issue. Throughout this book (and all of my other writings), I always use the term *not-for-profit,* rather than the more commonly used *nonprofit*. I do this for two reasons. The first is that the term not-for-profit is technically the correct one: The corporation is established in the IRS code as a corporation "not for profit." The second reason, and the more important one for this discussion, is that the term *nonprofit* sends the wrong message.

A nonprofit is an entity that loses money. Some examples would include Chrysler in the late 1970s, or Amazon.com in the first years of its rapid growth. Unfortunately, most not-for-profits are also nonprofits. What the 501(c)(3) is, however, is a corporation formed, under law passed by Congress, to pursue a variety of areas such as education, religion, social services, the arts, and so forth. Here is the key:

> *Nowhere, in any state or federal law or regulation, does it say that a not-for-profit must lose money or break even financially. In fact, in the IRS code, it says that "the* **profits** *of the corporation shall not inure to the benefit of (various people)"* (emphasis added).

Thus, having profits is fine with the law, and with IRS regulations. Still don't believe me? Look at it this way: Congress gave not-for-profits a tax break. Not-for-profits don't have to pay income tax on funds earned related to their mission statement. So, your organization has a tax exemption from paying taxes on "income." But it is not an income tax as an individual thinks of such a tax—paying a portion of your income. No, it is a *business* income tax. Businesses pay taxes on a portion of their profits (which the IRS terms their *income*—hence the confusion). Thus, your organization really has an exemption from paying taxes on your profits. Here's the key: If you couldn't make a profit, you wouldn't need the tax exemption!

In fact, what Congress intended was for your organization to keep your profits and reinvest them in the community! What have our funders done? In the main, take your profits back. Thus, the less they can pay, the better, and if a not-for-profit is "making money" or has a reserve, that is immediately suspect and cause for a reduction in funding for the next funding cycle, a special audit, or both. This is not only absurd, but so far out of date it makes my head spin. The real amazement is that all of us in the not-for-profit community have allowed it to continue this long.

Not only is it okay for not-for-profits to make money, I contend that not-for-profits *must* make money in most, if not every year, if they are to do their job right. Only financially stable organizations will be able to react quickly to changing needs in their communities. Only financially stable organizations will be able to recruit and retain excellent staffs, take risks on behalf of their clientele, and do their job as it needs to be done.

Finally, only financially stable not-for-profits will be able to stop the cycle of dependence on government for hand-to-mouth funding. (For more on this, see Chapter 10.)

Profit is accepted in every other sector of our economy, even in some sectors of the not-for-profit economy (e.g., hospitals). Why, then, should profit and the stability, flexibility, and quality that it produces be such a pejorative when it is applied to not-for-profits in general?

Again, I fear misinterpretation and misquoting here. I am not contending that not-for-profits should make money just to make money, or just to buy nice offices or pay high salaries. The profits should be reinvested in the mission in the way that each organization's board and staff see best maximizes the use of those funds to accomplish the mission.

4. COMPETITION IS OKAY

Imagine that the owner of a new fast food franchise came to a zoning hearing in your town and asked the zoning commission to rezone a parcel of land so that she could build a burger stand at the same intersection where another fast food restaurant already operated. Now imagine the zoning commission turning the zoning request down because it "duplicates an existing service." The franchise owner would scream bloody murder and sue, and win, with a great deal of popular support in the community, because we have a long and successful tradition of free enterprise and competition. Now, and this is not so hard to envision, imagine that same franchise owner sitting on a funding panel at your United Way and voting to turn down a funding request for a new program because it "duplicates an existing program already operating in the community."

It happens all the time. Agencies, particularly in social services, are regularly given geographic monopolies by their government funders. This is done to avoid duplication and in the spirit of efficiency and economy. It is amazing to me that we let this start and let it continue when all of the evidence from every corner of the globe shows that competition (if profits are allowed and retained) will encourage better service, at more economical prices than monopolies.

In short, competition for customers is okay, and should be encouraged. I am not naive enough to say that this should be done wholesale next fiscal year. The staffs and boards of not-for-profits are well trained as monopolies, and a transition time is needed and will be rocky for some. Much of the advice in this book is designed to get them ready for just such competition.

C. SPECIFIC ACTION ITEMS

This list of action items is offered as an agenda for change for the five major groups that need to act now: the government, foundations, United Ways, the community at large, and the staffs and boards of our not-for-profits. All of them are designed to mesh with the four overall philosophical changes listed in this chapter.

To be fair, I also must note here that some governments, some foundations, and some United Ways are already doing many if not all of the things I suggest below. In fact, with the exception of the idea of national management certification for not-for-profits, there is little here that has not already been tested and found to work. Thus, as you read these suggestions, don't put them aside, saying "Never happen," or "Would never work." They already are happening and already do work in other communities. What you need to do is to make them work in yours.

Government (Federal, State, County, Local)

1. *End the policy of "use it or lose it".* Let not-for-profits bid on work that you want done, and then, if they do what you contracted for, and have money left over afterward, let them keep it. If you bid the contract fairly, and the contractor did what you asked, why should they have to return what they didn't spend? All this encourages is waste, fraud, or both. (*Note:* the federal government is making major strides here, while the states in general are lagging far behind.)

2. *End monopolies.* Let the not-for-profits you fund bid against each other and against for-profits. Open the markets up. To do this well, you will need to learn how to write contracts and requests for proposals in new ways, and you will have to link the end of monopolies to the end of "use it or lose it," but it will work. You will, in the end, get better services, better quality, and more productivity.

3. *Encourage productivity and quality.* Compensate contractors if they meet high quality and productivity standards—ones that are set forth in the contract. Even small financial incentives can bring up standards rapidly. Again, this has to be linked with the end of "use it or lose it," or you will lose any beneficial effect.

4. *Pay on time, and pay fair scale.* We are no longer in an era of tight government budgets. Surpluses abound. Of course, there is still

the popular prohibition on new taxes, but you can raise fees and not do this. Paying less than cost is a short-term solution that creates (and has created) a long-term problem: chronically underfunded agencies that are perpetually dependent on the government.

5. *Reduce or end the use of matching fund requirements.* The theory of the match is that it shows agency or community commitment and the likelihood of program continuity later on if funding ceases. In reality, this requirement impoverishes not-for-profits and/or encourages them to cheat by allowing "in-kind" contributions—those of time or overhead that are already paid for—often by another government agency. Can you imagine the same government asking Dell to sell a PC at 25% *below* cost? That's exactly what a 25% match does. Stop it.

6. *Develop a universal accounting and audit format.* For every type of funding, a not-for-profit often has to go through a different set of bookkeeping and year-end audit and accounting forms. Sometimes this means one agency has to do 10 separate types of forms. As you can imagine, this does not result in administrative efficiencies. I refuse to believe that with all the expertise in this country, governments and CPAs cannot come up with a universal set of accounting and year-end program audit protocols that would save millions of dollars in administrative oversight costs each year.

Foundations

1. *Require management certification for funding.* I put this on the foundation's agenda because they could commission such a certification effort more easily than the government. My vision here is of a management certification such as the Commission on the Accreditation of Rehabilitation Facilities (CARF) for not-for-profits. All agencies that could meet the certification would be certified for three years, and that would make them eligible (or more competitive) for foundation funds, and could even be a prerequisite for funding continuation. Certification could also be made a competitive edge for government and/or United Way funding. I suggest that the foundations link up with the graduate programs in not-for-profit management, such as the University of San Francisco, Case Western Reserve, and Yale, to develop the certification.

2. *Encourage and fund seed projects with business outcomes.* Program-related investments (PRIs) do this to some extent and are the

most laudable development from the foundations of the past decade, in my view. However, foundations can go further to encourage financial empowerment, and seeding outside business ventures are one way to do that.

3. *Stop the practice of "use it or lose it."* See number 1 under Government.

4. *Stop or reduce match requirements.* See number 5 under Government.

United Ways

1. *Stop funding deficits.* Many United Ways have policies of funding only deficits, and all this does is encourage future deficits. If you accept my theory of not-for-profit transactions—that donors are buying services—then United Ways should purchase the most needed services, whether or not the agency is making money.

2. *Demand management certification.* See number 1 under Foundations.

3. *Encourage Competition.* Do not refuse funding just because a service is duplicated: Let agencies compete to provide the best service. Demand quality, but even with higher quality competition will ultimately lower your cost, and will probably weed out the weak and inflexible agencies. This *will* be painful. People *will* scream, but the community *will* be better off for it.

The American Public (and the Press)

1. *Stop assuming that all not-for-profits are welfare recipients.* They aren't. There are efficient, effective, and productive not-for-profits and inefficient, underproductive ones, just like in the for-profit sector, and the ratio is probably about the same.
   Corollary assumption: That all not-for-profits steal. They don't. I've never seen a study done, but I wouldn't be surprised if the rate of theft and corruption in the not-for-profit sector is less than the proprietary or governmental sectors. It's just that when a not-for-profit staff or board member steals and it makes the papers, it is big news. At any rate, the public's and press's demands for incredibly

expensive scrutiny of every dollar spent—spending millions to prevent the theft of thousands—is not only counterproductive, it is
insulting to the hundreds of thousands of dedicated and honest not-
for-profit staff and board that are serving us well. Reasonable accounting and checks and balances both within and outside not-for-
profits are important, but we've got things way out of proportion
now, and our tax dollars are not well spent in this area.

2. *When you serve on a board, don't check your common sense or
business expertise at the door.* I've lost count of how many times
I've watched good, solid businesspeople make incredibly dumb decisions for a not-for-profit "because we aren't really a business." Just
because the organization is not in it for the money doesn't mean
you suspend common sense in making policy decisions. You are on
the board to contribute your wisdom, expertise, experience, and
perspective to the discussion: Don't leave home without them.

3. *Demand productivity, flexibility, and quality from your not-for-
profits.* Just because it has "always been that way" is no excuse for
stodgy management and outdated programming. Be as demanding
of your not-for-profits as you are of stores and businesses you patron-
ize. If you donate money, you are a customer: Demand quality.

What you can do

If the items above are to become reality, you need to help. As a
not-for-profit staff member, there are things you need to be doing to
reinforce these new ideas and make them work in your community. While
everything that I have tried to convey in this book moves you and your
organization toward that end, I can distill it into two short phrases:

1. *Be businesslike.* Not cold, or profit driven, but businesslike. The
more you act like a business, the more you will be treated like
one. This includes dressing appropriately, using business language
(markets, cash flow, quality management), and the like. Join the
chamber, and get active. Not-for-profit staffs regularly complain that
they "don't get any respect." Part of this wound is self-inflicted.
Remember, you earn your money—you are not a charity. Go out
and act like it, and you will start to be treated accordingly.

2. *Be competitive—accept the marketplace and try to adapt.* This is, I know, a big change, but if the governments and foundations end "use it or lose it" and end monopolies, you'll have to get with it sooner or later. I suggest sooner.

D. AN EXHORTATION

These agenda items are only a start. Until all parties involved buy into the major philosophies, we won't make significant progress. Until not-for-profits learn and practice the skills and policies outlined in this book, they won't become the lean, creative, and productive social entrepreneurs that would so benefit the social fabric of our society. Until the public sees our not-for-profits as more than charities, they will delay realizing the full potential that this vital sector of our economy has to assist and contribute to the nation as a whole.

However, none of us has to wait for the others to get on board before starting the change. Each board member can demand better policies, a strategic plan, better financial oversight, and quality control. Each mission-based manager can value the line staff, act as if every action has an impact on the organization's marketing, and not recoil from the thought of competition. Each government agency can end the policy of "use it or lose it," even if another program does not. Each United Way can demand management training and excellence, even if there is not yet a national certification. Each citizen can trust the boards and staff to do good works and provide reasonable oversight. If each of us did, we would be well on our way. The sooner each of us start, the better for all of us, and for the communities we serve.

RECAP

In this chapter, we went over the key issues that we all need to work on to fix what is broken in the not-for-profit-sector. First, I reiterated my beliefs regarding the fact that your organization is a mission-based business, that you earn all your income, and that it is essential for you to make money as a good steward. Then, I focused in on core beliefs that need to change at the funder level and made a series of suggestions for each of the major funder groups (government, foundations, United Ways) as well as ways the public and your organization can move the agenda ahead. We are in this together, and need to solve the problems together. Don't delay!

Questions for Discussion

1. Which of our funders should see this chapter first? How should we approach them?
2. Should we foster a larger discussion in our community? Can we talk to a sympathetic reporter? Are our board and staff in agreement with these ideas?
3. How can we pass these ideas on to our state and national groups?

14

Final Words

I hope that you feel that you are on your way to becoming an even better mission-based manager than you were at the beginning of this book. I have tried to give you the benefit of my experiences and observations about what not-for-profits nationwide are doing to get more mission for their money, to be more businesslike in pursuit of their mission.

We are at an important crossroads for America's not-for-profits, and thus for your organization as well. We can't go back to the federal largesse of the 1970s. Even though we have budget surpluses, we don't want to ever be that dependent again. We can't stay as we are—still behind in technology, assuming that the money we need will magically show up. Too many people in our communities are depending on us to provide more and better services. We must go forward, but how? Will your organization choose the path of becoming a mission-based business? Or will you continue to think of yourself and your organization as a charity? Will you aggressively pursue the use of all of the resources available to you, including lessons from the for-profit sector? Or will you continue to do business as usual?

The answer is, of course, up to you, your staff, and your board. But if you choose the path of being a mission-based manager and want to manage a mission-oriented business, you have already been exposed to the keys in this book. One last time, let's review the characteristics that your organization needs to have to be successful and thrive in the coming years. In parentheses after each characteristic you will find the number of the chapter(s) where that characteristic is discussed in detail:

1. A viable mission (Chapter 4)
2. A businesslike board of directors (Chapter 5)
3. A strong, well-educated staff (Chapter 6)

4. Wired and technologically savvy (Chapter 7)
5. Social entrepreneurs (Chapter 8)
6. A bias for marketing (Chapter 9)
7. Financially empowered (Chapter 10)
8. A vision for where they are going (Chapter 11)
9. A tight set of controls (Chapter 12)

You may have found that many or even all of the characteristics I tout as necessary to your vitality are already present in your organization. If so, congratulations: Your organization will probably continue to provide services well into the next century. But wait. Is it *your* opinion only that says that you are already doing all of these things? Or did you see about the perspective of the staff and board? If it was just your opinion, remember that you do not always see things with total objectivity. Check with others, including some funders. Find out if they see your organization evidencing the same characteristics in the same way.

In Chapter 1, I suggested that you read this book as a team: Have all the senior managers read the same one or two chapters and then discuss what ideas you can or should adopt in your organization. If you didn't do that, now that you are through the entire book, try team reading. Get a group of your senior staff together and have them read a chapter or two a week, discussing them at a regular staff meeting. Going over any management text in this fashion is the best way to get the most good out of the book. You might also want to use the *Mission-Based Management Workbook*, which has been specifically designed to help you implement the ideas in the book.

To me, the fact that you have been willing to read an entire book on managing your organization is clear evidence that you want to become a mission-based manager. But will you turn the investment of the hours you took out of your busy schedule to read this text to good use? Will you continue to put in the effort to become a mission-based manager who runs a mission-based organization? Many of the changes needed are behavioral: Developing a bottoms-up management style takes some serious change for some people. Communicating with the attitude that the key is what people hear, and not what you say, takes some adjusting to. Developing a culture of new ideas, in which all are encouraged, and changing methods of thinking to ask all the markets what they want instead of "knowing what they need" are disciplines that are difficult to stick to.

Psychologists that I have talked to say that a behavioral change takes two years to "take." That is, if someone adopts a lifestyle of exercise and healthy eating after years of being a couch potato full of junk food, it takes two full years before that new lifestyle becomes a habit rather than a major effort.

I suspect that it is longer for an organization. All the changes that you want to facilitate will need to be adapted to by *all* (or at least a sizable majority of) your staff and board, and that in itself will take a while. Only when they make that adaptation does the two-year clock start ticking. You need to be there leading by example, encouraging, cajoling, showing, evaluating. You are the key to the success or failure.

I sincerely hope that you succeed. Our nation and your community need every one of the not-for-profits that can make the transition from charity to mission-based business. Our national needs and wants in education, the arts, social services, research, and religion are growing, not waning, and it will take a full roster of mission-based managers to bring these organizations into their fullest potential. The new century provides a new opportunity to renew our commitment to our mission in new, more effective ways. The ways of the mission-based manager *are* more effective.

Mission-based managers are different. They see the mission first—the outcome of their organization's services—in very human terms. As a mission-based manager, don't ever lose that perspective. It is what sets you apart from your for-profit peers. Yes, it makes your job that much tougher, but it makes the satisfaction of your job that much greater. It is what makes all the work worth it.

Remember that the services you provide are all provided *by* a person, and they all are provided *to* a person. In between those two people is your mission: the what and why of your organization. The mission is what brings those two people together. You are the champion of that mission both in your organization and in your community. With the skills you have learned here, you should find great success. Good luck.

Index